BRITISH RAILWAYS ATLAS 1947

THE LAST DAYS OF THE BIG FOUR

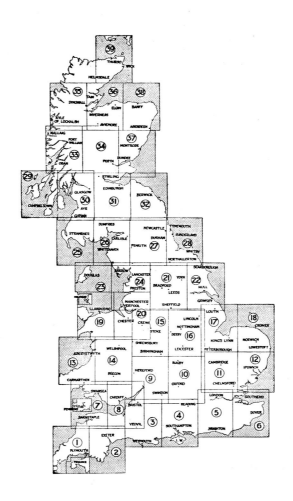

IAN ALLAN *Publishing*

Explanation

Great Western Railway	*Yellow*
London, Midland & Scottish Railway ...	*Red*
London & North Eastern Railway ...	*Blue*
Southern Railway	*Green*
Other Lines	*Indicated by name*

A number bracketed in the margin indicates the continuation map.

SCALE OF MILES

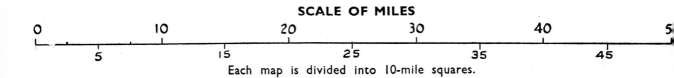

Each map is divided into 10-mile squares.

First published 1948
Reprinted 1987
This impression 1996

ISBN 0 7110 2438 3

Published by Ian Allan Publishing

an imprint of Ian Allan Ltd, Terminal House,
Station Approach, Shepperton, Surrey TW17 8AS.
Printed by Ian Allan Printing Ltd, Coombelands
House, Addlestone, Surrey KT15 1HY.

SECTIONAL MAPS OF THE BRITISH RAILWAYS

This atlas was originally published in 1948 as a permanent record of the British railway system as it was at the end of private ownership in December 1947. The book has been out of print for many years and the publishers are pleased to be able to make it available again in paperback form.

It will be seen that each map is divided into 10 mile squares identified by longitudinal letters and lateral numerals, so that from the Index all stations and principal junctions can be located by map number, letter and numerical reference. Stations in the index are shown in Roman type, whilst junctions and other points where there is no station are shown in italics.

Stations are normally indexed under their town name, but where there are characteristic additional names, the index will show them both under the town and such names as Thorpe (Norwich), Paragon (Hull) etc. Non-characteristic sub-titles such as Central, City, Exchange are not directly entered and one entry, eg Leeds will cover both Leeds Central and Leeds City stations. However, where a sub-title is compounded in the title of a locality the entry is direct, eg South Canterbury under S in contrast to Canterbury East under C.

Dual titles are cross-indexed, eg Claxby & Usselby is indexed both under C and U, but the map reference appears only under the first named station.

Plurality of stations and railway companies at a single place are exemplified thus:

(a) Bicester, GWR & LMS. Symbol (&) between owning companies to indicate two separate stations, separately owned.
(b) Birkenhead, BJ, *CLC, *GWR, etc. Comma (,) between owning companies to indicate separate stations, each individually owned. The CLC & GWR stations here are non-passenger, see Note*.
(c) Saunderton, GWR/LNER. Oblique (/) to indicate one station, jointly owned and used.
(d) Brecon, **GWR**/LMS. One station, owned by the company listed in bold type, but also used by the other.
(e) Aylesbury, GWR/LNER/LPTB & LMS. Two stations, of which one is "triple-joint" and the other is exclusively owned and used by LMS.

The above categories do not necessarily apply to goods stations at the places concerned.

Track Junctions — Those readily traceable by reference to an adjoining station, eg, Aynho Jc, GWR are not specifically indexed.

WHERE IS IT ON THE MAP?

Example from Index; Framlingham, LNER, code 12, C3. Answer: on Map 12, in the square found by following Section C across until it meets the vertical column No 3.

NOTES AND ABBREVIATIONS

*	... No passenger service	Jc(s)	... Junction(s)	NSLR	... N. Sunderland Light Ry	SMR	... Snowdon Mountain Ry (rack railway, n.g.)
§	... Closed to all traffic	KESR	... Kent & East Sussex Ry	OAGB	... Oldham, Ashton & Guide Bridge Joint Ry (LMS/LNER)	SR	... Southern Ry
AJ	... Axholme Joint Ry (LNER/LMS)	LMS	... London, Midland & Scottish Ry			SSMW	... South Shields, Marsden & Whitburn (Coll.) Ry
BJ	... Birkenhead Joint Ry (GWR/LMS)	LNER	... London & North Eastern Ry	OI	... Otley & Ilkley Joint Ry (LMS/LNER)	SVY	... Severn & Wye Joint Ry (GWR/LMS)
CLC	... Cheshire Lines Committee (LMS/LNER)	LOR	... Liverpool Overhead Ry	Plat	... Platform, = "Halt"	SW	... Shrewsbury & Welshpool Joint Ry (GWR/LMS)
		LPTB	... London Passenger Transport Board	RCT	... Rye & Camber Tramy (n.g.)		
Coll(s)	... Colliery (-ies)	ME	... Manx Electric Ry (n.g.)	RHDR	... Romney, Hythe & Dymchurch Light Ry (n.g.)	SY	... South Yorkshire Joint Ry (LNER/LMS)
Corris	... Corris (n.g.) section, GWR	Mer	... Mersey Ry	RER	... Ravenglass & Eskdale Ry (n.g.)	Tal.	... Tal-y-Llyn Ry (n.g.)
DA	... Dundee & Arbroath Joint Ry (LMS/LNER)	MGN	... Midland & Gt Northern Jt Ry (LMS/LNER)			VR	... Vale of Rheidol (n.g.) section, GWR
DVL	... Derwent Valley Light Ry	MJ	... Methley Joint Railway (LMS/LNER)	SBH	... Snailbeach Dist. Rys (n.g.)	VT	... Vale of Towy Joint Ry
ECH	... Easton & Church Hope Ry (Portland)	MN	... Mid-Notts Jt Ry (LMS/LNER)	SD	... Somerset & Dorset Joint Ry (LMS/SR)		
EKR	... East Kent Ry	MSJA	... Manchester, South Jc, & Altrincham Ry (LMS/LNER)	Sdg(s)	... Siding(s)	WL	... Welshpool & Llanfair n.g. section, GWR
ER	... Easingwold Ry			SH	... Shrewsbury & Hereford Joint Ry (GWR/LMS)	WM	... Wrexham & Minera Joint Ry (GWR/LMS)
GWR	... Great Western Ry	Mum. R	... Mumbles Electric Ry	SK	... Swinton & Knottingley Joint Ry (LMS/LNER)		
HJ	... Halesowen Joint Ry (GWR/LMS)	n.g.	... Narrow gauge			WUT	... Wisbech & Upwell Tramy.
IMR	... Isle of Man Ry (n.g.)	NSJ	... Norfolk & Suffolk Joint Ry (LNER/MGN)	SM	... Shropshire & Montgomeryshire Ry		

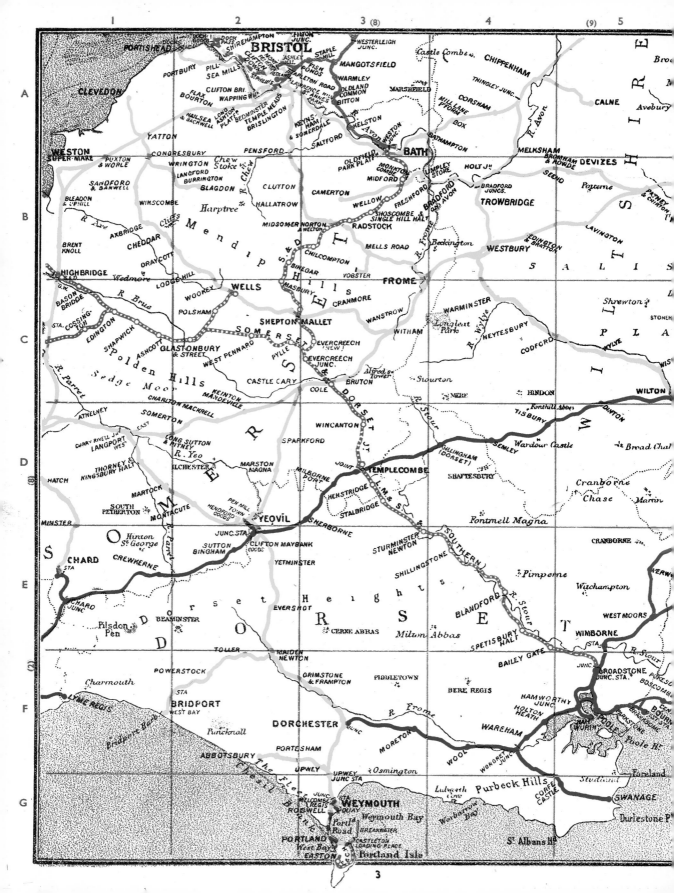

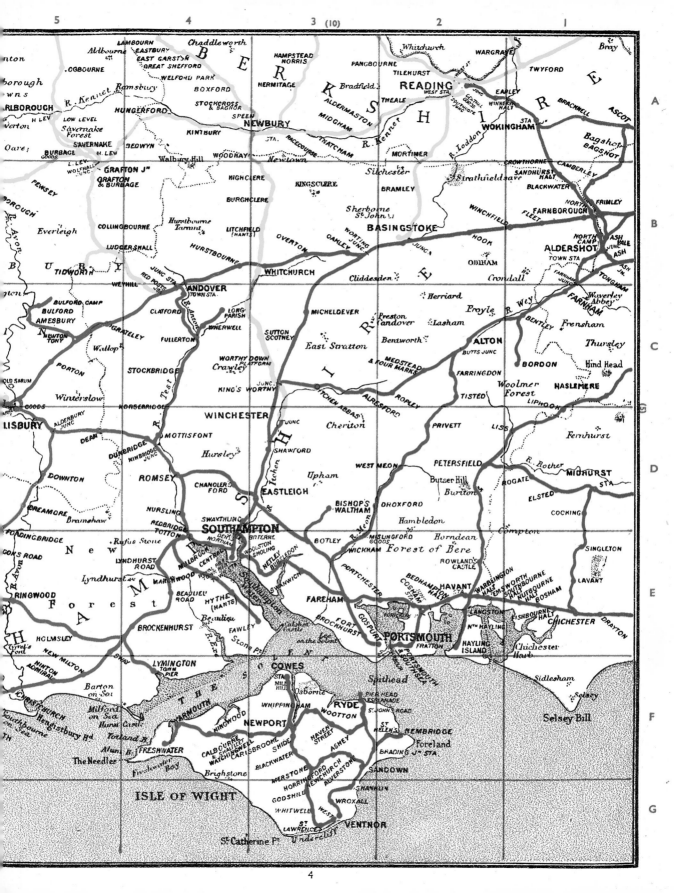

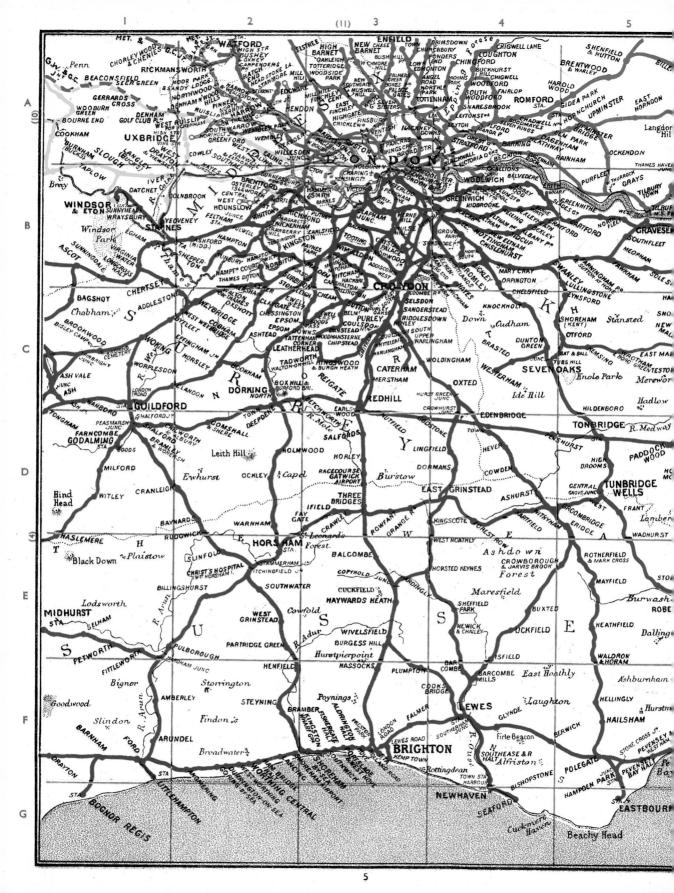

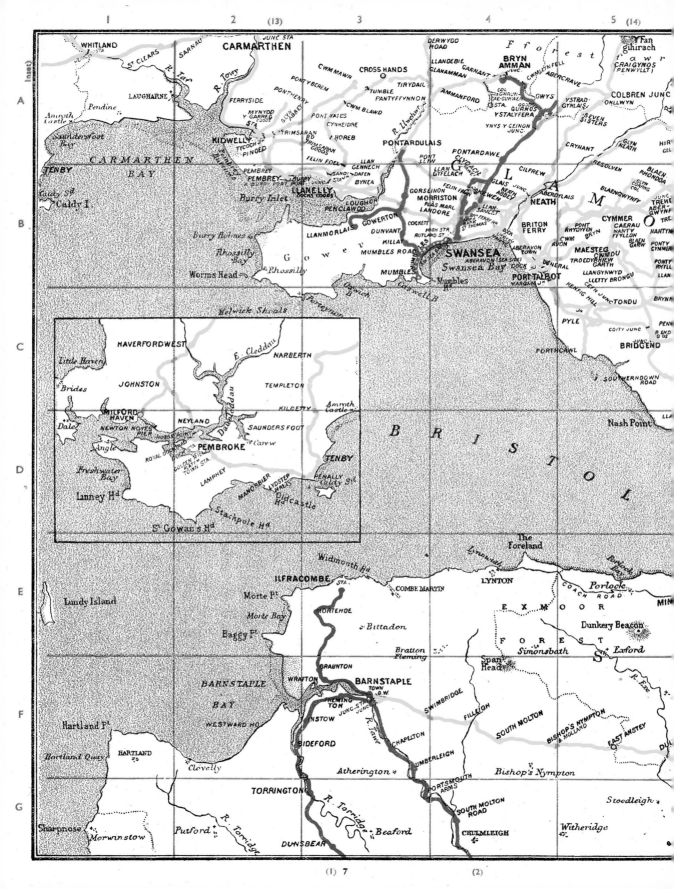

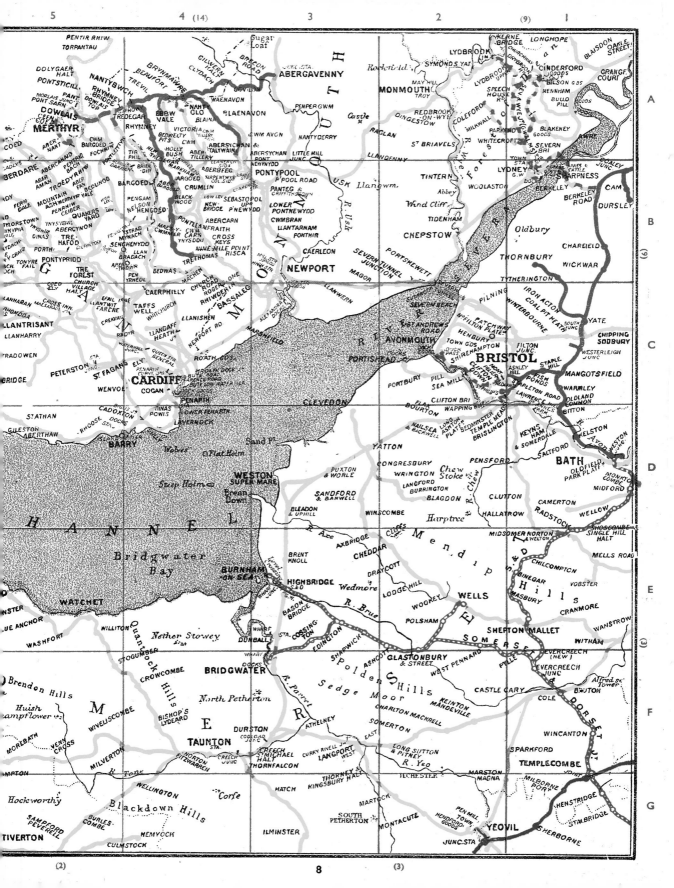

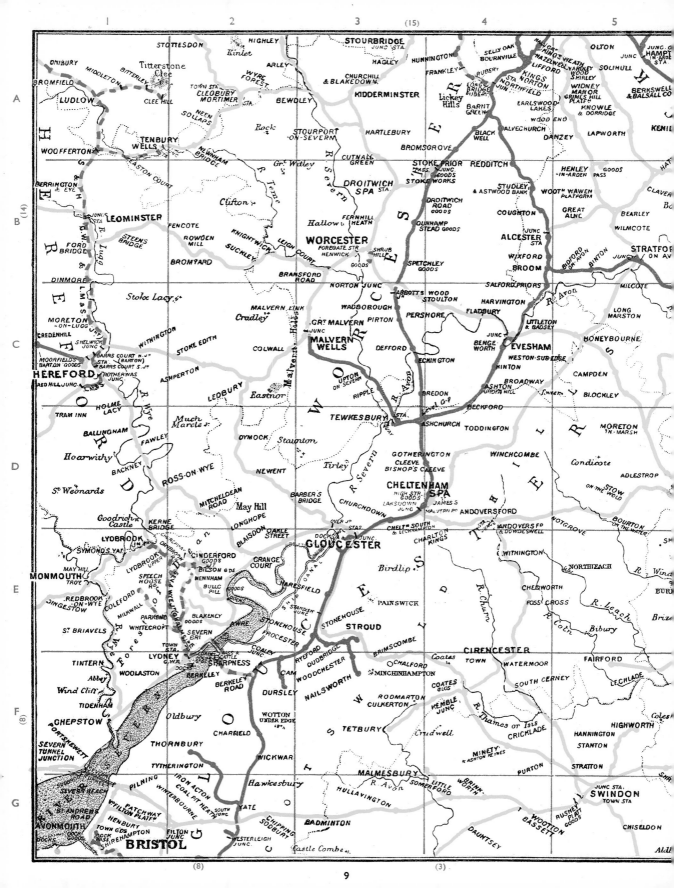

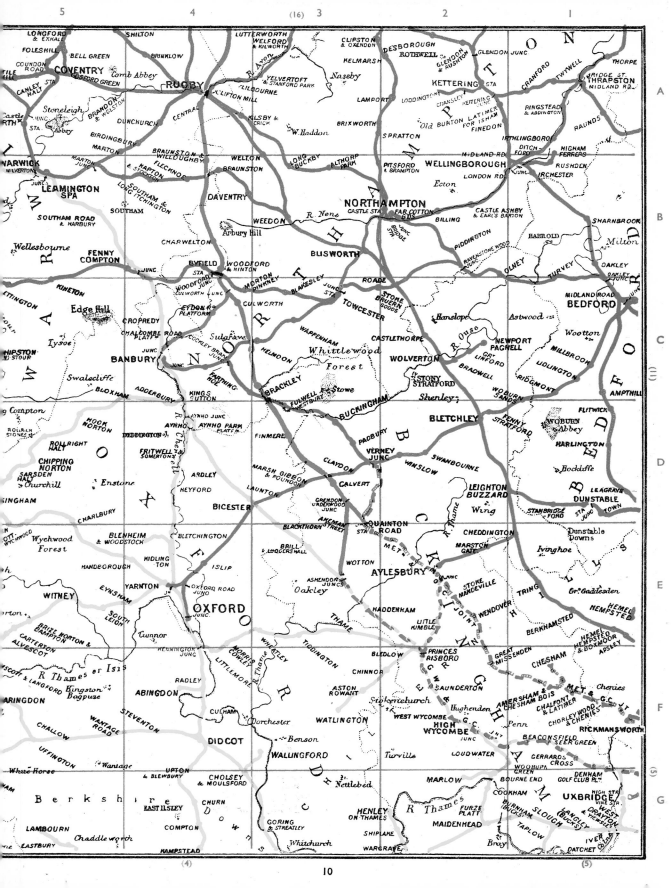

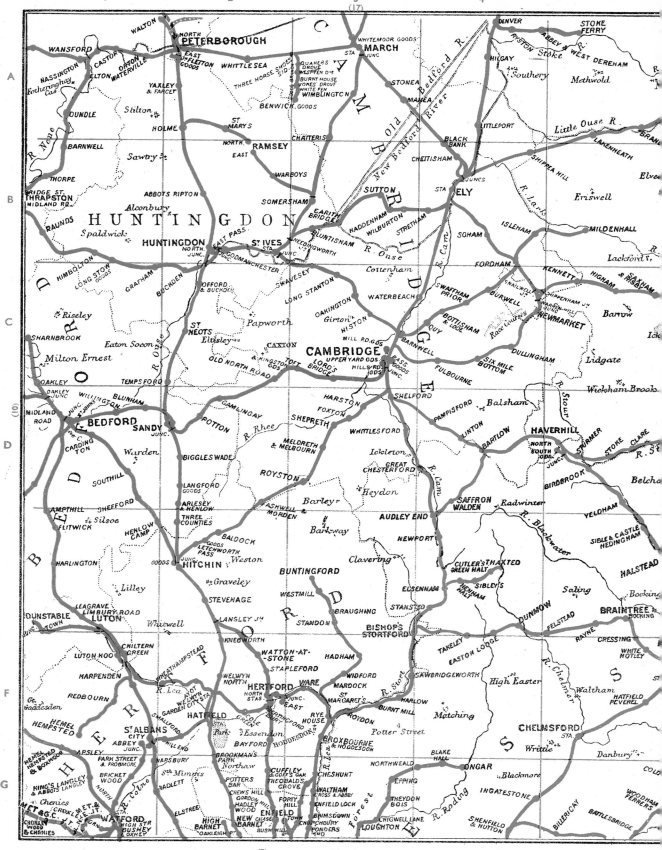

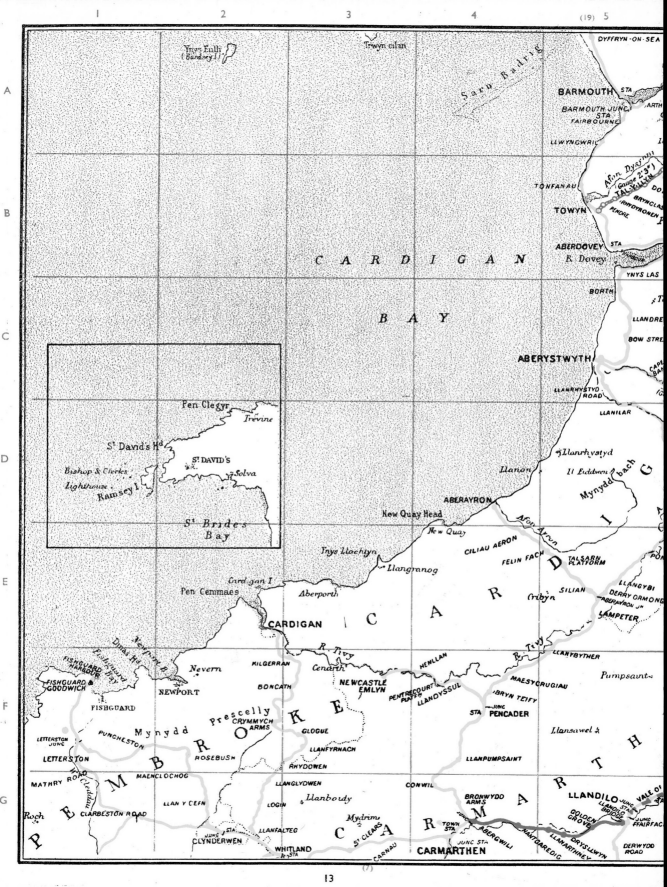

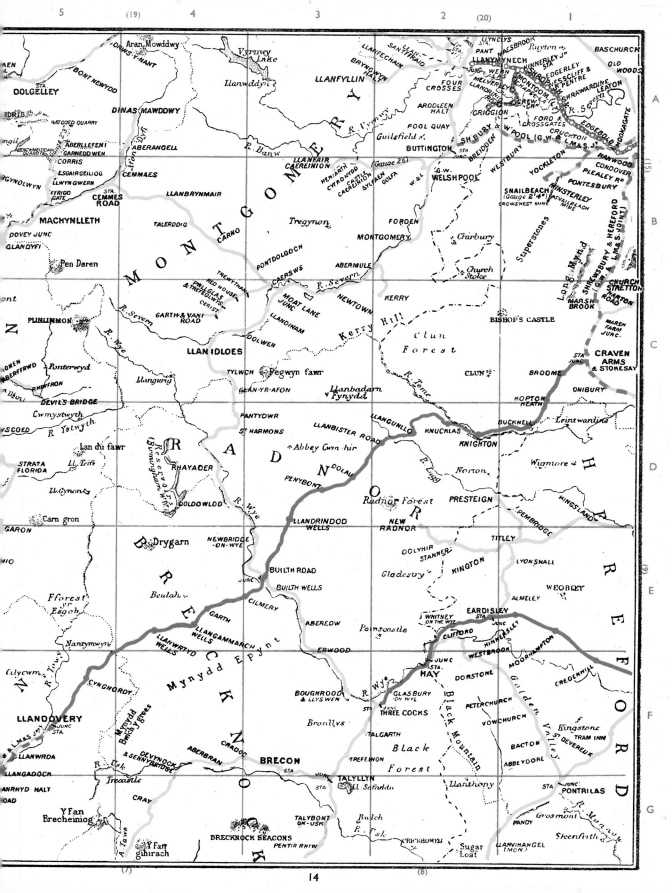

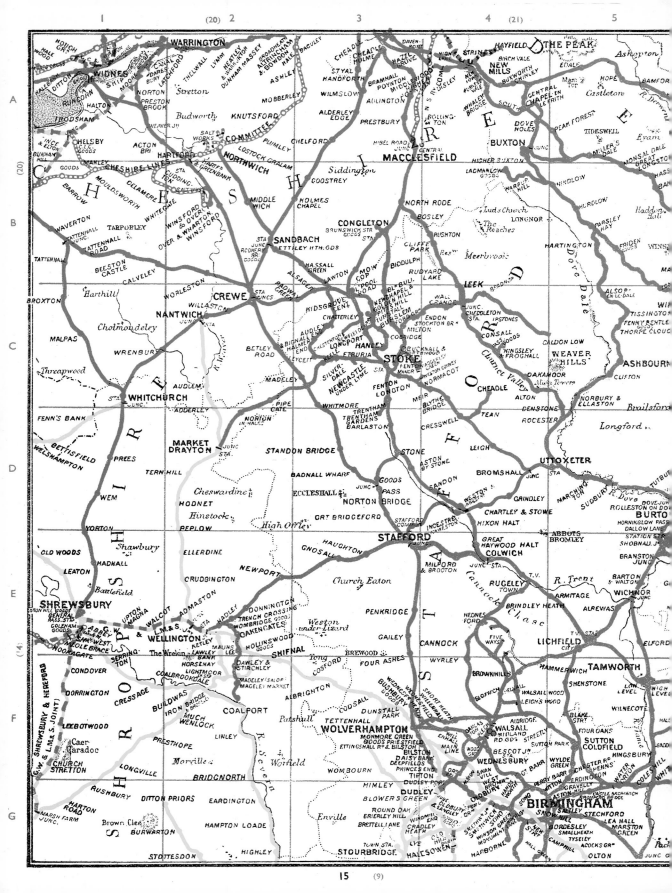

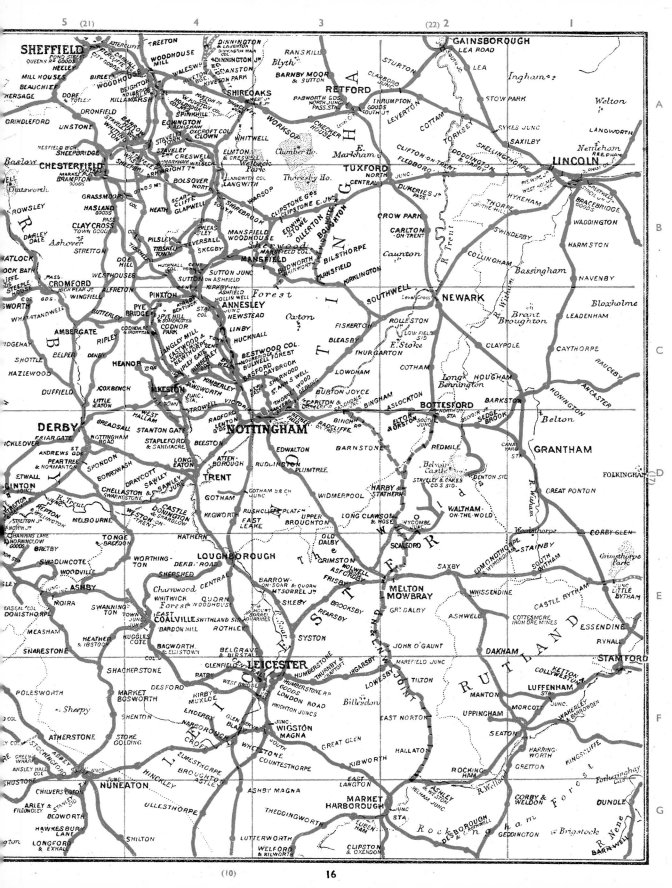

A

B

C

D

E

F

G

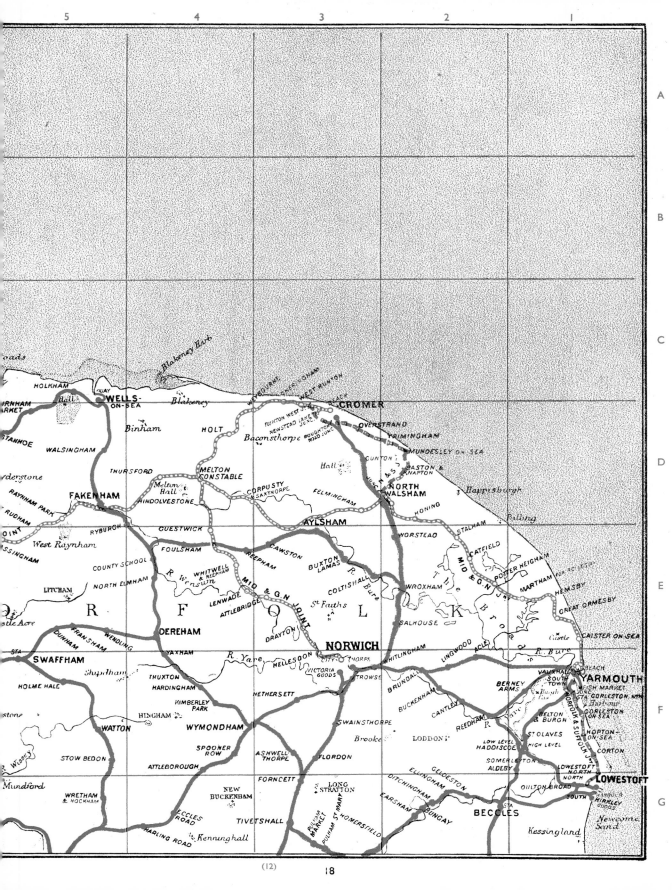

Map grid columns: 1 2 3 4 5

Row labels: A B C D E F G

Inset map (top left):

The Skerries
Cemaes
Carmel Hd
Church B
Llanfaethlu
Holyhead Bay
HOLYHEAD
PIER
South Stack
STA.
Bodedern
VALLEY
HOLY ISLD
RHOSNEIGR

Main map:

Cemaes
Bull B.
Pt Lynus
AMLWCH
RHOSGOCH
Penysarn
Dulas B.
Moelfre I.
Llanfaethlu
LLANERCHYMEDD
Bodedern
REDWHARF BAY & BENLLECH
Redwharf B.
Puffin I.
Great Ormes Head
LLANDUDNO
Conway Bay
LLANDUDNO JN.
COLWYN BAY
OLD COLWYN
TOWYD PIER
RHYL
STA.
PRESTATYN
TALAC
MELIDEN
DYSERTH
LLANGWYLLOG
PENTRAETH
ANGLESEY
LLANGEFNI
BEAUMARIS
Beaumaris Bay
CONWAY
GLAN CONWAY
LLANDULAS
ABERGELE
RHUDDLAN
StASAPH
RHOSNEIGR
TY CROES
HOLLAND ARMS
LLANFAIR
PORT PENRHYN
Penrhyn Cas.
PENMAEN-MAWR
LLANFAIR-FECHAN
Bettws y Abergele
R. Elwy
TREFNANT
BODORGAN
CAERWEN
Britannia Bri.
MENAI BRI.
BANGOR
TREBORTH
FELIN HEN
ABER
R. Conway
TALY CAFN & EGLWYS BACH
Llanfair-Talhaiarn
DENBIGH
STA.
JUNC.
STA.
Abertfraw
Menai Strait
PORT DINORWIC
TREGARTH
BETHESDA
Nant Frarcon
DOLGARROG
Llansannan
LLANRHAIADR
Llanddwyn I.
GRIFFITH'S CROSSING
Carnedd Llewelyn
Llyn Owlyd
LLANRWST & TREFRIW
RHEWL
CAERNARVON
PONTRHYTHALLT
CWM-Y-GLO
Ll. Padarn
N
Llyn Owlyd
D
E
N
RUTH
Aber Menai
LLANBERIS
Llyn Owen
Mynydd Hiraethog
BETTWS-Y-COED
EYAR
CAERNARVON
DINAS
LLANWNDA
SNOWDON
PASS
Y Glydr
Capel Curig
Clocaenog
B
BAY
GROESLON
Moel Siabod
R. Alwen
NANT CLWYD
PENYGROES
Llyn Cwellyn
SLATE QUARRIES
SNOWDON
Ll. Llydaw
PONT-Y-PANT
Pentre Voelas
DERWEN
Clynnog
NANTLLE
Nant Gwynant
Ll. Gwynant
DOLWYDDELEN
R. Alwen
Truyntal
Nant Gwynant
Ll. Dinas
ROMAN BRIDGE
Cerrig-y-Druidion
GWYDDELWERN
Yr Eifl
PANT GLAS
Pass of Aberglaslyn
BLAENAU FESTINIOG
Llyn Conway
R. Conway
CORWEN
JUNC.
STA.
BRYNKIR
STA.
STA.
CYNWYD
YNYS
PORTMADOC
MINFFORDD
MANOD
WERN, GOODS
CRICCIETH
FESTINIOG
ARENIG
FRONGOCH
R. Dee
LLANDRILLO
LLANGYBI
CHWILOG
STA.
PENRHYNDEUDRAETH
CWM PRYSOR
LLANUWCHLLYN
ABERERCH
AFON WEN
PENYCHAIN
TALSARNAU
MAENTWROG ROAD
Aremig
BALA
LLANDDERFEL
PWLLHELI
Traeth Mawr
TRAWSFYNYDD
Bala Lake
BALA JUNC.
E
Cader
Llanbedrog
HARLECH
Rhinog fawr
A. Llio
N
Pistyll
PEDAIR FFORDO
PENYBONTFAWR
St Tudwal's Is
LLANBEDR & PENSARN
Mochras
A. Mawddach
Rhaiadr
Rhobell fawr
I
O
B
LLANGYNOG
M
E
R
DYFFRYN-ON-SEA
Aran Benllyn
Aran Mowddwy
DRWS-Y-NANT
LLANUWCHLLYN
Vyrnwy Lake
H

(13)   19   (14)

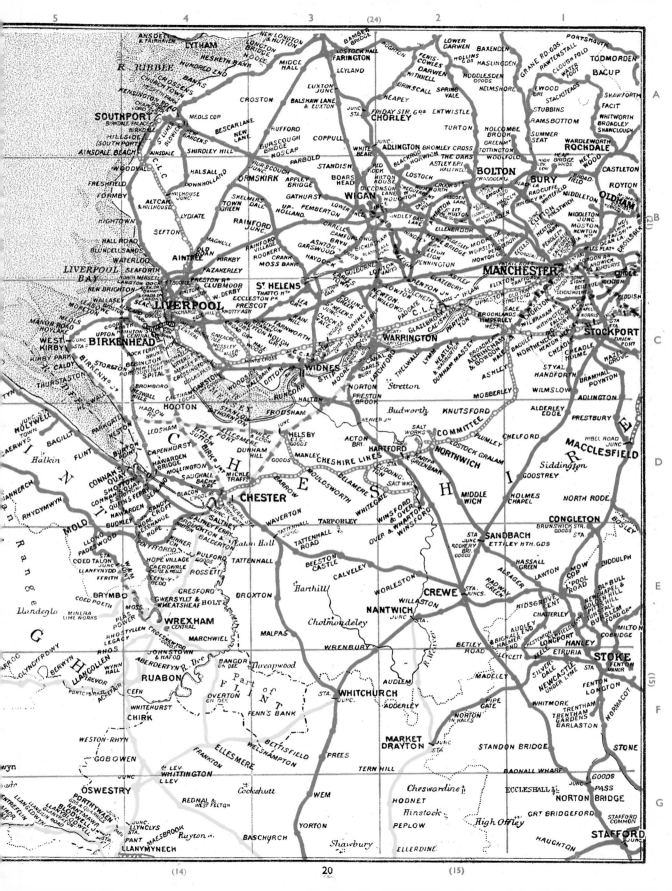

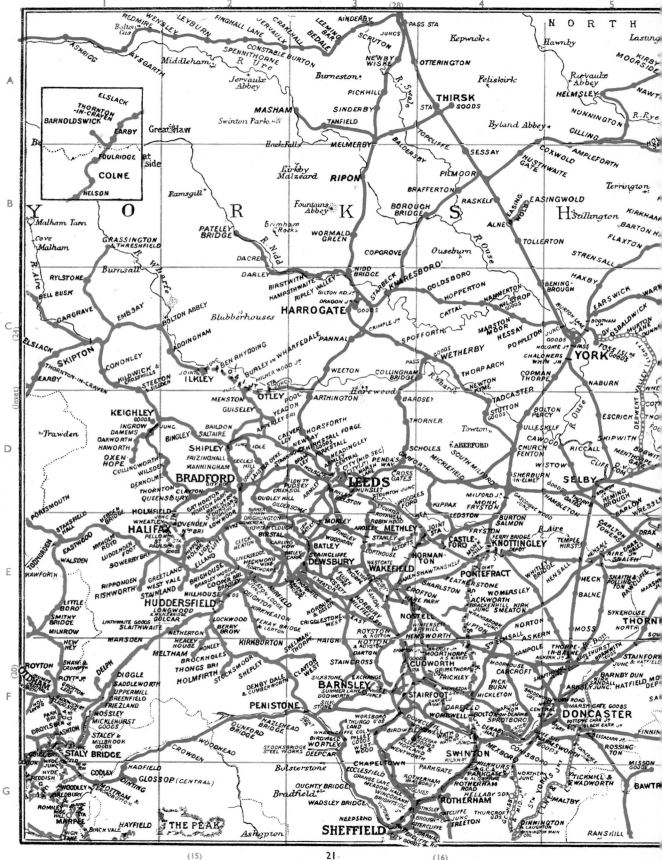

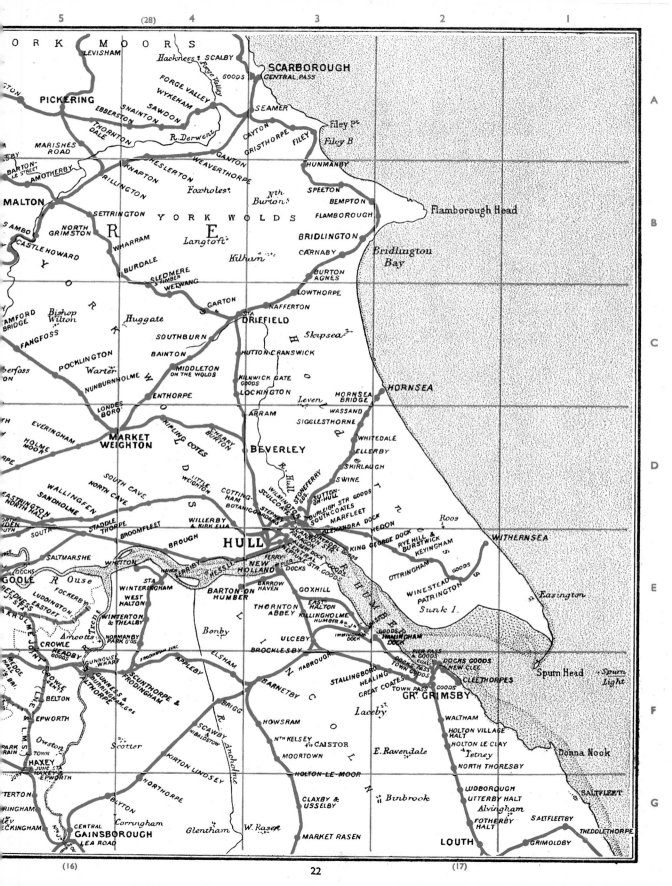

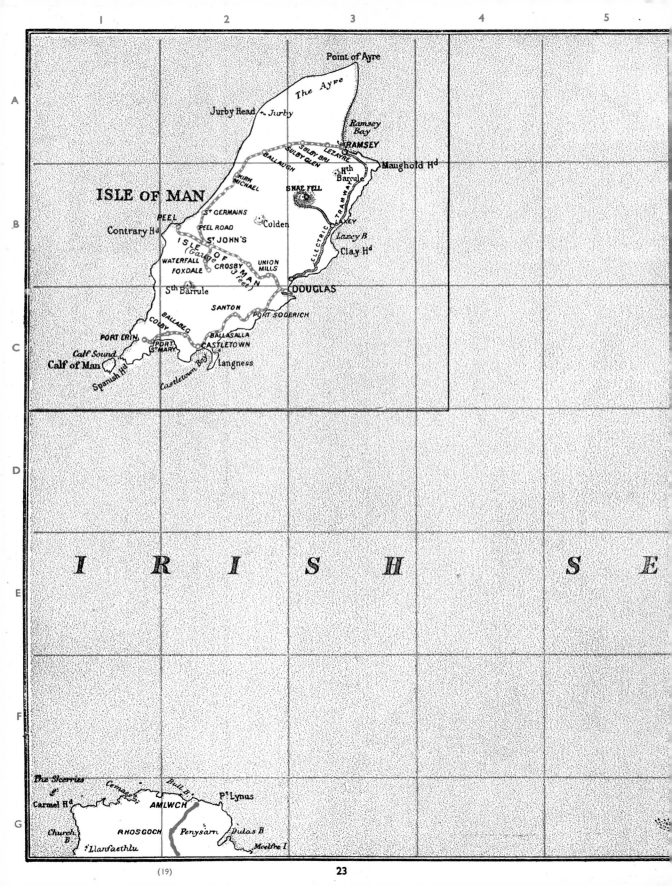

ISLE OF MAN

Point of Ayre

The Ayre

Jurby Head ~ Jurby

Ramsey Bay

S.BLBY BRI   LEZAYRE   RAMSEY

SULBY GLEN

BALLAUGH   Nth Barrule   Maughold Hd

KIRK MICHAEL   SNAE FELL

ST GERMAINS   Colden

PEEL   PEEL ROAD   LAXEY

Contrary Hd   ST JOHN'S   Laxey B

ISLE OF MAN   Clay Hd

(3 feet)

WATERFALL   CROSBY   UNION MILLS

FOXDALE

Sth Barrule   DOUGLAS

SANTON   PORT SODERICH

BALLABEG

COLBY   BALLASALLA

PORT ERIN   PORT St MARY   CASTLETOWN

Calf Sound   Langness

Calf of Man   Spanish Hd   Castletown Bay

I R I S H   S E

The Skerries   Bull B.   Pt Lynus

Carmel Hd   Cemaes   AMLWCH

Church B.   RHOSGOCH   Penysarn   Dulas B.

Llanfaethlu   Moelfre I.

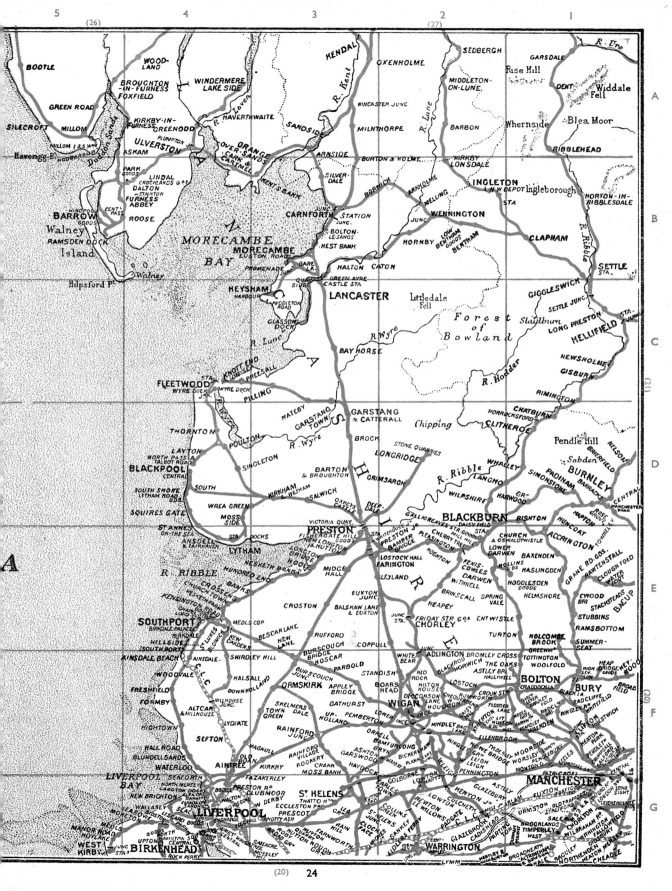

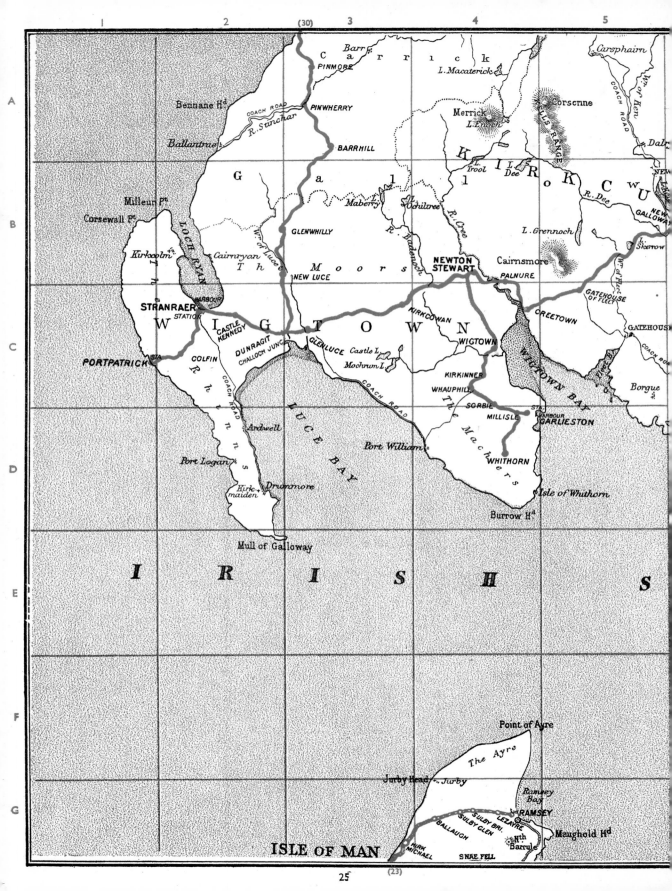

A

B

C

D

E

F

G

Carsphairn

Barr.

PINMORE

Carrick

L. Macaterick

Bennane Hd

COACH ROAD

PINWHERRY

Merrick

Corscrine

R. Stinchar

Ballantrae

BARRHILL

L. Enoch

KELLS RANGE

Wr of Ken

COACH ROAD

Dalr

Milleur Pt

Corsewall Pt

G

a

l

l

L. Trool

L. Dee

R. Kirko

K

C

W

U

Maberry

Ochiltree

R. Cree

NEW

GALLOWAY

Kirkcolm

LOCH RYAN

Cairnryan

GLENWHILLY

R. Bladenoch

L. Grennoch

L. Skerrow

The

Wr of Luce

Moors

NEW LUCE

NEWTON

STEWART

Cairnsmore

Wr of Fleet

STRANRAER

HARBOUR

STATION

PALNURE

GATEHOUSE

OF FLEET

CREETOWN

W

I

G

T

O

W

N

KIRKCOWAN

CASTLE

KENNEDY

DUNRAGIT

CHALLOCH JUNC

GLENLUCE

Castle L.

WIGTOWN

WIGTOWN BAY

GATEHOUSE

PORTPATRICK

STA

COLFIN

Mochrum L.

KIRKINNER

Borgue

COACH ROAD

Rhu

Ardwell

LUCE BAY

WHAUPHILL

The

Machers

SORBIE

MILLISLE

STA

HARBOUR

GARLIESTON

Port Logan

Drummore

COACH ROAD

Port William

WHITHORN

ns

Kirk-

maiden

Isle of Whithorn

Burrow Hd

Mull of Galloway

I R I S H

S

Point of Ayre

The Ayre

Jurby Head

Jurby

Ramsey

Bay

RAMSEY

LEZAYRE

SULBY BRI.

SULBY GLEN

BALLAUGH

Maughold Hd

KIRK

MICHAEL

Nth

Barrule

SNAE FELL

ISLE OF MAN

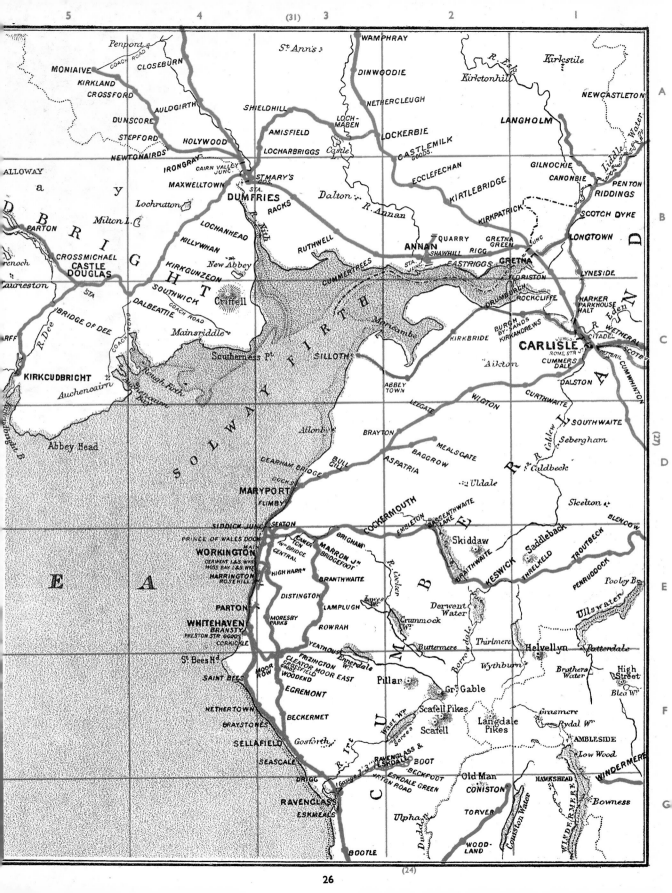

A
B
(27)
C
D
E
F
G

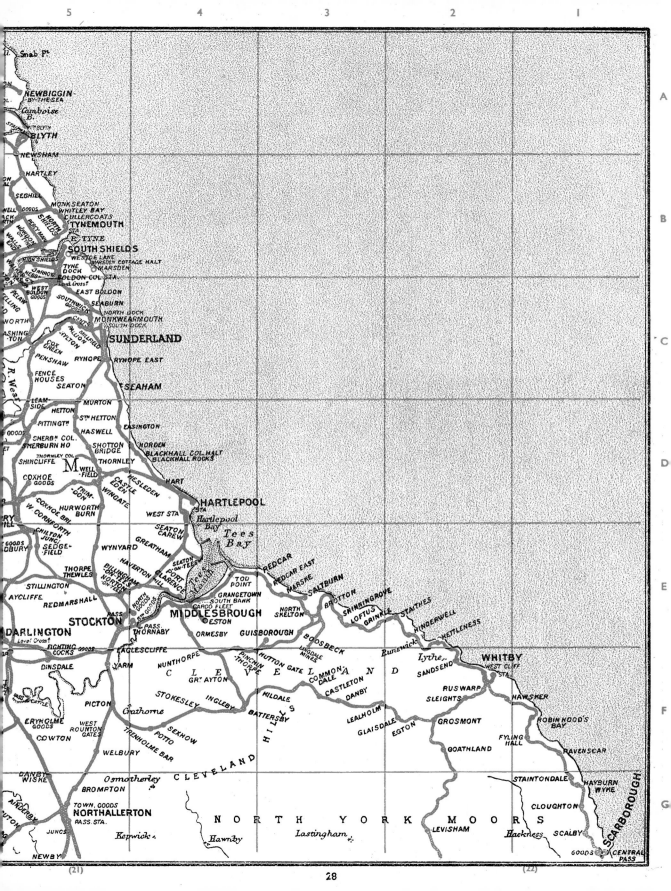

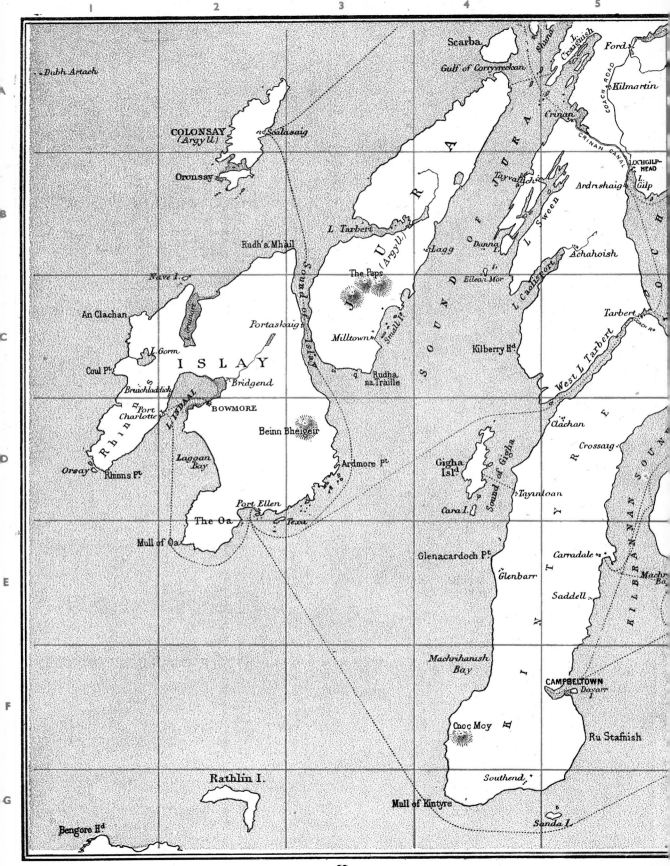

. Dubh Artach

COLONSAY
(Argyll)
↝ Scalasaig

Oronsay

Scarba
Gulf of Corryyreckan

L. Craignish
Ford

COACH ROAD
Kilmartin

Crinan

J U R A

Tayvallich

CRINAN CANAL

Ardrishaig

LOCHGILP-
HEAD
L. Gilp

Rudh'a Mhail

L. Tarbert

JURA
(Argyll)

Lagg
Danna I.

L. Sween

Achahoish

Nave I.

The Paps

Eilean Mor

L. Caolisport

Tarbert

COACH RD

An Clachan

Primaur

Portaskaig

Milltown

Small I.

Rudha
na Traille

Kilberry Hd

West L. Tarbert

I S L A Y

L. Gorm

Coul Pt

Bridgend

Bruichladdich

LINDAAL

BOWMORE

Beinn Bheigeir

Clachan

Port
Charlotte

Rhinns

Laggan
Bay

Ardmore Pt

Gigha
Isld

Sound of Gigha

Crossaig

Orsay

Rhinns Pt

Port Ellen

Texa

The Oa

Cara I.

Taynloan

Mull of Oa

Glenacardoch Pt

Carradale

Machr
Ba

Glenbarr

Saddell

KILBRANNAN SOUND

Machrihanish
Bay

CAMPBELTOWN
Davaar
I

Cnoc Moy

Ru Stafnish

Rathlin I.

Southend

Mull of Kintyre

Sanda I.

Bengore Hd

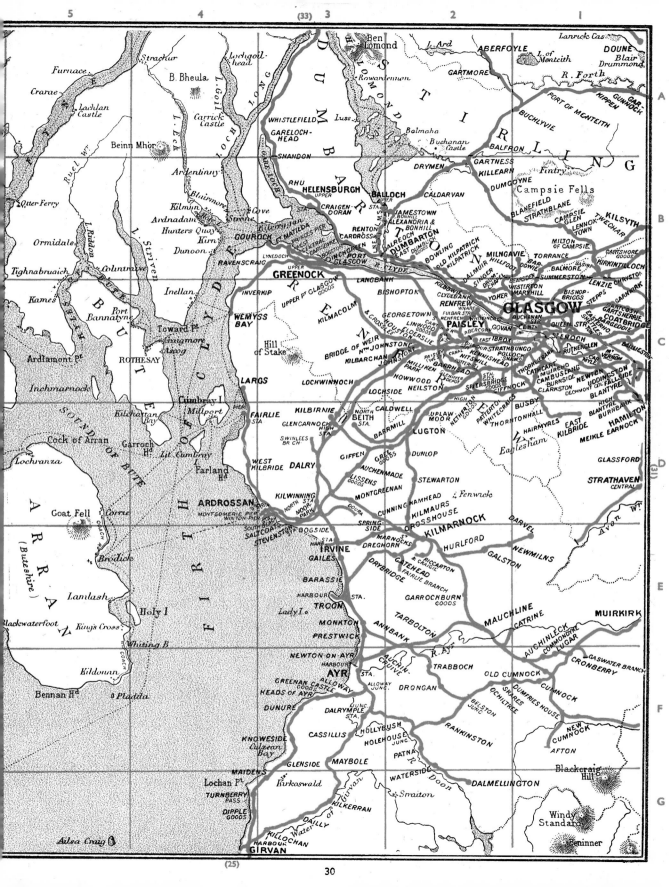

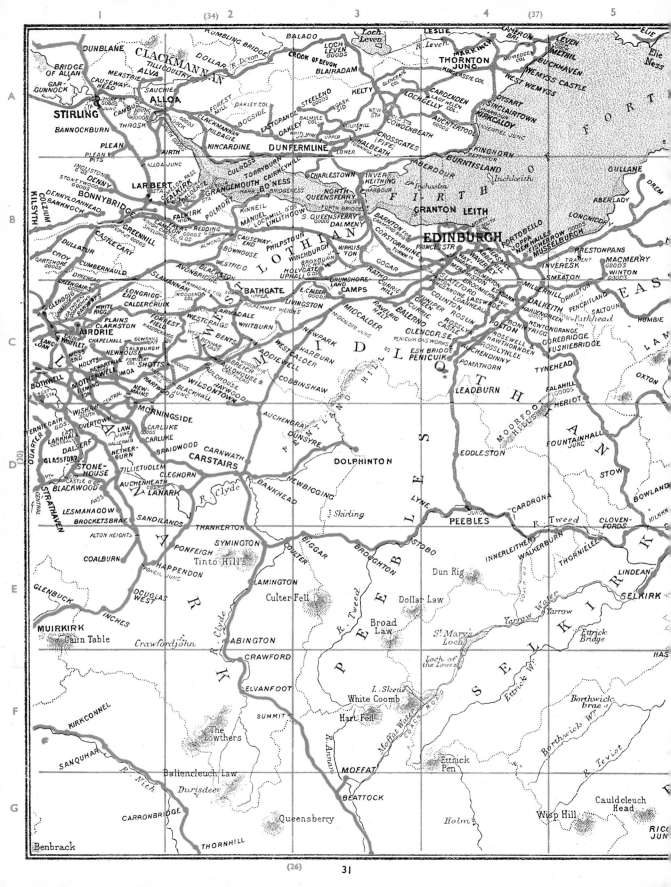

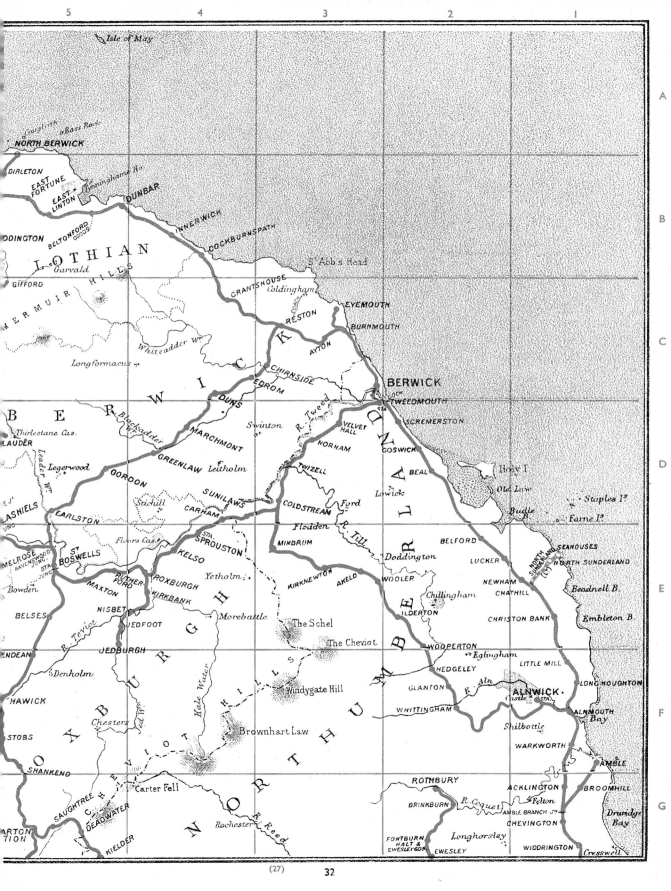

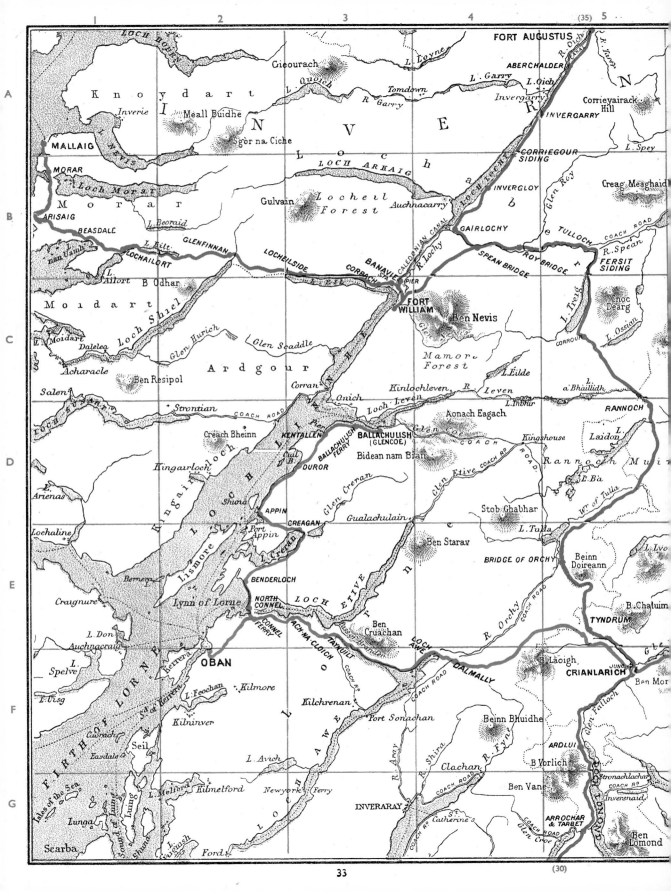

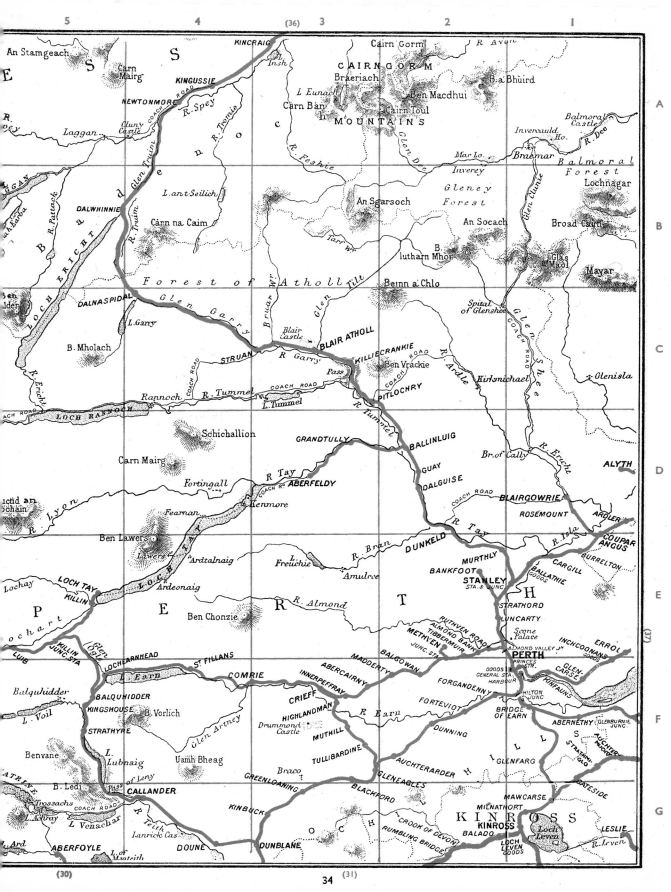

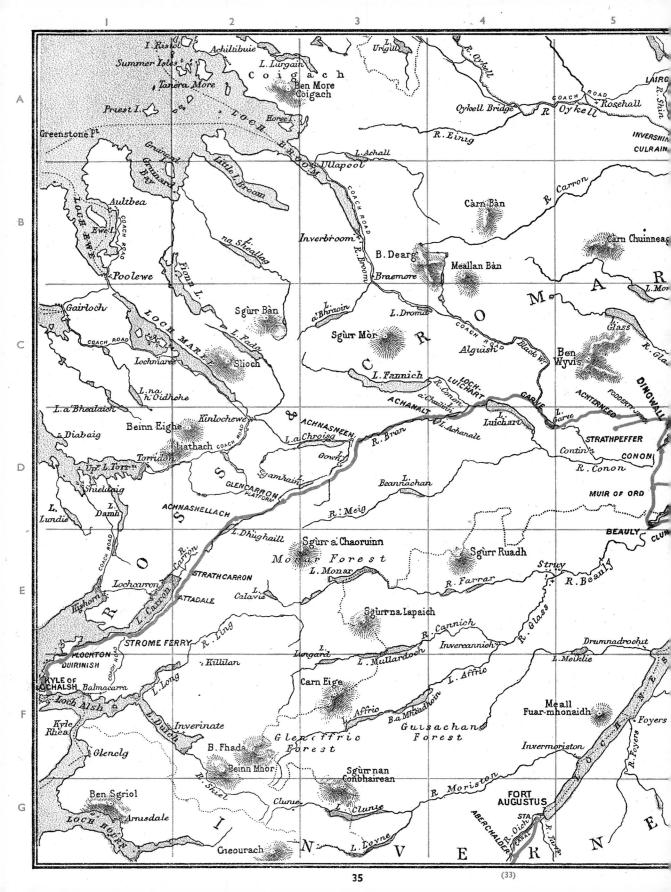

(33)

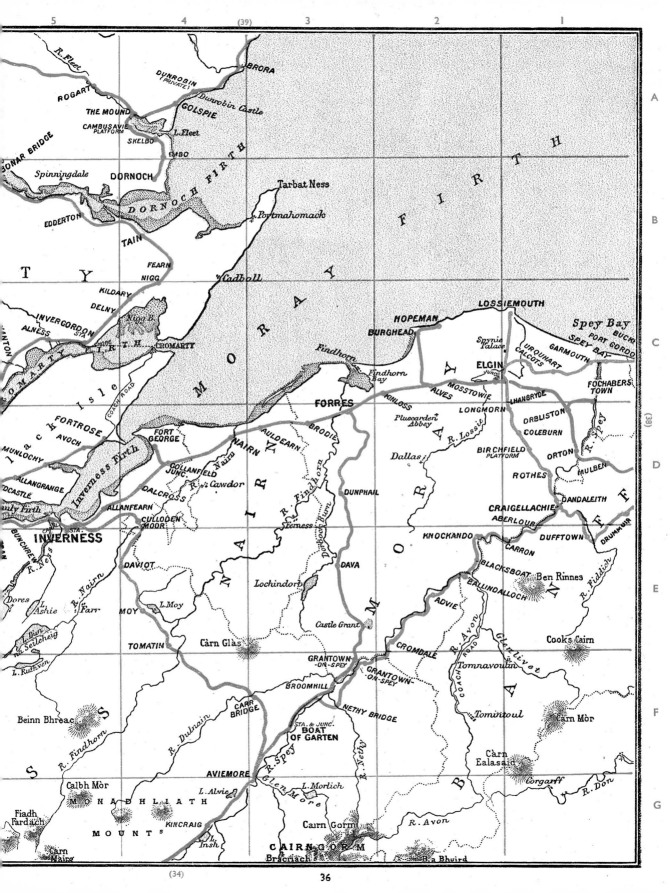

R. Fleet
ROGART
BRORA
DUNROBIN (PRIVATE)
Dunrobin Castle
THE MOUND
GOLSPIE
CAMBUSAVIE PLATFORM
SKELBO
L. Fleet
EMBO
BONAR BRIDGE
Spinningdale
DORNOCH
DORNOCH FIRTH
Tarbat Ness
EDDERTON
Portmahomack
TAIN
A

MORAY FIRTH

TY
Y
FEARN
NIGG
Cadboll
KILDARY
DELNY
INVERGORDON STA.
ALNESS
Nigg B.
LOSSIEMOUTH
HOPEMAN
BURGHEAD
Spynie Palace
URQUHART
CALCOTS
Spey Bay
PORT GORDON
GARMOUTH
BUCHI
SPEY BAY
CROMARTY FIRTH
CROMARTY
Findhorn
ELGIN JUNC.
Y
ALVES
MOSSTOWIE
LONGMORN
LHANBRYDE
FOCHABERS TOWN
Black Isle
COACH ROAD
Findhorn Bay
FORRES
KINLOSS
Pluscarden Abbey
R. Lossie
ORBLISTON
COLEBURN
R. Spey
(38)
FORTROSE
AVOCH
FORT GEORGE
BRODIE
AULDEARN
Dallas
BIRCHFIELD PLATFORM
ORTON
MULBEN
MUNLOCHY
NAIRN
COLLANFIELD JUNC.
Nairn
R. Cawdor
DUNPHAIL
ROTHES
DANDALEITH
ALLANGRANGE
DALCROSS
R. Findhorn
CRAIGELLACHIE
ABERLOUR
F
EDCASTLE
ALLANFEARN
CULLODEN MOOR
Ferness
DUFFTOWN
DRUMMUIR
uly Firth
STA.
INVERNESS
DAVIOT
Dorbock Burn
DAVA
KNOCKANDO
CARRON
BLACKSBOAT
Ben Rinnes
R. Fiddich
BUNCHREW
R. Ness
Dores
L. Ashie
R. Nairn
R. Farr
MOY
L. Moy
Lochindorb
Castle Grant
ADVIE
CROMDALE
R. Avon
BALLINDALLOCH
Glenlivet
Cooks Cairn
E
L. Dun nc Seilcheig
L. Ruthven
TOMATIN
Càrn Glas
GRANTOWN-ON-SPEY
GRANTOWN-ON-SPEY
Tomnavoulin
Càrn Mòr
MONADHLIATH
BROOMHILL
NETHY BRIDGE
COACH ROAD
Tomintoul
Beinn Bhreac
CARR BRIDGE
STA. & JUNC.
BOAT OF GARTEN
R. Nethy
Càrn Ealasaid
Corgarff
R. Don
Calbh Mòr
AVIEMORE
R. Spey
L. Alvie
Glenmore
L. Morlich
R. Avon
Fiadh Fardach
MOUNTs
L. Inch
CAIRNGORM
Cairn Gorm
Càrn Maira
Bracriach
B a Bhuird

INDEX

TO

STATIONS

SHOWN ON THESE MAPS

(Explanation Page III)

ABBEY—BELMONT

A

Abbey (St. Albans), L.M.S., 11, F1.
• Abbey (Shrewsbury), S.M., 15, E1.
•Abbey & W. Dereham, L.N.E.R., 17, F5.
•Abbeydore, G.W.R., 14, F1.
Abbeyhill, L.N.E.R., 31, B4.
Abbey St.(Nuneaton),L.M.S., 16, F5.
Abbey Town, L.N.E.R., 26, C2.
Abbey Wood, S.R., 5, B4.
Abbotsbury, G.W.R., 3, F2.
Abbot's Langley, see King's Langley.
Abbots Ripton, L.N.E.R.,11, B2.
Abbots Wood Jc., L.M.S./G.W.R., 9, C3.
Aber, L.M.S., 19, D3.
Aberaman, G.W.R., 8, B5.
•Aberangell, G.W.R., 14, A4.
Aberavon, G.W.R., 7, B4.
Aberayron, G.W.R., 13, D4.
Aberayron Jc., G.W.R., 13, E5.
Aberbargoed (Mon.), G.W.R., 8, B4.
Aberbeeg, G.W.R., 8, B4.
Aberbran Halt, G.W.R., 14, F4.
Abercairny, L.M.S., 34, F3.
Abercanaid, G.W.R., 8, B5.
Abercarn, G.W.R., 8, B4.
§Aberchalder, L.N.E.R., 33, A5.
Abercorn (Paisley), L.M.S., 30, C2.
•Abercrave, G.W.R., 7, A5.
Abercwmeiddaw Quarry, Corris, 14, A5.
Abercynon, G.W.R., 8, B5.
Aberdare, G.W.R., 8, B5.
Aberdeen, L.N.E.R./L.M.S., 38, G2.
•Aberderfyn, G.W.R., 20, F4.
Aberdour, L.N.E.R., 31, B4.
Aberdovey, G.W.R., 13, B5.
Aberdylais, G.W.R., 7, B4.
Aberedw, G.W.R., 14, E3.
Abererch, G.W.R., 19, F1.
Aberfan, G.W.R., 8, B5.
Aberfeldy, L.M.S., 34, D3.
•Aberffrwd, V.R., 14, C5.
Aberfoyle, L.N.E.R., 30, A2.
Abergavenny, G.W.R. & L.M.S., 8, A3.
Abergavenny Jc., G.W.R./L.M.S., 8, A3.
Abergele, L.M.S., 19, D4.
Abergwili, L.M.S., 13, G4.
Abergwynfi, G.W.R., 7, B5.
•Abergynolwyn, Tal., 13, B5.
•Aberlady, L.N.E.R., 31, B5.
•Aberllefeni, Corris, 14, A5.
Aberlour, L.N.E.R., 36, D1.
Abermule, G.W.R., 14, B3.
Abernant, G.W.R., 8, A5.
Abersychan, G.W.R., 8, A3.
•Abersychan & Talywain, L.M.S./G.W.R., 8, A4.
Aberthaw, G.W.R., 8, D5.
Abertillery, G.W.R., 8, B4.
Abertridwr, G.W.R., 8, B4.
Aberystwyth, G.W.R. & •V.R., 13, C5.
Abingdon, G.W.R., 10, F4.
Abington, L.M.S., 31, E2.
Aboyne, L.N.E.R., 37, A2.
Aby, L.N.E.R., 17, A3.
Accrington, L.M.S., 24, E1.
Achanalt, L.M.S., 35, D4.
Ach-na-cloich, L.M.S., 33, E3.
Achnasheen, L.M.S., 35, D3.
Achnashellach, L.M.S., 35, D2.
Achterneed, L.M.S., 35, D5.
Acklington, L.N.E.R., 32, B1.
Ackworth, S.K., 21, E4.
Acle, L.N.E.R., 18, F2.
Acocks Green, G.W.R., 15, G5.
Acrefair, G.W.R., 20, F5.
Acton, G.W.R. & L.M.S., 5, B3.
:Acton Bridge, L.M.S., 20, D3.
Adderbury, G.W.R., 10, D4.
Adderley (Salop),G.W.R., 15 D2.
Addiewell, L.M.S. & •L.N.E.R., 31, C2.
Addingham, L.M.S., 21, C2.
Addington (Northants), see Ringstead.
Addiscombe, S.R., 5, B3.
Addlestone, S.R., 5, C2.
Adisham, S.R., 6, C2.
Adlestrop, G.W.R., 9, D5.
Adlington (Cheshire), L.M.S., 15, A3.
Adlington (Lancs), L.M.S., 20, A3.
Admaston, G.W.R./L.M.S., 15, E2.
Advie, L.N.E.R., 36, E2.
Afon Wen, G.W.R./L.M.S., 19, F1.
Afton, L.M.S., 30, F1.
Ainderby, L.N.E.R., 28, G5.
Ainsdale, L.M.S., 20, A4.
Ainsdale Beach, C.L.C., 20, A4.
Aintree, L.M.S. & C.L.C., 20, B4.
Airdrie, L.N.E.R. & •L.M.S., 31, C1.
Aire Jc., L.N.E.R., 21, E5.
Airmyn & Rawcliffe, L.N.E.R., 21, E5.
Airth, L.M.S., 31, A2.
•Akeld, L.N.E.R., 32, E3.
•Akeman St., L.N.E.R., 10, E3.
Albany Park, S.R., 5, B4.
•Albert Dock (Hull),L.N.E.R., 22, E3.
Albion, L.M.S., 15, F4.
Albion Coll., G.W.R., 8, B5.
Albrighton, G.W.R., 15, F3.
Albury, see Chilworth.
Alcester, L.M.S./•G.W.R., 9, B4.
Aldeburgh, L.N.E.R., 12, C1.
Aldeby, L.N.E.R., 18, F1.
Alderbury Jc., S.R., 4, D5.
Alderley Edge, L.M.S., 15, A3.
Aldermaston, G.W.R., 4, A3.
Aldershot, S.R., 4, B1.
Aldridge, L.M.S., 15, F4.
Aldrington Halt, S.R., 5, F3.
Aldwarke, see Parkgate, L.N.E.R.
•Alexandra Dock (Hull), L.N.E.R., 22, E3.
Alexandra Dock (Liverpool), L.M.S., 20, C4.
Alexandra Docks (Newport), G.W.R., 8, C3.
Alexandria & Bonhill, L.M.S./L.N.E.R., 30, B3.
Alford (Aberdeen), L.N.E.R., 38, F4.
Alford Town (Lincs.), L.N.E.R., 17, B3.
Alfreton, L.M.S., 16, C4.
Algarkirk, L.N.E.R., 17, D2.
Allanfearn, L.M.S., 36, D5.
Allangrange, L.M.S., 36, D5.
•Allendale, L.N.E.R., 27, C3.
Allerton, L.M.S. & C.L.C., 20, C4.
Allhallows-on-Sea, S.R., 6, B5.
Alloa, L.N.E.R./L.M.S., 31, A2.
Alloa (Goods), L.M.S., 31, A2.
Alloa Jc., L.M.S., 31, B1.
•Alloway, L.M.S., 30, F3.
§Almeley, G.W.R., 14, E1.
Almondbank, L.M.S., 34, E2.
Almond Jc., L.N.E.R., 31, B2.
Almond Valley Jc., L.M.S., 34, E2.
Alne, L.N.E.R., 21, B4.
Alness, L.M.S., 36, C5.
Alnmouth, L.N.E.R., 32, F1.
Alnwick, L.N.E.R., 32, F1.
Alresford (Essex), L.N.E.R., 12, E4.
Alresford (Hants.) S.R., 4, C3.
Alrewas, L.M.S., 15, E5.
Alsager, L.M.S., 15, C3.
Alsop-en-le-Dale, L.M.S., 15, C5.
Alston, L.N.E.R., 27, D2.
Altcar & Hillhouse, C.L.C., 20, B4.
Althorne, L.N.E.R., 12, G5.
Althorpe, L.N.E.R., 22, F5.
Althorp Park, L.M.S., 10, B3.
Altnabreac, L.M.S., 39, D2.
Altofts, L.M.S., 21, E4.
Alton (Hants.), S.R., 4, C2.
Alton (Staffs.), L.M.S., 15, C4.
•Alton Heights (Lanark), L.M.S., 31, E1.
Altrincham & Bowdon, M.S.J.A./C.L.C., 20, C2.
Alva, L.N.E.R., 31, A1.
Alvechurch, L.M.S., 9, A4.
Alverstone (I.W.), S.R., 4, F3.
Alverthorpe, L.N.E.R., 21, E3.
Alves, L.M.S., 36, C2.
Alvescot, G.W.R., 10, E5.
Alyth (Perth), L.M.S., 37, D1.
Alyth Jc., (Angus), L.M.S., 37, D1.
Ambergate, L.M.S., 16, C5.
Amberley, S.R., 5 F1.
•Amble, L.N.E.R., 32, F1.
Amble Branch Jc., L.N.E.R., 32, G1.
Amersham & Chesham Bois, L.N.E.R./L.P.T.B., 10, F1.
Amesbury, S.R., 4, C5.
•Amesley, L.N.E.R., 27, C5.
Amisfield, L.M.S., 26, A3.
Amlwch, L.M.S., 19, C1.
Ammanford, G.W.R., 7, A4.
•Amotherby, L.N.E.R., 22, B5.
Ampleforth, L.N.E.R., 21 B5.
Ampthill, L.M.S., 10, C1.
Ancaster, L.N.E.R., 16, C1.
Andover Jc., S.R., 4, C4.
,, Town, S.R., 4, C4.
Andoversford, G.W.R., 9, D4.
Andoversford & Dowdeswell, G.W.R., 9, D4.
Anfield, see Walton (Lancs.).
Angel Road, L.N.E.R., 5, A3.
Angerton, L.N.E.R., 27, A4.
Angmering, S.R., 5, F2.
Annan, L.M.S., 26, B2.
Annan Quarry, L.M.S., 26, B2.
Annbank, L.M.S., 26, E2.
Annesley, L.M.S. & •L.N.E.R., 16, C4.
Annfield Plain, L.N.E.R., 27, C5.
Annitsford, L.N.E.R., 27, B5.
Ansdell & Fairhaven, L.M.S., 24, E4.
Ansley Hall Coll., L.M.S., 16, F5.
•Anston, L.M.S./L.N.E.R., 16, A4.
Anstruther, L.N.E.R., 37, G3.
Apperley Bridge, L.M.S., 21, D2.
Appin, L.M.S., 33, D2.
Appleby (Lincs.), L.N.E.R., 22, F4.
Appleby (Westmorland), L.M.S. & L.N.E.R., 27, E2.
Appledore (Kent), S.R., 6, E4.
Applehurst Jc., L.N.E.R., 21, F5.
Appleton, L.M.S. 20, C3.
Appley Bridge, L.M.S., 20, B3.
Apsley, L.M.S., 10, E1.
•Arbirlot, D.A., 37, D3.
Arbroath, D.A., 37, D3.
Arddleen Halt, G.W.R., 14, A2.
Ardingly, S.R., 5, E3.
Ardleigh, L.N.E.R., 12, E4.
Ardler, L.M.S., 37, D1.
Ardley, G.W.R., 10, D4.
Ardlui, L.N.E.R., 33, F5.
Ardrossan, L.M.S., 30, D3.
Ardsley, L.N.E.R., 21, E3.
Ardwick, L.N.E.R., 20, B1.
Arenig, G.W.R., 19, F4.
Argoed, L.M.S., 8, B4.
Arisaig, L.N.E.R., 33, B1.
Arkholme, L.M.S., 24, B2.
Arksey, L.N.E.R., 21, F5.
Arkwright Town, L.N.E.R., 16, B4.
Arlesey & Henlow, L.N.E.R., 11, D2.
Arley (Worcs.), G.W.R., 9, A2.
Arley & Fillongley, L.M.S., 16, G5.
Armadale, L.N.E.R., 31, C2.
Armadale Colliery, L.N.E.R., 31, C2.
Armathwaite, L.M.S., 27, D1.
Armitage, L.M.S., 15, E5.
Armley, L.N.E.R./L.M.S. & L.M.S., 21, D3.
Arnage, L.N.E.R., 38, E2.
Arnside, L.M.S., 24, A3.
Arpley (Warrington), L.M.S., 20, C2.
Arram, L.N.E.R., 22, D3.
Arrochar&Tarbet, L.N.E.R., 33, G5.
Arthington, L.N.E.R., 21 D3.
Arthog, G.W.R., 13, A5.
Arundel, S.R., 5, F1.
Ascot, S.R., 5, B1.
Ascott -under - Wychwood, G.W.R., 10, E5.
Asfordby, L.M.S., 16, E3.
Ash, S.R., 5, C1.
Ashbourne, L.M.S., 15, C5.
Ashburton, G.W.R., 2, C4.
Ashbury, S.R., 1, B5.
Ashburys, L.N.E.R., 20, B1.
Ashby (de-la-Zouch), L.M.S., 16, E5.
Ashby Magna, L.N.E.R., 16, G4.
Ashchurch, L.M.S., 9, D3.
Ashcott, S.D., 3, C1.
Ashendon Jc., G.W.R./L.N.E.R., 10, E3.
Ashey (I.W.), S.R., 4, F3.
Ashford (Kent), S.R., 6, D4.
Ashford (Middx.), S.R., 5, B2.
Ashington, L.N.E.R., 27 A5.
Ash Jc., S.R., 5, C1.
Ashley (Ches.), C.L.C., 20, C2.
Ashley & Weston (Northants), L.M.S., 16, G2.
Ashley Heath, S.R., 3, E5.
Ashley Hill, G.W.R., 8, C1.
Ashperton, G.W.R., 9, C2.
Ashtead, S.R., 5, C2.
Ashton (Devon), G.W.R., 2, C3.
Ashton (Lancs.), L.M.S., L.N.E.R., O.A.G.B., 21, F1.
Ashton-in-Makerfield, L.N.E.R., 20, B3.
Ashton Keynes, see Minety.
Ashton-under-Hill, L.M.S., 9, C4.
Ash Town, E.K.R., 6, C2.
Ashurst, S.R., 5, D4.
Ash Vale, S.R., 5, C1.
Ashwater, S.R., 1, B5.
Ashwell (Rutland), L.M.S., 16, E2.
Ashwell & Morden (Cambs.), L.N.E.R., 11, D2.
•Ashwellthorpe, L.N.E.R.,12, A3.
Askam, L.M.S., 24, A4.
Askern, L.M.S., 21, E5.
Askern Jc., L.M.S./L.N.E.R., 21, F5.
Askrigg, L.N.E.R., 27, G3.
Aslockton, L.N.E.R., 16, C2.
Aspall&Thorndon, L.N.E.R., 12, C3.
Aspatria, L.M.S., 26, D3.
Astley, L.M.S., 20, B2.
Astley Bridge (Goods), L.M.S., 20, B2.
Aston (Warwicks.), L.M.S., 15, G5.
•Aston-by-Stone, L.M.S., 15, D4.
Aston Rowant, G.W.R., 10, F3.
Astwood Bank, see Studley.
•Aswarby, L.N.E.R., 17, D1.
Athelney, G.W.R., 8, F3.
Atherstone, L.M.S., 16, F5.
Atherton, L.M.S., 20, B2.
Attadale, L.M.S., 35, E2.
Attenborough, L.M.S., 16, D4.
•Attercliffe, L.N.E.R., 16, A5.
Attercliffe Rd., L.M.S., 16 A5.
Attleborough, L.N.E.R., 18, F4.
Attlebridge, M.G.N., 18, E3.
Auchendinny, L.N.E.R., 31, C4.
Auchengray, L.M.S., 31, D2.
Auchenheath, L.M.S., 31, D1.
•Auchenmade, L.M.S., 30,D3.
Auchincruive, L.M.S., 30, F2.
Auchindachy, L.N.E.R., 38, D5.
Auchinleck, L.M.S., 30, F1.
§Auchmacoy, L.N.E.R., 38, E2.
Auchmuty Mills, L.N.E.R., 37, G1.
Auchnagatt, L.N.E.R., 38, D2.
Auchterarder, L.M.S., 34, F2.
Auchterhouse, L.M.S., 37, E1.
Auchterless, L.N.E.R., 38, D3.
Auchtermuchty, L.N.E.R., 37, F1.
Auchtertool (Goods), L.N.E.R., 31, A4.
Audlem, G.W.R., 15, C2.
•Audley & Bignall End, L.M.S., 15, C3.
Audley End, L.N.E.R., 11, E4.
Auldbar Rd., L.M.S., 37, D2.
Auldearn, L.M.S., 36, D3.
Auldgirth, L.M.S., 26, A4.
•Aultmore, L.M.S., 38, D5.
Authorpe, L.N.E.R., 17, A3.
Aviemore, L.M.S., 36, D5.
•Avonbridge, L.N.E.R., 31, B2.
Avonmouth Dock, G.W.R./L.M.S., 8, C2.
Avonwick, G.W.R., 2, D4.
Awre, G.W.R., 9, E2.
Awsworth, L.N.E.R., 16, C4.
Axbridge, G.W.R., 8, E3.
Axminster, S.R., 2, B1.
Aycliffe, L.N.E.R., 28, E5.
Aylesbury, G.W.R./L.N.E.R./L.P.T.B. & L.M.S., 10, E2.
Aylesford, S.R., 6, C5.
Aylesham Halt, S.R., 6, C2.
Aylsham, L.N.E.R., 18, E3.
Aylsham, M.G.N., 18, D3.
Aynho, G.W.R., 10, D4.
Aynho Park Plat., G.W.R., 10, D4.
Ayot, L.N.E.R., 11, F2.
Ayr, L.M.S., 30, F3.
Aysgarth, L.N.E.R., 27, G4.
Ayton, L.N.E.R., 32, C3.

B

Babworth(Goods), L.N.E.R., 16, A3.
Backney, G.W.R., 9, D1.
Backwell, see Nailsea.
Backworth, L.N.E.R., 28, B5.
•Bacton, G.W.R., 14, F1.
Bacup, L.M.S., 20, A1.
Baddesley Coll., L.M.S., 16, F5.
Badminton, G.W.R., 9, G3.
•Badnall Wharf, L.M.S., 15, D3.
Badsey, see Littleton.
•Baggrow, L.M.S., 26, D2.
Baggilt, L.M.S., 20, D5.
Bag Lane (Atherton), L.M.S., 20, B2.
Bagnor, see Stockcross.
Bagshot, S.R., 5, C1.
Baguley, C.L.C., 20, C1.
Bagworth & Ellistown, L.M.S. 16, E4.
Baildon, L.M.S./L.N.E.R., 21, D2.
Bailey Gate, S.D., 3, E4.
Baillieston, L.M.S., 30, C1.
Bainton, L.N.E.R., 22, C4.
Bakewell, L.M.S., 15, B5.
Bala, G.W.R., 19, F4.
Bala Jc., G.W.R., 19, F4.
Balado, L.N.E.R., 34, G2.
Balby Jc., L.N.E.R., 21, F5.
Balcombe, S.R., 5, E3.
Baldersby, L.N.E.R., 21, B3.
Balderton, G.W.R., 20, E4.
Baldock, L.N.E.R., 11, E2.
Baldovan, L.M.S., 37, E2.
Baldragon, L.M.S., 37, E2.
•Balerno, L.M.S., 31, C3.
Balfron, L.N.E.R., 30, A2.
Balgowan, L.M.S., 34, F2.
Balham, S.R., 5, B3.
Ballabeg, I.M.R., 23, C2.
Ballachulish (Glencoe), L.M.S., 33, D3.
Ballachulish Ferry, L.M.S., 33, D3.
Ballasalla, I.M.R., 23, C2.
Ballater, L.N.E.R., 37, A1.
Ballathie (Goods), L.M.S., 34, E1.
Ballaugh, I.M.R., 23, A2.
Ballindalloch, L.N.E.R., 36, E2.
Ballingham, G.W.R., 9, D1.
Ballinluig, L.M.S., 34, D2.
Balloch, L.M.S./L.N.E.R., 30, B3.
Balmore, L.N.E.R., 30, B1.
Balmule Colliery, L.N.E.R., 31, A3.
Balne, L.N.E.R., 21, E5.
Balquhidder, L.M.S., 34, F5.
Balsall Common, see Berkswell.
Balshaw Lane & Euxton, L.M.S., 24, E3.
Bamber Bridge, L.M.S., 24, E2.
Bamford, L.M.S., 15, A5.
Bamfurlong, L.M.S., 20, B3.
Bampton (Devon), G.W.R., 8, G5.
Bampton (Oxon.), see Brize Norton.
Banavie, L.N.E.R., 33, C3.
Banbury, G.W.R./L.N.E.R., & L.M.S., 10, C4.
Banchory, L.N.E.R., 37, A4.
Banff, L.N.E.R., 38, C4.
Banff Bridge, L.N.E.R., 38, C4.
Bangor, L.M.S., 19, D2.
Bangor-on-Dee, G.W.R., 20, F4.
Bankfield (L'pool), Goods, L.M.S., 20, C4.
•Bankfoot, L.M.S., 34, E2.
•Bankhead, L.M.S., 31, D2.
•Banknock, L.N.E.R., 31, B1.
Banks, L.M.S., 20, A4.
Bank Top (Darlington), L.N.E.R., 28, F5.
Bannockburn, L.M.S., 31, A1.
Banstead, S.R., 5, C3.
Banwell, see Sandford.
Barassie, L.M.S., 30, E3.
Barber's Bridge, G.W.R., 9, D2.
Barbon, L.M.S., 24, A2.
Barcombe, S.R., 5, F4.
Barcombe Mills, S.R., 5, F4.
Bardney, L.N.E.R., 17, B1.
Bardon Hill, L.M.S., 16, E4.
Bardon Mill, L.N.E.R., 27, B2.
•Bardowie, L.N.E.R., 30, B1.
Bardsey, L.N.E.R., 21, D3.
Bare Lane, L.M.S., 24, B3.
•Bargeddie, L.N.E.R., 30, C1.
Bargoed, G.W.R., 8, B4.
§Barham, S.R., 6, C2.
Barking, L.M.S./L.P.T.B., 5, A4.
Barkston, L.N.E.R., 16, C1.
Barlaston, L.M.S., 15, D3.
Barlow, L.N.E.R., 21, E5.
•Barmby, L.N.E.R., 21, E5.
Barming, S.R., 6, C5.
Barmouth, G.W.R., 13, A5.
Barmouth Jc., G.W.R., 13 A5.
Barnack, see Uffington.
Barnard Castle, L.N.E.R., 27, E4.
Barnby Dun, L.N.E.R., 21, F5.
Barnby Moor & Sutton, L.N.E.R., 16, A3.
Barnehurst, S.R., 5, B4.
Barnes, S.R., 5, B3.
Barnetby, L.N.E.R., 22, F3.
Barnham (Suffolk),L.N.E.R., 12, B5.
Barnham (Sussex), S.R., 5, F1.
Barnhill, L.M.S., 37, E2.
Barnoldswick, L.M.S., 21, inset.
Barnsley, L.M.S./L.N.E.R., 21, F3.
Barnstaple, S.R. & G.W.R., 7, F3.
Barnstaple Jc., S.R./G.W.R., 7, F3.
Barnstone, L.M.S./L.N.E.R. 16, D3.
Barnt Green, L.M.S., 9, A4.
Barnton, L.M.S., 31, B3.
Barnwell (Cambs.),L.N.E.R., 11, C3.
Barnwell (Northants.), L.M.S., 11, B1.
Barracks (Burnley), L.M.S., 24, D1.
Barras, L.N.E.R., 27, F3.
Barrasford L.N.E.R., 27, B3.
Barrhead, L.M.S., 30, C2.
Barrhead, South (Goods) L.M.S., 30, C2.
Barrhill, L.M.S., 25, A3.
Barrmill, L.M.S., 30, D3.
Barrow (Ches.), C.L.C., 20, D3.
Barrowden, *see* Wakerley.
Barrow Haven, L.N.E.R., 22, E3.
Barrow Hill & Staveley Works, L.M.S., 16, A4.
See also Staveley Works.
Barrow-in-Furness, L.M.S., 24, B5.
Barrow-on-Soar & Quorn, L.M.S., 16, E3.
See also Quorn, L.N.E.R.
Barr's Court Jcs., G.W.R. L.M.S., 9, C1.
Barry, G.W.R., 8, D5.
Barry Docks, G.W.R., 8, D4.
Barry Island, G.W.R., 8, D4.
Barry Links, D.A., 37, E3.
Barry Pier, G.W.R., 8, D4.
Bartlow, L.N.E.R., 11 D4.
Barton (Goods), L.N.E.R. 27, F5.
•Barton & Broughton, L.M.S., 24, D3.
Barton & Walton, L.M.S., 15, E5.
•Barton Hill, L.N.E.R., 21, B5.
•Barton-le-street, L.N.E.R., 22, B5.
Barton-on-Humber, L.N.E.R., 22, E4.
Baschurch, G.W.R., 20, G4.
Basford (Notts.), L.M.S. & L.N.E.R., 16, C4.
Basingstoke, S.R. & G.W.R., 4, B2.
Bason Bridge, S.D., 8, E3.
Bassaleg, G.W.R./L.M.S., 8, C3.
Bassenthwaite Lake, L.M.S., 26, D2.
Bat & Ball (Sevenoaks), S.R., 5, C5.
Bath, G.W.R. & L.M.S./S.D., 3, A3, 3, Is. D., A3.
Bathampton, G.W.R., 3, A4.
Bathgate, L.N.E.R., 31, C2.
Batley, L.M.S. & L.N.E.R., 21, E3.
Batley Carr, L.N.E.R., 21, E3.
Battersby, L.N.E.R., 28, F4.
Battle, S.R., 6, F5.
Battlesbridge, L.N.E.R., 6, A5.
Bawtry, L.N.E.R., 21, G5.
Baxenden, L.M.S., 24, E1.
Bayford, L.N.E.R., 11, F2.
Bay Horse, L.M.S. 24, C3.
Baynards, S.R., 5, D2.
Beaconsfield, G.W.R. L.N.E.R., 10, F1.
Beal, L.N.E.R., 32, D2.
Bealings, L.N.E.R., 12, D3.
Beamish ,L.N.E.R., 27, C5.
Bearley, G.W.R., 9, B5.
•Bearpark L.N.E.R., 27, D5
Bearsden, L.N.E.R., 30, B2.
Bearsted & Thurnham, S.R., 6, C5.
§Beasdale, L.N.E.R., 33, B1
Beattock, L.M.S., 31, G3.
Beauchief, L.M.S., 16, A5.
Beaufort, L.M.S., 8, A4.
Beaulieu Road, S.R., 4, E4.
Beauly, L.M.S., 35, E5.
Bebington & New Ferry B.J., 20, C4.
Bebside, L.N.E.R., 28, A5.
Beccles, L.N.E.R., 12, A2.
Beckenham (Jc.), S.R., 5, B4.
•Beckermet, L.M.S., 26, F3.
§Beckfoot, R.E.R., 26, F2.
Beckford, L.M.S., 9, C4.
Beckingham, L.N.E.R., 22, G5.
•Beckton, L.N.E.R., 5, A4.
Bedale, L.N.E.R., 27, G5.
Bedford, L.M.S., 10, C1.
Bedhampton Halt, S.R., 4 E2.
Bedlington, L.N.E.R., 27,A5.
Bedlinog, G.W.R., 8, B5.
Bedminster, G.W.R., 8, D2.
Bedwas, G.W.R., 8 B4.
Bedwellty Pits, L.M.S., 8,A4.
Bedworth, L.M.S., 16, G5.
Bedwyn, G.W.R., 4, A4.
Beechburn, L.N.E.R., 27, D5.
Beeston (Notts.), L.M.S., 16 D4.
Beeston (Yorks.), L.N.E.R., 21, D3.
Beeston Castle, L.M.S., 20 E3.
Beighton, L.N.E.R., 16, A4.
Beith, L.M.S., 30, D3.
Bekesbourne, S.R., 6, C2.
Belford, L.N.E.R., 32, E2.
Belgrave & Birstall, L.N.E.R., 16, E4.
Bell Busk, L.M.S., 21, C1.
Belle Vue, L.M.S./L.N.E.R., 20, B1.
•Bell Green, L.M.S., 10, A5.
Bellingham (N. Tyne), L.N.E.R., 27, A3.
Belmont (Middx.), L.M.S., 5, A2.
Belmont (Surrey), S.R., 5, C3.

BELPER—BUTE ROAD

Belper, L.M.S. 16, C5.
Belses, L.N.E.R., 32, E5.
Belston Jc., L.M.S., 30, F2.
Belton, A.J., 22, F5.
Belton & Burgh, L.N.E.R., 18, F1.
Beltonford (Goods), L.N.E.R., 32, B5.
Belvedere, S.R., 5, B4.
Belvoir Jc., L.N.E.R., 16, D2.
Bembridge, (I.W.) S.R., 4, F2.
Bempton, L.N.E.R., 22, B3.
Benderloch, L.M.S., 33, E2.
Benfleet, L.M.S., 6, A5.
Bengeworth, L.M.S., 9, C4.
Benhar East, L.N.E.R., 31, C2.
Benhar West, L.M.S., 31, C2.
Beningborough, L.N.E.R., 21, C5.
Benllech, *see* Red Wharf Bay.
Ben Rhydding, O.I., 21, C2.
Bensham, L.N.E.R., 27, C5.
Bentham, L.M.S., 24, B2.
Bentley (Hants.), S.R., 4, C1.
Bentley (Suffolk), L.N.E.R., 12, E4.
Benton, L.N.E.R., 27, B5l
Bents, L.N.E.R., 31, C2.
•Benwick Goods Branch, L.N.E.R., 11, A3.
Bere Alston, S.R., 1, D
Bere Ferrers, S.R., 1, D
Berkeley, S.V.Y., 9, F2.
Berkeley Road, L.M.S./ S.V.Y., 9, F2.
Berkhamsted, L.M.S., 10, E1.
Berkswell & Balsall Common, L.M.S., 9, A5.
erney Arms, L.N.E.R., 18, F1.
Berrington, G.W.R., 15, F1.
Berrington & Eye, S.H., 9, B1.
Berry Brow, L.M.S., 21, E2.
Berwick (Sussex), S.R., 5, F4.
Berwick-on-Tweed, L.N.E.R., 32, C3.
Berwyn, G.W.R., 20, F5.
Bescar Lane, L.M.S., 20, A4.
Bescot, L.M.S., 15, F4.
Bessacar Jc., L.N.E.R./ L.M.S., 21, F5.
Bestwood Coll., L.N.E.R., 16, C4.
Betchworth, S.R., 5, C3.
Bethesda, L.M.S., 19, D2.
§Betley Road, L.M.S., 15, C2.
Bettisfield, G.W.R., 20, F3.
Bettws-y-Coed, L.M.S., 19, E4.
Beverley, L.N.E.R., 22, D3.
Bewdley, G.W.R., 9, A3.
Bexhill, S.R., 6, F5.
Bexley, S.R., 5, B4.
Bexleyheath, S.R., 5, B4.
Bicester, G.W.R. & L.M.S., 10, D4.
Bickershaw, L.N.E.R., 20, B2.
Bickleigh, G.W.R., 2, D5.
Bickley, S.R., 5, B4.
Biddenden, K.E.S.R., 6, D4.
•Biddulph, L.M.S., 15, B3.
Bideford, S.R., 7, F3.
•Bidford-on-Avon, L.M.S., 9, B5.
Bidston, **L.M.S.**/L.N.E.R., 20, C4.
Biggar, L.M.S., 31, E3.
Biggleswade, L.N.E.R., 11, D2.
Biglis Jc., G.W.R., 8, D4.
Bignall End, *see* Audley.
Bilbster, L.M.S., 39, D4.
•Billacombe, G.W.R., 2, D5.
Billericay, L.N.E.R., 5, A5.
Billing, L.M.S., 10, B2.
•Billingboro' & Horbling, L.N.E.R., 17, D1.
Billingham-on-Tees, L.N.E.R., 28, E4.
Billingshurst, S.R., 5, E2.
Bilson (Goods), G.W.R., 9, E2.
Bilston, G.W.R., 15, F4.
See also Ettingshall Road.
•Bilsthorpe, M.N., 16, B3.
Bilton Road Jc., L.N.E.R., 21, C3.
Binegar, S. D., 3, B2.
Bingham, L.N.E.R., 16, C3.
Bingham Road (Notts.), L.N.E.R./L.M.S., 16, D3.
Bingley, L.M.S., 21, D2.
•Binton, L.M.S., 9, B5.
Birchfield Platform, L.N.E.R., 36, D1.
Birchington-on-Sea, S.R., 6, B2.
Birch Vale, L.M.S./L.N.E.R., 15, A4.
Birdbrook, L.N.E.R., 11, D5.
Birdingbury, L.M.S., 10, A4.
Birdwell, L.N.E.R., 21, F3.
Birdwell & Pilley (Goods), L.M.S., 21, F3.
Birkdale, L.M.S. 20, A4.
Birkdale Palace, C.L.C., 20, A4.
Birkenhead, B.J., •C.L.C., •G.W.R., •L.M.S., Mer., •L.N.E.R., 20, C4.
Birkenshaw, L.N.E.R., 21, E2.
Birley Coll., L.N.E.R., 16, A5.
Birmingham, G.W.R. & L.M.S., 15, —
Birnam, *see* Dunkeld.
Birnie Rd., L.N.E.R., 37, C4.
Birstall (Leics.), *see* Belgrave.
Birstall (Yorks.), L.M.S., 21, E2.
Birstwith, L.N.E.R., 21, C3.
Birtley, L.N.E.R., 27, C5.
Bishop Auckland, L.N.E.R., 27, E5.
Bishopbriggs, L.N.E.R., 30, C1.
§Bishopsbourne, S.R., 6, C3.
Bishop's Cleeve, G.W.R., 9, D4.
Bishop's Lydeard, G.W.R., 8, F4.
Bishop's Nympton & Molland, G.W.R., 7, F5.
Bishop's Stortford, L.N.E.R. 11, E3.
•Bishop's Waltham, S.R., 4, D3.
Bishopstone, S.R., 5, G4.
Bishopton, L.M.S., 30, C2.
•Bisley Camp, S.R., 5, C1.
Bittaford Platform, G.W.R., 2, D5.
Bitterley, S.H., 9, A1.
Bitterne, S.R., 4, E3.
Bitton, L.M.S., 8, D1.
Blaby, L.M.S., 16, F4.
Black Bank, L.N.E.R., 11, B4.
•Black Bull, L.M.S., 15, C3.
Blackburn, L.M.S., 24, D2.
Black Carr Jc., L.N.E.R., 21, F5.
Blackdown, *see* Mary Tavy.
Blackford, L.M.S., 34, F3.
Blackhall Jc., L.N.E.R., 31, C2.
Blackhall Colliery Halt, L.N.E.R., 28, D4.
Blackhall Rocks, L.N.E.R., 28, D4.
Blackheath (London), S.R., 5, B4.
Blackhill, L.N.E.R., 27, C4.
Black Lane (Radcliffe), L.M.S., 20, B1.
Black Mill, G.W.R., 7, C5.
Blackpool, L.M.S., 24, D4.
Blackrod, L.M.S., 20, B2.
•Blackston, L.N.E.R., 31, B2.
Blackthorn, G.W.R., 10, E3.
Blackwater (Hants.), S.R., 4, B1.
Blackwater (I.W.), S.R., 4, F3.
•Blackwall, L.N.E.R., 5, B4.
Blackwell (Worcs.), L.M.S., 9, A4.
Blackwood (Lanark), L.M.S., 31, D1.
Blackwood (Mon.), L.M.S. & •G.W.R., 8, B4.
Blacksboat, L.N.E.R., 36, E2
Blacon, L.N.E.R., 20, D4.
Blaenau Festiniog, G.W.R. & L.M.S., 19, F3.
Blaenavon, G.W.R. & •L.M.S., 8, A4.
•Blaenclydach, G.W.R., 8, B5.
Blaengarw, G.W.R., 7, B5.
Blaengwynfi, G.W.R., 7, B5.
Blaenrhondda, G.W.R., 7, B5
•Blagdon, G.W.R., 8, D2.
Blaina, G.W.R., 8, A4.
•Blairadam, L.N.E.R., 31, A3.
Blair Atholl, L.M.S., 34, C3.
Blairgowrie, L.M.S., 34, D1.
Blaisdon, G.W.R., 9, E2.
Blakedown, *see* Churchill.
Blake Hall, L.N.E.R., 11 G4.
Blakeney (Goods) G.W.R., 9, E2.
Blakesley, L.M.S., 10, C3.
Blake Street, L.M.S., 15, F5.
Blanchland (Goods), L.N.E.R., 27, D4.
Blandford, S.D., 3, E4.
Blanefield, L.N.E.R., 30, B2.
Blankney & Metheringham L.N.E.R., 17, B1.
Blantyre, L.M.S., 30, C1.
Blaydon, L.N.E.R., 27, C5.
Bleadon & Uphill, G.W.R. 8, D3.
Bleasby, L.M.S., 16, C3.
Bledlow, G.W.R., 10, F2.
Blencow, L.M.S., 26, E1.
Blenheim & Woodstock, G.W.R., 10, E4.
Bletchington, G.W.R., 10, E4.
Bletchley, L.M.S., 10, D2.
Blewbury, *see* Upton, G.W.R.
•Blidworth & Rainworth, L.M.S., 16, B3.
Blisworth, L.M.S., 10, B3.
Blockley, G.W.R., 9, C5.
Blodwell Jc., G.W.R., 20, G5.
Blowers Green, G.W.R., 15, F4.
•Blowick, L.M.S., 20, A4.
Bloxham, G.W.R., 10, C4.
Bloxwich, L.M.S., 15, F4.
Blue Anchor, G.W.R., 8, E5.
Blundellsands, L.M.S., 20, B4.
Blunham, L.M.S., 11, D1.
•Bluntisham, L.N.E.R., 11 B3.
Blyth, L.N.E.R., 28, A5.
Blythe Bridge, L.M.S., 15, C4.
Blyton, L.N.E.R., 22, G5.
•Boarhills, L.N.E.R., 37, F3.
Boars Head, L.M.S., 20, B3.
Boat of Garten, L.M.S./ L.N.E.R., 36, F3.
Bocking, *see* Braintree.
§Boddam, L.N.E.R., 38, D1.
Bodfari, L.M.S., 19, D5.
Bodiam, K.E.S.R., 6, E5.
Bodmin, G.W.R. & S.R., 1, D3.
Bodmin Road, G.W.R., 1, D3.
Bodorgan, L.M.S., 19, D1.
Bognor Regis, S.R., 5, G1.
Bogside (Fife), L.N.E.R., 31, A2.
Bogside (Renfrew), L.M.S., 30, E3.
Bogston, L.M.S., 30, B3.
Boldon Coll., L.N.E.R., 28, B5.
Bollington, L.M.S./L.N.E.R., 15, A4.
Bolsover, L.N.E.R. & •L.M.S., 16, B4.
Bolton, L.M.S., 20, B2.
Bolton Abbey, L.M.S., 21, C2.
Bolton-le-Sands, L.M.S., 24, B3.
Bolton-on-Dearne, S.K., 21, F4.
Bolton Percy, L.N.E.R., 21, D4.
Bonar Bridge, L.M.S., 36, B5
Boncath, G.W.R., 13, F3.
Bonds Main Coll., L.M.S. & L.N.E.R., 16, B4.
Bo'ness, L.N.E.R., 31, B2.
Bonhill, *see* Alexandria.
Bonnybridge, •L.M.S. & L.N.E.R., 31, B1.
Bonnyrigg, L.N.E.R., 31, C4.
Bontnewydd, G.W.R., 14, A5.
Bookham, S.R., 5, C2.
Boosbeck, L.N.E.R., 28, E3.
•Boot, R.E.R., 26, F2.
Bootham Jc., L.N.E.R., 21, C5.
Bootle (Cumb.), L.M.S., 26, G3.
Bootle (Lancs.), L.M.S., 20, C4.
Bordesley, G.W.R., 15, G5.
Bordon, S.R., 4, C1.
Boroughbridge, L.N.E.R., 21, B4.
Borough Green, *see* Wrotham.
Borrobol Platform, L.M.S., 39, F1.
Borrowash, L.M.S., 16, D5.
Borth, G.W.R., 13, C5.
Borwick, L.M.S., 24, B3.
Boscarne Jc., S.R./G.W.R., 1, D3.
Boscombe, S.R., 3, F5.
Bosham, S.R., 4, E1.
Bosley, L.M.S., 15, B4.
Boston, L.N.E.R., 17, C3.
Botanic Gardens, L.N.E.R., 22, D3.
Bothwell, L.M.S., 31, C1.
Botley, S.R., 4, E3.
Bottesford, L.N.E.R., 16, C2.
Bottisham & Lode, L.N.E.R. 11, C4.
Boughrood & Llyswen, G.W.R., 14, F3.
Boughton, L.N.E.R., 16, B3.
Bourne, **L.N.E.R.**/L.M.S./ M.G.N., 17, E1.
Bourne End, G.W.R., 10, G2.
Bournemouth, S.R. & **S.R.**/ S.D., 3, F5.
Bournville, L.M.S., 9, A4.
Bourton-on-the-Water, G.W.R., 9, D5.
Bovey, G.W.R., 2, C4.
Bow (Devon), S.R., 2, B4.
Bowdon, *see* Altrincham.
Bower, L.M.S., 39, C3.
Bowes. L.N.E.R., 27, F4.
•Bowes Park, L.N.E.R., 5, A3.
•Bowhouse, L.N.E.R., 31, B2.
Bowland, L.N.E.R., 31, D5.
Bowling, L.M.S. & L.N.E.R., 30, B2.
Bowling Jc., L.M.S., 21, D2.
Bow Street, G.W.R., 13, C5.
Box, G.W.R., 3, A4.
Boxford, G.W.R., 4, A4.
Boxhill & Burford Bridge, S.R., 5, C2.
Boxmoor, *see* Hemel Hempsted.
•Boyce's Bridge, W.U.T., 17, F4.
Braceborough Spa Halt, L.N.E.R., 17, E1.
Bracebridge (Goods), L.N.E.R., 16, B2.
Brackenhill Jc., S.K., 21, E4.
Brackley, L.M.S., 10, C4.
,, L.N.E.R., 10, C3.
Bracknell, S.R., 4, A1.
Bradbury, L.N.E.R., 28, E5.
Bradfield, L.N.E.R., 12, E4.
Bradford, **L.M.S.**/L.N.E.R., •L.M.S., •L.N.E.R. 21, D,2.
Bradford Jc., G.W.R., 3, B4.
Bradford-on-Avon, G.W.R., 3, B4.
Brading Jc., (I.W.), S.R., 4, F2.
Bradley, L.M.S., 21, E2.
Bradley Fold, L.M.S., 20, B2.
Bradley Wood Jc., L.M.S., 21, E2.
Bradninch, *see* Hele.
•Bradnop, L.M.S., 15, C4.
Bradwell, L.M.S., 10, C2.
Brafferton, L.N.E.R., 21, B4.
Braidwood, L.M.S., 31, D1.
Braintree & Bocking, L.N.E.R., 11, E5.
Braithwaite, L.M.S., 26, E2.
Bramber, S.R., 5, F2.
Bramford, L.N.E.R., 12, D4.
Bramhall, L.M.S., 15, A3.
Bramley (Hants.), G.W.R., 4, B2.
Bramley (Yorks.), L.N.E.R., 21, D3.
Bramley & Wonersh, S.R., 5 D1.
Brampford Speke Halt, G.W.R., 2, B3.
Brampton (Derby) Goods, L.M.S., 16, B5.
Brampton (Northants.), *see* Pitsford.
Brampton (Suffk.), L.N.E.R., 12, B2.
Brampton Jc. (Cumb.), L.N.E.R., 27, C1.
Bramwith (Goods), L.N.E.R., 21, F5.
Brancepeth, L.N.E.R., 27, D5.
Brancliffe Jc., L.N.E.R./ L.M.S., 16, A4.
Brandon (Durham), L.N.E.R 27, D5.
Brandon (Norfk.), L.N.E.R., 11, A5.
Brandon & Wolston, L.M.S., 10, A5.
Branksome, **S.R.**/S.D., 3, F5.
Bransford Road, G.W.R., 9 B3.
Branston Jc., L.M.S., 15, E5.
Branston & Heighington, L.N.E.R., 17, B1.
Bransty (Whitehaven), L.M.S., 26, E4.
•Branthwaite, L.M.S., 26, E3.
Brasted, S.R., 5, C4.
Bratton, *see* Edington.
Braughing, L.N.E.R., 11, E3
Braunston, L.M.S., 10, B4.
Braunston & Willoughby, L.N.E.R., 10, B4.
Braunton, S.R., 7, F3.
Braystones, L.M.S., 26, F3.
Brayton, L.M.S., 26, D2.
Brayton Jc., L.N.E.R., 21 D5.
Breadsall, L.N.E.R., 16, D5.
Breamore, S.R., 4, D5.
Brechin, L.M.S., 37, C3.
Brecon, **G.W.R.**/L.M.S., 14, F3.
Brecon Rd., L.M.S., 8, A3.
Bredbury, L.M.S./L.N.E.R., 21, G1.
Bredon (Leics.), *see* Tonge.
Bredon (Worcs.), L.M.S., 9, C3.
Breich, L.M.S., 31, C2.
Breidden, S.W., 14, A2.
Brent (Devon), G.W.R. 2, D4.
Brentford, S.R. & •G.W.R., 5, B2.
Brent Knoll, G.W.R., 8, E3.
Brentor, S.R., 1, C5.
Brentwood & Warley, L.N.E.R., 5, A5.
Bretby Wharf, L.M.S., 16, E5.
Brettell Lane, G.W.R., 15, G3.
Bretton, *see* Broughton.
Bricket Wood, L.M.S., 11, G1.
Bridestowe, S.R., 2, B5.
§Bridge, S.R., 6, C3.
Bridgend, G.W.R., 7, C5.
Bridgend & Coity (Goods), G.W.R., 7, C5.
•Bridgefoot, L.M.S., 26, E3.
Bridge of Allan, L.M.S., 31, A1.
Bridge of Dee, L.M.S., 26, C5.
Bridge of Dun, L.M.S., 37, C3
Bridge of Earn, L.N.E.R., 34, F1.
Bridge of Orchy, L.N.E.R. 33, E5.
Bridge of Weir, L.M.S., 30, C3.
Bridgerule, *see* Whitstone.
Bridgeness, L.N.E.R., 31, B2.
Bridge St. (Northampton), L.M.S., 10, B2.
Bridge Street (Thrapston), L.M.S., 10, A1.
Bridgnorth, G.W.R., 15, F2.
Bridgwater, G.W.R. & S.D., 8, F3.
Bridlington, L.N.E.R., 22, B3.
Bridport, G.W.R., 3, F2.
Brierfield, L.M.S., 24, D1.
Brierley Hill, G.W.R., 15, G3.
Brierley Jc., L.M.S./L.N.E.R., 21, F4.
Brigg, L.N.E.R., 22, F4.
Brigham, L.M.S., 26, E3.
Brighouse, L.M.S., 21, E2.
Brightlingsea, L.N.E.R., 12, F4.
Brighton, S.R., 5, F3.
Brightside, L.M.S., 21, G3.
Brill & Ludgershall, G.W.R., 10, E3.
Brimscombe, G.W.R., 9, E3.
Brimsdown, L.N.E.R., 11, G3.
Brindley Heath, L.M.S., 15, E4.
Brinkburn, L.N.E.R., 32, G2.
Brinklow, L.M.S. 10, A2.
Brinkworth, G.W.R., 9, G4.
Brinscall, L.M.S., 24, E2.
Brislington, G.W.R., 8, D1.
Bristol, G.W.R./ L.M.S., L.M.S., •G.W.R., 8, C2.
Britannia Bridge, L.M.S., 19, D2.
Brithdir, G.W.R., 8, B4.
Briton Ferry, G.W.R., 7, B4.
•Briton Ferry Road, G.W.R., 7, B4.
Brixham, G.W.R., 2, D3.
Brixton, S.R., 5, B3.
•Brixton Road, G.W.R., 2, E5.
Brixworth, L.M.S., 10, A3.
Brize Norton & Bampton, G.W.R., 10, E5.
Broadbottom, *see* Mottram.
Broad Clyst, S.R., 2, B3.
Broadfield, L.M.S., 20, B1.
Broad Green, L.M.S., 20, C4.
Broadheath, L.M.S., 20, C2.
•Broadley, L.M.S., 20, A1.
Broadstairs, S.R., 6, B1.
Broadstone, **S.R.**/S.D., 3, F5.
Broad Street, L.M.S., 5, A3.
Broadway, G.W.R., 9, C4.
•Brock, L.M.S., 24, D3.
Brockenhurst, S.R., 4, E4.
Brocketsbrae, L.M.S., 31, D1.
Brockford & Wetheringsett, L.N.E.R., 12, C4.
Brockholes, L.M.S., 21, F2.
Brocklesby, L.N.E.R., 22, E3.
Brocton, *see* Milford, L.M.S.
Brodie, L.M.S., 36, D3.
Brodsworth Coll., L.N.E.R., 21, F4.
Bromborough, B.J., 20, C4.
Bromfield, S.H., 9, A1.
•Bromford Bridge, L.M.S., 15, G5.
Bromham & Rowde, G.W.R., 3, B5.
Bromley Cross, L.M.S., 20, A2.
Bromley North (Kent), S.R., 5, B4.
Bromley South (Kent), S.R., 5, B4.
Brompton, L.N.E.R., 28, G5.
Bromsgrove, L.M.S., 9, A4.
Bromshall Jc., L.M.S./ L.N.E.R., 15, D4.
Bromyard, G.W.R., 9, B2.
Bronwydd Arms, G.W.R., 13, G4.
Brookland Halt, S.R., 6, E4.
Brooklands (Ches.), M.S.J.A., 20, C1.
Brookman's Park, L.N.E.R., 11, G2.
Brooksby, L.M.S., 16, E3.
Brookwood, S.R., 5, C1.
Broom (Jc.), L.M.S., 9, B4.
Broome, L.M.S., 14, C1.
Broomfield Jc., L.M.S./ L.N.E.R., 37, C4.
Broomfleet, L.N.E.R., 22, E4.
Broomhill (Inverness), L.M.S., 36, F3.
Broomhill (North'd.), L.N.E.R., 32, G1.
Broomieknowe, L.N.E.R., 31, C4.
Broomielaw, L.N.E.R., 27, E4.
Brora, L.M.S., 39, G2.
Broseley, *see* Iron Bridge.
Brotton, L.N.E.R., 28, E3.
Brough, L.N.E.R., 22, E4.
Broughton (Lancs.), *see* Barton.
Broughton (Peebles), L.M.S., 31, E3.
Broughton & Bretton, L.M.S., 20, D4.
Broughton Astley, L.M.S., 16, G4.
Broughton-in-Furness, L.M.S., 24, A5.
Broughton Lane, L.N.E.R., 21, G4.
Broughty Ferry D.A., 37, E2.
Brownhills, L.M.S., 15, F4.
Broxbourne & Hoddesdon, L.N.E.R., 11, F3.
Broxburn Oil Works, L.N.E.R., 31, B3.
Broxton, L.M.S., 20, E3.
Brucklay, L.N.E.R., 38, D2
Brundall, L.N.E.R., 18, F2.
•Brunswick (L'pool), C.L.C., & L.M.S., 20, C4.
Brunswick St. (Goods), L.M.S., 15, B3.
Bruton, G.W.R., 3, C3.
Brymbo, G.W.R./L.M.S. & •L.N.E.R., 20, E4.
•Bryn (Glam.), G.W.R., 7, B5.
Bryn (Lancs.), L.M.S., 20, B3.
Brynamman, G.W.R., & **L.M.S.**/G.W.R., 7, A4.
•Brynglas, Tal., 13, B5.
Bryngwyn Halt, G.W.R., 14, A2.
Brynkir, L.M.S., 19, F2.
Brynmawr, **L.M.S.**/G.W.R. 8, A4.
Brynmenyn, G.W.R., 7, C5.
Bryn Teify, G.W.R., 13, F4.
Bubwith, L.N.E.R., 21, D5.
Buchanan St. (Glasgow), L.M.S., 30, C1.
Buchlyvie, L.N.E.R., 30, A1.
Buckden, L.M.S., 11, C2.
See also Offord.
Buckenham, L.N.E.R., 18, F2.
Buckfastleigh, G.W.R., 2, D4.
Buckhaven, L.N.E.R., 31, A4.
Buckhurst Hill, L.N.E.R., 5, A4.
Buckie, L.N.E.R., 36, C1.
Buckingham, L.M.S., 10, D3
Buckley, L.N.E.R., 20, D4.
Bucknall & Northwood, L.M.S., 15, C3.
Bucknell, L.M.S., 14, D1.
Buckpool, L.N.E.R., 38, C5.
Bucksburn, L.N.E.R., 38, F2.
Buddon, D.A., 37, E3.
Bude, S.R., 1, A4.
Budleigh Salterton, S.R., 2 C2.
Bugle, G.W.R., 1, D2.
Buildwas, G.W.R., 15, F2.
Builth Road, G.W.R. & L.M.S., 14, E3.
Builth Wells, G.W.R., 14, E3.
Bulford, S.R., 4, C5.
Bulford Camp, S.R., 4, C5.
Bullgill, L.M.S., 26, D3.
Bullo Pill (Goods), G.W.R., 9, E2.
Bulwell, L.M.S. & L.N.E.R. 16, C4.
Bulwell Forest, L.N.E.R., 16, C4.
Bunchrew, L.M.S., 36, E5.
Bungay, L.N.E.R., 12, A2.
Buntingford, L.N.E.R., 11, E3.
Burbage, *see* Grafton.
Burbage (Goods), G.W.R., A5.
Burdale, L.N.E.R., 22, B4.
Bures, L.N.E.R., 12, E5.
Burford Bridge, *see* Box Hill.
Burgess Hill, S.R., 5, E3.
Burgh, *see* Belton.
Burgh-by-Sands, L.N.E.R., 26, C1.
Burghclere, G.W.R., 4, B3.
•Burghead, L.M.S., 36, C2.
Burgh Heath, *see* Kingswood.
Burgh-le-Marsh, L.N.E.R., 17, B4.
Burlescombe, G.W.R., 8, G5.
Burley-in-Wharfedale, O.I., 21, D2.
Burleigh St. (Goods), L.N.E.R., 22, D3.
Burmarsh Road Halt, R.H.D.R., 6, E3.
Burnbank, L.N.E.R., 30, C1.
Burneside, L.M.S., 27, G1.
•Burngullow, G.W.R., 1, D2.
Burnham (Bucks), G.W.R., 5, A1.
Burnham Market, L.N.E.R., 18, D5.
Burnham-on-Crouch, L.N.E.R., 12, G5.
Burnham-on-Sea, S.D., 8, E3
Burnley, L.M.S., 24, D1.
Burnmouth, L.N.E.R., 29, C3.
Burnside, L.M.S., 30, C1.
Burnt House (Goods) L.N.E.R., 11, A3.
Burntisland, L.N.E.R., 31, B4.
Burnt Mill, L.N.E.R., 11, F3.
Burrelton, L.M.S., 34, E1.
Burringham (Goods), *see* Gunness.
•Burrington, G.W.R., 8, D2.
Burry Port, G.W.R., 7, B2.
See also Pembrey.
Burscough Bridge, L.M.S., 20, A3.
Burscough Jc., L.M.S., 20, B4.
Bursledon, S.R., 4, E3.
Burslem, L.M.S., 15, C3.
Burston, L.N.E.R., 12, B4.
Burstwick, *see* Rye Hill.
Burton Agnes, L.N.E.R., 22, B3.
Burton & Holme, L.M.S., 24, B3.
Burton Joyce, L.M.S., 16, C3.
Burton Lane Jc., L.N.E.R., 21, C5.
Burton Latimer, L.M.S., 10, A2.
Burton Point, L.N.E.R., 20, D4.
Burton (on Trent), L.M.S. & •L.N.E.R., 15, D5.
Burton Salmon, L.N.E.R., 21, E4.
§Burwarton, G.W.R., 15, G2.
Burwell, L.N.E.R., 11, C4.
Bury, L.M.S., 20, B1.
Bury St. Edmunds, L.N.E.R., 12, C5.
Busby, L.M.S., 30, C1.
Bushbury Jc., L.M.S./G.W.R., 15, F3.
Bushey & Oxhey, L.M.S., 11, G1.
Bush Hill Park, L.N.E.R., 11, G3.
•Bute Road (Cardiff), G.W.R., 8, C4.

Bute Pier (Cardiff), G.W.R., 8, C4.
Butterknowle, L.N.E.R., 27, E4.
•Butterley, L.M.S., 16, C5.
Buttington, G.W.R./S.W., 14, A2.
Butts Jc., S.R., 4, C2.
Buxted, S.R., 5, E4.
Buxton, L.M.S., 15, A4.
Buxton Lamas, L.N.E.R., 28, E3.
Buxworth L.M.S., 15, A4.
Bwllfa Colls., G.W.R., 8, B5.
•Byers Green, L.N.E.R., 27, D5.
Byfield, L.M.S., 10, B4.
Byfleet, S.R., 5, C2.
Bynea, G.W.R., 7, B3

C

Cadeby Coll., L.M.S., 21, F4.
Cadeleigh, G.W.R., 2, A3.
Cadishead, C.L.C., 20, C2.
Cadoxton, G.W.R., 8, D4.
Caerau, G.W.R., 7, B5.
Caergwrle Castle & Wells, L.N.E.R., 20, E4.
Caerleon, G.W.R., 8, B3.
Caernarvon, L.M.S., 19, D2.
Caerphilly, G.W.R., 8, C4.
Caersws, G.W.R., 14, C3.
Caerwys, L.M.S., 20, D5.
Cairnbulg, L.N.E.R., 38, C1.
Cairneyhill, L.N.E.R., 31, B3.
Cairnie Jc., L.N.E.R., 38, D5.
Cairn Valley Jc., L.M.S., 26, B4.
Caister-on-Sea, M.G.N., 18, E1.
Calbourne & Shalfleet (I.W.), S.R., 4, F4.
Calcots, L.N.E.R., 36, C1.
•Caldarvan, L.N.E.R., 30, B2.
•Calder, L.M.S., 31, C1.
Caldercruix, L.N.E.R., 31, C1.
•Caldon Low, L.M.S., 15, C5.
Caldwell, L.M.S., 30, D2.
Caldy, B.J., 20, C5.
Callander, L.M.S., 34, G4.
•Callerton, L.N.E.R., 27, B5.
Callington, S.R., 1, C5.
Calne, G.W.R., 3, A5.
Calstock, S.R., 1, C5.
Calthwaite, L.M.S., 27, D1.
Calveley, L.M.S., 20, E3.
Calverley, L.M.S., 21, D2.
Calvert, L.N.E.R., 10, D3.
Cam, L.M.S., 9, F2.
§Camber, R.C.T., 6, E4.
Camberley, S.R., 4, B1.
Camborne, G.W.R., 1, E5.
Cambridge, L.N.E.R./L.M.S., 11, C3.
Cambus, L.N.E.R., 31, A1.
Cambusavie Plat., L.M.S., 36, A4.
Cambuslang, L.M.S., 30, C1.
Cambus o'May, L.N.E.R., 37, A2.
Camelford, S.R., 1, B3.
Camelon, L.N.E.R./L.M.S., 31, B2.
Camelon (Goods), L.N.E.R. & L.M.S., 31, B1.
Cameron Bridge, L.N.E.R., 37, G1.
Camerton (Cumb.), L.M.S., 26, E3.
•Camerton (Som.), G.W.R., 3, B3.
Campden, G.W.R., 9, C5.
•Camp Hill, L.M.S., 15, G4.
•Camps, L.M.S., 31, C3.
Camps, L.N.E.R., 31, C3.
Campsie Glen, L.N.E.R., 30, B1.
•Canada Dock, L.M.S., 20, C4.
Canal (Inverness), L.M.S., 36, E5.
Canal (Paisley), L.M.S., 30, C2.
Canal Yard (Grantham), L.N.E.R., 16, D1.
Canley Halt, L.M.S., 10, A5.
Cannock, L.M.S., 15, E4.
•Cannon St. (Hull), L.N.E.R., 22, E3.
Canonbie, L.N.E.R., 26, B1.
Canterbury, S.R., 6, C3.
Cantley, L.N.E.R., 18, F2.
•Capel, L.N.E.R., 12, D4.
•Capel Bangor, V.R., 13, C5.
Capenhurst, B.J., 20, D4.
Carbean, G.W.R., 1, D2.
Carbis, G.W.R., 1, D2.
Carbis Bay, G.W.R., 1, E4.
Carcroft, L.N.E.R., 21, F4.
Cardenden, L.N.E.R., 31, A4.
Cardiff, G.W.R., 8, —.
Cardigan, G.W.R., 13, F2.
Cardington, L.M.S., 11, D1.
Cardrona, L.N.E.R., 31, D4.
Cardross, L.N.E.R., 30, B3.
Careston, L.M.S., 37, C2.
Cargill, L.M.S., 34, E1.
Cargo Fleet, L.N.E.R., 28, E4.
Carham, L.N.E.R., 32, D4.
Carisbrooke (I.W.), S.R., 4, F3.
Cark & Cartmel, L.M.S., 24, B4.
•Carlinghow, L.M.S., 21, E3.
Carlisle, L.M.S./L.N.E.R., •L.M.S., •L.N.E.R., 26, C1.
Carlton & Netherfield, L.N.E.R., 16, C3.
See also Netherfield, L.M.S.
Carlton-on-Trent, L.N.E.R., 16, B2.
•Carlton Towers, L.N.E.R., 21, E5.
Carluke, L.M.S., 31, D1.
Carluke (Goods), L.N.E.R., 31, D1.
Carmarthen, G.W.R./L.M.S., 13, G4.
Carmont, L.M.S., 37, B4.
Carmyle, L.M.S., 30, C1.
•Carmyllie, D.A., 37, D3.
Carnaby, L.N.E.R., 22, B3.
Carn Brea, G.W.R., 1, E5.
Carnforth, L.M.S., 24, B3.
Carno, G.W.R., 14, B4.
Carnoustie, D.A., 37, E3.
Carnwath, L.M.S., 31, D2.
Carpenders Park, L.M.S., 5, A2.
Carr Bridge, L.M.S., 36, F3.
Carrog, G.W.R., 20, F5.
Carron, L.N.E.R., 36, E1.
Carronbridge, L.M.S., 31, G2.
Carshalton, S.R., 5, C3.
Carstairs, L.M.S., 31, D2.
Carterton, G.W.R., 10, E5.
•Cart Harbour (Paisley), L.M.S., 30, C2.
Cartmel, *see* Cark.
Cartsdyke, L.M.S., 30, B3.
Cassillis, L.M.S., 30, F3.
Castle (Lancaster), L.M.S., 24, C3.
Castle (Northampton), L.M.S., 10, B3.
Castle Ashby & Earls Barton, L.M.S., 10, B2.
Castle Bromwich, L.M.S., 15, G5.
Castle Bytham, L.M.S., 16, E1.
•Castle Caereinion, W.L., 14, B3.
Castle Cary (Som.), G.W.R., 3, C2.
Castlecary (Dumbarton), L.N.E.R., 31, B1.
•Castle Donington & Shardlow, L.M.S., 16, D4.
Castle Douglas, L.M.S., 26, C5.
Castle Eden, L.N.E.R., 28, D5.
Castleford, L.M.S. & L.N.E.R., 21, E4.
Castle Hedingham, *see* Sible.
•Castle Howard, L.N.E.R., 22, B5.
Castlemilk Goods, L.M.S., 26, B2.
Castle Kennedy, L.M.S., 25, C2.
Castlethorpe, L.M.S., 10, C2.
Castleton (Lancs.), L.M.S., 20, B1.
Castleton (Yorks.), L.N.E.R., 28, F3.
Castletown, I.M.R., 23, C2.
Castor, L.M.S., 11, A1.
•Catcliffe, L.N.E.R., 21, G4.
Caterham, S.R., 5, C3.
Catfield, M.G.N., 18, E2.
Cathcart, L.M.S., 30, C1.
Caton, L.M.S., 24, B3.
•Catrine, L.M.S., 30, E1.
Cattal, L.N.E.R., 21, C4.
Catterall, *see* Garstang.
Catterick Bridge, L.N.E.R., 27, F5.
Caudledown, G.W.R., 1, D2.
•Cauldcots, L.N.E.R., 37, D3.
Causeland, G.W.R., 1, D4.
•Causewayend, L.N.E.R., 31, B2.
Causewayhead, L.N.E.R., 31, A1.
Cavendish, L.N.E.R., 11, D5.
•Cawood, L.N.E.R., 21, D5.
Cawston, L.N.E.R., 18, E3.
Caythorpe, L.N.E.R., 16, C1.
Cayton, L.N.E.R., 22, A3.
Cefn, G.W.R., 20, F4.
Cefn Coed, G.W.R./L.M.S., 8, A5.
Cefn Jc., G.W.R., 7, C5.
Cefn-y-bedd, L.N.E.R., 20, E4
•Cemmaes, G.W.R., 14, B4.
Cemmes Rd., G.W.R., 14, B5.
§Cerist, G.W.R., 14, C4.
Chacewater, G.W.R., 1, E1.
Chadwell Heath, L.N.E.R., 5, A4.
Chailey, *see* Newick.
Chalcombe Road Platform, L.N.E.R., 10, C4.
Chalfont & Latimer, L.N.E.R./L.P.T.B., 10, F1.
Chalford, G.W.R., 9, F3.
Chalkwell, L.M.S., 6, A5.
Challoch Jc., L.M.S., 25, C3.
Chaloners Whin Jc., L.N.E.R., 21, C5.
Challow, G.W.R., 10, F5.
Chandlers Ford, S.R., 4, D4.
Chapel-en-le-Frith, L.M.S., 15, A4.
•Chapelhall, L.M.S., 31, C1.
•Chapel Lane, S.M., 14, A1.
Chapel St. (S'port), L.M.S., 20, A4.
Chapelton, S.R., 7, F3.
Chapeltown, L.M.S. & L.N.E.R., 21, G3.
Chappel & Wakes Colne, L.N.E.R., 12, E5.
Chard, S.R./G.W.R. & •S.R., 3, E1.
Chard Jc., S.R., 3, E1.
Charfield, L.M.S., 9, F2.
Charing, S.R., 6, D4.
Charing Cross, S.R. & L.P.T.B., 5, B3.
Charlbury, G.W.R., 10, D5.
•Charlestown, L.N.E.R., 31, B3.
Charlton, S.R., 5, B4.
Charlton Kings, G.W.R., 9, D4.
Charlton Mackrell, G.W.R., 3, D2.
Chartham, S.R., 6, C3.
•Chartley & Stowe, L.N.E.R., 15, D4.
Charwelton, L.N.E.R., 10, B4.
Chatburn, L.M.S., 24, D1.
Chatham, S.R., 6, B5.
Chathill, L.N.E.R., 32, E1.
Chatteris, L.N.E.R., 11, A3.
Chatterley, L.M.S., 15, C3.
Cheadle (Ches.), L.M.S. & C.L.C., 20, C1.
Cheadle (Staffs.), L.M.S., 15, C4.
Cheadle Hulme, L.M.S., 15, A3.
Cheam, S.R., 5, C3.
Cheddar, G.W.R., 3, B1.
Cheddington, L.M.S., 10, E1.
Cheddleton, L.M.S., 15, C4.
Chedworth, G.W.R., 9, E4.
Chelford, L.M.S., 15, A3.
•Chellaston & Swarkestone, L.M.S., 16, D5.
Chelmsford, L.N.E.R., 11, F5
Chelsfield, S.R., 5, C4.
Cheltenham Spa, G.W.R. & L.M.S., 9, D4.
Cheltenham South & Leckhampton, G.W.R., 9, D4.
Chenies, *see* Chorley Wood.
Chepstow, G.W.R., 8, B2.
Chequerbent, L.M.S., 20, B2.
•Checker House, L.N.E.R., 16, A3.
Cherry Burton, L.N.E.R., 22, D4.
Cherry Tree, L.M.S., 24, E2.
Chertsey, S.R., 5, B1.
Chesham, L.N.E.R./L.P.T.B., 10, F1.
Chesham Bois, *see* Amersham.
Cheshunt, L.N.E.R., 11, G3.
Chessington, S.R., 5, C2.
Chester, B.J./G.W.R./L.M.S. & C.L.C./L.N.E.R., 20, D4.
Chesterfield, L.M.S. & L.N.E.R., 16, B5.
Chester-le-Street, L.N.E.R., 27, C5.
Chester Road, L.M.S., 15, F5.
Chesterton, L.M.S., 15, C3.
Chestfield & Swalecliffe Halt, S.R., 6, B3.
Chettisham, L.N.E.R., 11 B4.
Chevington, L.N.E.R., 32, G1.
Chichester, S.R., 4, E1.
§Chigwell, L.N.E.R., 5, A4.
Chigwell Lane, L.N.E.R., 11, G3.
Chilcompton, S.D., 3, B3.
Chilham, S.R., 6, C3.
Chilsworthy Halt, S.R., 1, C5.
Chiltern Green, L.M.S., 11, F1.
Chilton Jc., L.N.E.R., 28, E5.
Chilvers Coton, L.M.S., 16, G5.
Chilworth & Albury, S.R., 5, D1.
Chingford, L.N.E.R., 5, A4.
Chinley, L.M.S., 15, A4.
Chinnor, G.W.R., 10, F2.
Chippenham, G.W.R., 3, A4.
Chippenham Jc., L.N.E.R., 11, C5.
Chipping Norton, G.W.R., 10, D5.
Chipping Sodbury, G.W.R., 9, G2.
Chipstead, S.R., 5, C3.
Chirk, G.W.R., 20, F4.
Chirnside, L.N.E.R., 32, C3.
Chirton, *see* Patney.
Chiseldon, G.W.R., 9, G5
Chislehurst, S.R., 5, B4.
Chollerton, L.N.E.R., 27, B3.
Cholsey & Moulsford, G.W.R., 10, G4.
Choppington, L.N.E.R., 27, A5.
Chorley, L.M.S., 24, E2.
Chorley Wood & Chenies, L.N.E.R./L.P.T.B., 10, F1.
Chorlton-cum-Hardy, C.L.C., 20, C1.
Christchurch, S.R., 4, F5.
Christon Bank, L.N.E.R., 32, E1.
Christow, G.W.R., 2, B4.
Christ's Hospital (West Horsham), S.R., 5, E2.
•Chryston, L.N.E.R., 30, C1.
Chudleigh, G.W.R., 2, C3.
Church & Oswaldtwistle, L.M.S., 24, E1.
•Churchbury, L.N.E.R., 11, G3.
Churchdown G.W.R./L.M.S., 9 D3
Church Fenton, L.N.E.R./L.M.S., 20, D4.
Churchill & Blakedown, G.W.R., 9, A3.
Church Road, G.W.R., 8, B3.
Church Stretton, S.H., 15, F1.
Churchtown, L.M.S., 20, A4.
Church Village Halt, G.W.R., 8, C5.
Churchway, G.W.R., 9, E2.
Churn, G.W.R., 10, G4.
Churston, G.W.R., 2, D3.
Chwilog, L.M.S., 19, F1.
Cilfrew, G.W.R., 7, B4.
•Cilfynydd, G.W.R., 8, B5.
Ciliau-Aeron, G.W.R., 13, E4.
Cilmery Halt, L.M.S., 14, E3.
Cinderford, S.V.Y., 9, E2.
Cirencester, G.W.R., 9, E4.
•Clackmannan, L.N.E.R., 31, A2.
Clacton-on-Sea & Holland-on-Sea, L.N.E.R., 12, F3.
Clandon, S.R., 5, C2.
Clapham Jc. (London), S.R., 5, B3.
Clapham (Yorks.), L.M.S., 24, B1.
Clarbeston Road, G.W.R., 13 G1.
Clarboro' Jc., L.N.E.R., 16, A2.
Clare, L.N.E.R., 11, D5.
•Clarence Road (Cardiff), G.W.R., 8, C4.
Clarence St. (Pontypool), G.W.R., 8, B3.
Clarkston (Lanark), L.N.E.R., 31, C1.
Clarkston (Renfrew), L.M.S., 30, C1.
Clatford, S.R., 4, C4.
Claverdon, G.W.R., 9, B5.
Claxby & Usselby, L.N.E.R., 22, G3.
Clay Cross, L.M.S., 16, B5.
Claydon (Bucks.), L.M.S., 10, D3.
Claydon (Suffolk), L.N.E.R., 12 D4.
Claygate, S.R., 5, C2.
Clay Mills, *see* Stretton.
Claypole, L.N.E.R., 16, C2.
Clayton, L.N.E.R., 21, D2.
Clayton West, L.M.S., 21, F.3.
•Cleator Moor East, L.M.S., 26, F3.
Cleckheaton, L.M.S., 21, E2.
Clee Hill, S.H., 9, A1.
Cleethorpes, L.N.E.R., 22 F2.
Cleeve, L.M.S., 9, D3.
Clegg St. (Oldham), O.A.G.B., 21, F1.
Cleghorn, L.M.S., 31, D2.
Cleland (late Omoa), L.M.S., 31, C1.
Clenchwarton, M.G.N., 17, E4.
Cleobury Mortimer, G.W.R., 9, A2.
§Cleobury Mortimer Town, G.W.R., 9, A2.
Clevedon, G.W.R., 8, D3.
Cliburn, L.N.E.R., 27, E1.
Cliff Common, L.N.E.R. & •D.V.L., 21, D5.
Cliffe, S.R., 6, B5.
Cliffe Park, L.M.S., 15, B4.
•Clifford, G.W.R., 14, E2.
Clifton (Derbys.), L.M.S., 15, C5.
•Clifton & Lowther, L.M.S., 27, E1.
Clifton Bridge, G.W.R., 8, C2.
Clifton Down, G.W.R./L.M.S., 8, C2.
Clifton Jc. (Lancs.), L.M.S., 20, B1.
Clifton Maybank (Goods), G.W.R., 3, E2.
Clifton Mill, L.M.S., 10, A4.
Clifton Moor, L.N.E.R., 27, E1.
Clifton-on-Trent, L.N.E.R., 16, B2.
Clipston & Oxenden, L.M.S., 10, A3.
Clipstone (Goods), L.N.E.R., 16, B3.
Clitheroe, L.M.S., 24, D1.
Clock Face, L.M.S., 20, C3.
Clocksbriggs, L.M.S., 37, D2.
Closeburn, L.M.S., 26, A4.
Clough Fold, L.M.S., 20, A1.
Cloughton, L.N.E.R., 28, G1.
Clovenfords, L.N.E.R., 31, E5.
Clown, L.M.S. & •L.N.E.R., 16, A4.
Clubmoor, C.L.C., 20, C4.
Clunes, L.M.S., 35, D5.
Clutton, G.W.R., 3, B2.
Clydach, L.M.S., 8, A4.
Clydach-on-Tawe, L.M.S., 7, B4.
Clydach Vale, G.W.R., 8, B5.
Clydebank, L.M.S. & L.N.E.R., 30, C2.
Clynderwen, G.W.R., 13, G2.
Coalbrookdale, G.W.R., 15, F2.
Coalburn, L.M.S., 31, E1.
Coaley Jc., L.M.S, 9, F2.
Coalpit Heath, G.W.R., 8, C1.
Coalport, G.W.R. & L.M.S., 15, F2.
Coalville, L.M.S., 16, E4.
Coanwood, L.N.E.R., 27, C2.
Coatbridge, L.M.S. & L.N.E.R., 30, C1.
•Coates (Glos.), G.W.R., 9, F4.
Cobbinshaw, L.M.S., 31, C2.
Cobham, S.R., 5, C2.
Cobridge, L.M.S., 15, C3.
Cockburnspath, L.N.E.R., 32, B4.
Cockermouth, L.M.S., 26, E3.
Cockett, G.W.R., 7, B4.
Cockfield, L.N.E.R., 12, C5.
Cockfield Fell, L.N.E.R., 27, E5.
•Cocking, S.R., 4, D1.
Cockley Brake Jc., L.M.S., 10, C4.
Codford, G.W.R., 3 C4.
Codnor Park, L.N.E.R., 16, C4.
Codnor Park & Ironville, L.M.S., 16, C5.
Codsall, G.W.R., 15, F3.
Coed Ely, G.W.R., 8, C5.
•Coed Poeth, G.W.R., 20, E5.
Coed Talon, L.M.S., 20, E5.
Cogan, G.W.R., 8, C4.
Cogload Jc., G.W.R., 8, F3.
Coity (Goods), *see* Bridgend.
Coity Jc., G.W.R., 7, C5.
Colbren Jc., G.W.R., 7, A5.
Colby, I.M.R., 23, C2.
Colchester, L.N.E.R., 12, E4.
Coldham, L.N.E.R., 17, F3.
•Cold Norton, L.N.E.R., 12, G5.
Coldstream, L.N.E.R., 32, D3.
Cole, S.D., 3, C3.
•Coleburn, L.N.E.R., 36, D1.
•Coleford, S.V.Y., 9, E1.
Coleford Jc., S.R., 2, B4.
Cole Green, L.N.E.R., 11, F2.
Coleham (Goods), S.H., 15, E1.
Coleshill, L.M.S., 15, G5.
Colfin, L.M.S., 25, C2.
•Colinton, L.M.S. 31, C4.
Collessie, L.N.E.R., 37, F1.
Collingbourne, G.W.R., 4, B5.
Collingham, L.M.S., 16, B2.
Collingham Bridge, L.N.E.R., 21, C4.
Collington Halt, S.R., 6, F5.
Collins Green, L.M.S., 20, C3.
Colliston, L.M.S., 37, D3.
Collyweston, *see* Ketton.
Colnbrook, G.W.R., 5, B2.
Colne, L.M.S., 21, inset.
Coltishall, L.N.E.R., 18, E3.
Colwall, G.W.R., 9, C2.
Colwich, L.M.S., 15, E4.
Colwyn Bay, L.M.S., 19, C4
Colyford, S.R., 2, B1.
Colyton, S.R., 2, B1.
•Colzium, L.N.E.R., 31, B1.
Combpyne, S.R., 2, B1.
Commondale, L.N.E.R., 28, F3.
Commondyke, L.M.S., 30, F1.
•Commonhead, L.N.E.R., 31, C1.
Compton, G.W.R., 10, G4.
Comrie, L.M.S., 34, F3.
Condover, S.H., 15, F1.
Congleton, L.M.S., 15, B3.
Congresbury, G.W.R., 8, D2.
Coningsby, L.N.E.R., 17, C2.
Conisborough, L.N.E.R., 21, F4.
Coniston, L.M.S., 26, G2.
Connah's Quay, L.M.S., 20, D4.
Connah's Quay & Shotton, L.N.E.R., 20, D4.
Connel Ferry, L.M.S., 33, E2.
Conon, L.M.S., 35, D5.
Cononley, L.M.S., 21, C1.
Consall, L.M.S., 15, C4.
Consett, L.N.E.R., 27, C5.
Constable Burton, L.N.E.R., 27, G5.
Conway, L.M.S., 19, D3.
Conwil, G.W.R., 13, G4.
Cooden Beach, S.R., 6, F5.
Cookham, G.W.R., 10, G2.
Cooksbridge, S.R., 5, F4.
Coombe, G.W.R., 1, D4.
Coombe Road, S.R., 5, C3.
Cooper Bridge, L.M.S., 21, E2.
Copgrove, L.N.E.R., 21, B3.
Copmanthorpe, L.N.E.R., 21, C5.
Copplestone, S.R., 2, A4.
Copyhold Jc., S.R., 5, E3.
Coppull, L.M.S., 20, A3.
Corbridge, L.N.E.R., 27, C4.
Corby Glen, L.N.E.R., 16, D1.
Corby & Weldon, L.M.S., 16, G1.
Corfe Castle, S.R., 3, G4.
Corkickle (Whitehaven), L.M.S., 26, E4.
Cornhill, L.N.E.R., 38, C4.
Cornwood, G.W.R., 2, D5.
Corpach, L.N.E.R., 33, C3.
Corpusty & Saxthorpe, M.G.N., 18, D4.
§*Corriegour Siding*, L.N.E.R., 33, B4.
•Corris, Corris, 14, B5.
Corrour, L.N.E.R., 33, C5.
Corsham, G.W.R., 3, A4.
Corstorphine, L.N.E.R., 31, B4.
Corton, N.S.J., 18, F1.
Corwen, G.W.R./L.M.S., 19 F5.
Coryton, G.W.R., 1, C5.
Cosford, G.W.R., 15, F3.
Cosham, S.R., 4, E2.
Cossington, S.D., 8, E3.
•Cotcastle, L.M.S., 31, D1.
Cotehill, L.M.S., 27, C1.
•Cotham, L.N.E.R., 16, C2.
Cotherstone, L.N.E.R., 27, E4.
Coton Hill (Goods), G.W.R., 15, E1.
Cottam, L.N.E.R., 16, A2.
Cottesmore Iron Mines, L.M.S., 16, E1.
Cottingham, L.N.E.R., 22, D3.
•Cottingwith D.V.L., 21, D5.
Coughton, L.M.S., 9, B4.
Coulsdon North, S.R., 5, C3.
,, South, S.R., 5, C3.
Coulter, L.M.S., 31, E3.
•Coundon, L.N.E.R., 27, E5.
Coundon Road, L.M.S., 10, A5.
Counter Drain, M.G.N., 17, E2.
Countesthorpe, L.M.S., 16, F3.
County School, L.N.E.R., 18, • E4.
Coupar Angus, L.M.S., 34, E1.
Cove Bay, L.M.S., 38, G2.
Coventry, L.M.S., 10, A5.
Cowbit, L.N.E.R., 17, E2.
Cowbridge, G.W.R., 8, C5.
Cowden, S.R., 5, D4.
Cowdenbeath, L.N.E.R., 31, A3.
Cowes (I.W.), S.R., 4, F3.
Cowley, G.W.R., 5, A2.
Cowley Bridge Jc., G.W.R., S.R., 2, B3.
Cowton, L.N.E.R., 28, F5.
•Coxbench, L.M.S., 16, C5.
Cox Green, L.N.E.R., 28, C5.
Coxhoe (Goods), L.N.E.R., 28, D5.
Coxhoe Bridge, L.N.E.R., 28, D5.
•Coxlodge, L.N.E.R., 27, B5.
Coxwold, L.N.E.R., 21, B5.
Craddock Lane (Bolton) Goods, L.M.S., 20, B2.
Cradley Heath, G.W.R., 15, G3.
Cradoc, G.W.R., 14, F4.
Craigellachie, L.N.E.R., 36, D1.
Craigendoran, L.N.E.R., 30, B3.
Craigie, *see* Riccarton, L.M.S.
Craigo, L.M.S., 37, C3.
Craig-y-nos (Penwyllt), G.W.R., 7, B5.
Crail, L.N.E.R., 37, F3.
Crakehall, L.N.E.R., 27, G5.
Cramlington, L.N.E.R., 27, B5.
Cranbrook, S.R., 6, D5.
Crane St. (Pontypool), G.W.R., 8, B3.
Cranford (Northants), L.M.S., 10, A1.
Crank, L.M.S., 20, B3.
Cranleigh, S.R., 5, D2.
Cranmore, G.W.R., 3, C3.
Cransley, L.M.S., 10, A2.
Crathes, L.N.E.R., 37, A4.
Craven Arms & Stokesay, S.H., 14, C1.
Crawford, L.M.S., 31, F2.
Crawley, S.R., 5, D3.
Cray, G.W.R., 14, G4.
Crayford, S.R., 5, B4.
Creagan, L.M.S., 33, E3.
Credenhill, L.M.S., 9, C1.
Crediton, S.R., 2, B4.
Creech Jc., G.W.R., 8 F4.
Creech St. Michael Halt, G.W.R., 8, F3.
Creetown, L.M.S., 25, C4.
Creigiau, G.W.R., 8, C5.
Cressage, G.W.R., 15, F1.
Cressing, L.N.E.R., 11, F5.
Cressington, C.L.C., 20, C4.
Cresswell (Staffs.), L.M.S., 15, D4.
Creswell (Derbys.) *see* Elmton
•Creswell & Welbeck, L.N.E.R., 16, B4.
Crewe, L.M.S./G.W.R., 15, C2.
•Crew Green, S.M., 14, A1.
Crewkerne, S.R., 3, E1.
Crews Hill, L.N.E.R., 11, G2.
Crianlarich, L.M.S. & L.N.E.R., 33, F5.
Criccieth, G.W.R., 19, F2.
Crick, *see* Kilsby.
Cricklade, G.W.R., 9, F4.
Cricklewood, L.M.S., 5, A3.
Crieff, L.M.S., 34 F3.
•Criggion, S.M., 14, A2.
Crigglestone, L.M.S., 21, E3.
Crimple Jc., L.N.E.R., 21, C3
Crocklands (Goods), L.M.S., 24, B4.
Croes Newydd (Goods), G.W.R., 20, E4.
Croft, L.M.S., 16, F4.
Crofthead, *see* Fauldhouse, L.N.E.R.
Crofton, L.M.S., 21, E4.
Croft Spa, L.N.E.R., 28, F5.
Cromdale, L.N.E.R., 36, E2.
Cromer, L.N.E.R. 18, D3.

CROMER BEACH—EVERINGHAM

Cromer Beach, M.G.N., 18, D3.
Cromford, L.M.S., 16, C2.
Crompton, *see* Shaw.
Cronberry, L.M.S., 30, F1.
Crook, L.N.E.R., 27, D5.
Crook of Devon, L.N.E.R., 34, G2.
Crook St. (Bolton) Goods, L.M.S., 20, B2.
Cropredy, G.W.R., 10, C4.
Crosby, L.M.R., 23, B2.
Crosby Garrett, L.M.S., 27, F2.
Crossens, L.M.S., 20, A4.
Crossfield (Goods), L.M.S., 26, F3.
•Crossford, L.M.S., 26, A5.
Crossgates (Fife), L.N.E.R., 31, A3.
Crossgates (Salop), *see* Ford (Salop).
Cross Gates (Yorks.), L.N.E.R., 21, D3.
Cross Hands, G.W.R., 7, A3.
Crosshills, *see* Kildwick.
Crosshouse, L.M.S., 30, E2.
Cross Inn, G.W.R., 8, C5.
Cross Keys, G.W.R., 8, B4.
Crosslee, *see* Houston.
Crossmichael, L.M.S., 26, B5.
Croston, L.M.S., 24, E3.
Crowborough & Jarvis Brook, S.R., 5, E4.
Crowcombe, G.W.R., 8, F4.
Crowden, L.N.E.R., 21, G2.
Crowhurst, S.R., 6, F5.
Crowhurst Jc., S.R., 5, D4.
•Crowle, A.J., 22, E5.
Crowle Central, L.N.E.R., 22, F5.
Crow Park, L.N.E.R., 16, B2.
Crowsnest Mine, S.B.H., 14, B1.
Crowthorne, S.R., 4, B1.
Croxley Green, L.M.S., & L.N.E.R./L.P.T.B., 11, G1.
Croy, L.N.E.R., 31, B1.
•Cruckton, S.M., 14, A1.
§Cruden Bay, L.N.E.R., 38, E1.
Crudgington, G.W.R., 15, E2.
Crumlin, G.W.R., 8, B4.
Crumpsall, L.M.S., 20, B1.
Crymmych Arms, G.W.R., 13, F2.
Crynant, G.W.R., 7, A5.
Crystal Palace, S.R., 5, B3.
Cuddington, C.L.C., 20, D3.
Cudworth, L.M.S., & •L.N.E.R., 21, F4.
Cuffley & Goff's Oak, L.N.E.R., 11, G2.
Culcheth, L.N.E.R., 20, C2.
Culgaith, L.M.S., 27, E1.
Culham, G.W.R., 10, F4.
Culkerton, G.W.R., 9, F3.
Cullen, L.N.E.R., 38, C5.
Cullercoats, L.N.E.R., 28, B5.
Cullingworth, L.N.E.R., 21, D2.
Culloden Moor, L.M.S., 36, D4.
Cullompton, G.W.R., 2, A2.
Culmstock, G.W.R., 2, A2.
Culrain, L.M.S., 35, A5.
•Culross, L.N.E.R., 31, B2.
Culter, L.N.E.R., 38, G3.
Cults, L.N.E.R., 38, G2.
Culworth, L.N.E.R., 10, C4.
Cumbernauld, L.M.S., 31, B1.
Cumberworth, *see* Denby Dale.
Cummersdale, L.M.S., 26, C1.
Cummertrees, L.M.S., 26, B3.
Cumnock, L.M.S., 30, F1.
Cumwhinton, L.M.S., 26, C1.
Cunninghamhead, L.M.S., 30, D3.
Cupar, L.N.E.R., 37, F2.
•Currie, L.M.S., 31, C3.
Currie Hill, L.M.S., 31, C3.
Curry Rivell Jc., G.W.R., 3, D1.
Curthwaite, L.M.S., 26, C1.
•Cuthlie, D.A., 37, D3.
Cutler's Green Halt, L.N.E.R., 11, E4.
Cutnall Green, G.W.R., 9, A3.
Cuxton, S.R., 6, B5.
Cwm, G.W.R., 8, A4.
Cwmavon (Glam.), G.W.R., 7, B5.
Cwmavon (Mon.), G.W.R. & •L.M.S., 8, A3.
Cwm Bargoed, G.W.R., 8, A5.
•Cwmblawd, G.W.R., 7, A3.
Cwmbran, G.W.R., 8, B3.
Cwmcarn, G.W.R., 8, B4.
Cwmdu, G.W.R., 7, B5.
Cwmllynfell, L.M.S., 7, A4.
Cwmmawr, G.W.R., 7, A3.
Cwm Prysor, G.W.R., 19, F3.
Cwm Tillery Coll., G.W.R., 8, A4.
•Cwm-y-Glo, L.M.S., 19, E2.
•Cyfronydd, W.L., 14, B3.
Cymmer, G.W.R., 7, B5.
Cynghordy, L.M.S., 14, F5.
•Cynheidre, G.W.R., 7, A3.
Cynwyd, G.W.R., 19, F5.

D

Dacre, L.N.E.R., 21, B2.
•Dafen, G.W.R., 7, B3.
Dagenham, L.M.S./L.P.T.B., 5, A4.
Dagenham Dock, L.M.S., 5, A4.
Daggons Road, S.R., 4, E5.
Dailly, L.M.S., 30, G3.
Dairsie, L.N.E.R., 37, F2.
Daisy Bank, G.W.R., 15, G4.
Daisyfield, L.M.S., 24, D2.
Daisy Hill, L.M.S., 20, B2.
Dalbeattie, L.M.S., 26, C4.
Dalcross, L.M.S., 36, D4.
Dalderse (Goods), L.N.E.R., 31, B2.
Dalguise, L.M.S., 34, D2.
•Dalkeith, L.N.E.R., 31, C4.
•Dallow Lane, L.M.S., 15, D5.
Dalmally, L.M.S., 33, F4.
Dalmellington, L.M.S., 30, G2.
Dalmeny, L.N.E.R., 31, B3.
Dalmuir, L.M.S. & L.N.E.R., 30, C2.
Dalnaspidal, L.M.S., 34, C4.
Dalreoch, L.M.S./L.N.E.R., 30, B3.
Dalry, L.M.S., 30, D3.
Dalrymple, L.M.S., 30, F3.
•Dalrymple Jc., L.M.S., 30, F3.
Dalserf, L.M.S., 31, D1.
Dalston (Cumb.), L.M.S., 26, C1.
Dalton, L.M.S., 24, B4.
Dalwhinnie, L.M.S., 34, B5.
Damems, L.M.S., 21, D1.
Danby, L.N.E.R., 28, F3.
Danby Wiske, L.N.E.R., 28, G5.
Dandaleith, L.N.E.R., 36, D1.
Danzey, G.W.R., 9, A5.
Darcy Lever, L.M.S., 20, B2.
Daresbury, B.J., 20, C3.
Darfield, L.M.S., 21, F4.
Darfeld Main Coll., L.N.E.R., 21, F4.
Darlaston, L.M.S., 15, F4.
Darley, L.N.E.R., 21, C2.
Darley Dale, L.M.S., 16, B5.
Darlington, L.N.E.R., 28, E5.
Darnall, L.N.E.R., 16, A4.
Darran, G.W.R., 8, B4.
•Darras Hall, L.N.E.R., 27, B5.
Darsham, L.N.E.R., 12, B2.
Dartford, S.R., 5, B5.
Darton, L.M.S., 21, F3.
Darvel, L.M.S., 30, E1.
Darwen, L.M.S., 24, E2.
Datchet, S.R., 5, B1.
Dauntsey, G.W.R., 9, G4.
Dava, L.M.S., 36, E3.
Davenport, L.M.S., 15, A3.
Daventry, L.M.S., 10, B4.
Daviot, L.M.S., 36, E4.
Dawley & Stirchley, L.M.S., 15, F2.
Dawlish, G.W.R., 2, C3.
Dawlish Warren, G.W.R., 2, C3.
Daybrook, L.N.E.R., 16, C3.
Deadwater, L.N.E.R., 32, G5
Deal, S.R., 6, C1.
Dean, S.R., 4, D5.
Dean Lane, L.M.S., 20, B1.
Dearham Bridge, L.M.S., 26, D3.
Dechmont Coll., L.M.S., 30, C1.
Deepcar, L.N.E.R., 21, F3.
•Deepdale, L.M.S., 24, D3.
Deepdene, S.R., 5, C2.
Deepfields, L.M.S., 15, F4.
Defford, L.M.S., 9, C3.
Deganwy, L.M.S., 19, C3.
•Deighton, L.M.S., 21, E2.
Delabole, S.R., 1, C3.
Delamere, C.L.C., 20, D3.
Delny, L.M.S., 36, C5.
Delph, L.M.S., 21, F1.
Denaby Halt, L.M.S., 21, F4.
Denbigh, L.M.S., 19, D5.
•Denby, L.M.S., 16, C5.
Denby Dale & Cumberworth, L.M.S., 21, F3.
Denham, G.W.R./L.N.E.R., 10, F1.
Denham Golf Club Plat., G.W.R./L.N.E.R., 10, F1.
•Denhead, D.A., 37, D3.
Denholme, L.N.E.R., 21, D2.
Denny, L.M.S., 31, B1.
•Dennyloanhead, L.N.E.R., 31, B1.
Denstone, L.M.S., 15, C5.
Dent, L.M.S., 24, A1.
Denton (Lancs.), L.M.S., 20, C1.
Denton Siding, L.N.E.R., 16, D2.
•Denver, L.N.E.R., 17, F4.
Derby, L.M.S. & L.N.E.R., 16, D5.
Derby Road (Ipswich). L.N.E.R., 12, D3.
•Derby Road (Loughboro'), L.M.S., 16, E4.
Dereham, L.N.E.R., 18, E4.
Deri Jc., G.W.R., 8, B4.
Derry Ormond, G.W.R., 13, E5.
Dersingham, L.N.E.R., 17, D5.
Derwen, L.M.S., 19, E5.
Derwenthaugh (Goods), L.N.E.R., 27, C5.
Derwent Iron & Steel Works (Workington), L.M.S., 26, E3.
Derwydd Rd., G.W.R., 13, G5.
Desborough & Rothwell, L.M.S., 16, G2.
Desford, L.M.S., 16, F4.
Dess, L.N.E.R., 37, A3.
•Devil's Bridge, V.R., 14, C5.
Devizes, G.W.R., 3, B5.
Devonport, G.W.R.,& S.R., 1, D5.
Devynock & Sennybridge, G.W.R., 14, F4.
Dewsbury, L.M.S & L.N.E.R., 21, E3.
Dewshill Pit, L.M.S., 31, C1.
Dicconson Lane, L.M.S., 20, B2.
Didcot, G.W.R., 10, F4.
Didsbury, L.M.S., 20, C1.
Digby, L.N.E.R., 17, C1.
Diggle, L.M.S., 21, F1.
Dinas (Caern'v'n), L.M.S., 19, E1.
Dinas (Rhondda), G.W.R., 8, B5.
•Dinas Mawddwy, G.W.R., 14, A4.
Dinas Powis, G.W.R., 8, D4.
Dingestow, G.W.R., 8, A2.
Dingwall, L.M.S., 35, D5.
Dinmore, S.H., 9, B1.
Dinnet, L.N.E.R., 37, A2.
•Dinnington & Laughton, S.Y., 16, A4.
Dinnington Coll., S.Y., 16, A4.
Dinsdale, L.N.E.R., 28, F5.
Dinting, L.N.E.R., 21, G1.
Dinton, S.R., 3, C5.
Dinwoodie, L.M.S., 26, A3.
Dipple (Goods), L.M.S., 30, G4.
Dirleton, L.N.E.R., 32, B5.
Disley, L.M.S., 15, A4.
Diss, L.N.E.R., 12, B4.
•Distington, L.M.S., 26, E3.
•Ditchford, L.M.S., 10, A1.
Ditchingham, L.N.E.R., 12, A2.
Ditton, L.M.S., 20, C3.
§Ditton Priors, G.W.R., 15, G1.
Docking, L.N.E.R., 17, D5.
Dock St. (Newport) Goods, G.W.R., 8, C3.
Doddington & Harby, L.N.E.R., 16, B2.
Dodworth, L.N.E.R., 21, F3.
Doe Hill, L.M.S., 16, B4.
Dogdyke, L.N.E.R., 17, C2.
Dolau, L.M.S., 14, D3.
Doldowlod, G.W.R., 14, D4.
Dolgarrog, L.M.S., 19, D3.
Dolgelley, G.W.R., 14, A5.
•Dolgoch, Tal., 13, B5.
Dollar, L.N.E.R., 31, A2.
•Dolphinton, L.M.S., 31, D3.
Dolwen, G.W.R., 14, C4.
Dolwyddelen, L.M.S., 19, E3.
Dolygaer Halt, G.W.R., 8, A5.
Dolyhir, G.W.R., 14, E2.
Doncaster, L.N.E.R., 21, F5.
Donington-on-Bain, L.N.E.R., 17, A2.
Donington Road, L.N.E.R., 17, D2.
•Donisthorpe, L.M.S., 16, E5.
Donnington, L.M.S., 15, E2.
Dorchester, G.W.R. & S.R., 3, F3.
Dore & Totley, L.M.S., 16, A5.
Dorking North, S.R., 5, C2.
,, Town, S.R., 5, C2.
Dormans, S.R., 5, D4.
Dornoch, L.M.S., 36, B4.
Dorridge, *see* Knowle.
Dorrington, S.H., 15, F1.
•Dorstone, G.W.R., 14, F2.
Doublebois, G.W.R., 1, D4.
Douglas, I.M.R. & M.E., 23, C2.
Douglas West, L.M.S., 31, E1
Doune, L.M.S., 34, G4.
Doura, L.M.S., 30, D3.
Dousland, G.W.R., 2, C5.
Dovecliffe, L.N.E.R., 21, F4.
Dove Holes, L.M.S., 15, A4.
Dove Jc., L.M.S., 15, D5.
Dover, S.R., 6, D2.
Dovercourt Bay, L.N.E.R., 12, E3.
Dovey Jc., G.W.R., 14, B5.
Dowdeswell, *see* Andoversford.
Dowlais, G.W.R. & L.M.S., 8, A5.
Dowlais Top, G.W.R., 8, A5.
Downham, L.N.E.R., 17, F4.
•Downholland, L.M.S., 20, B4
Downton, S.R., 4, D5.
Dragon Jc., L.N.E.R., 21, C3.
•Drax, L.N.E.R., 21, E5.
Drax Hales, L.N.E.R., 21, E5.
Draycott (Derbys.), L.M.S., 16, D4.
Draycott (Som.), G.W.R., 3, B2.
Drayton (Nor.), M.G.N., 18, E3.
•Drayton (Sussex), S.R.,4,E1.
Dreghorn, L.M.S., 30, E3.
Drem, L.N.E.R., 31, B5.
Driffield, L.N.E.R., 22, C4.
Drigg, L.M.S., 26, F3.
Drighlington, L.N.E.R., 21, E2.
•Drinnick Mill, G.W.R., 1, D2.
Droitwich Rd. (Goods), L.M.S., 9, B4.
Droitwich Spa, G.W.R./L.M.S., 9, B3.
Dronfield, L.M.S., 16, A5.
Drongan, L.M.S., 30, F2.
Dronley, L.M.S., 37, E1.
Droxford, S.R., 4, D2.
Droylsden, L.M.S., 21, F1.
Drum, L.N.E.R., 37, A4.
Drumburgh, L.N.E.R., 26, C2.
Drumchapel, L.N.E.R., 30, C2.
Drumlithie, L.M.S., 37, B4.
Drummuir, L.N.E.R., 36, D1
Drumshoreland, L.N.E.R., 31, B3.
Drws-y-Nant, G.W.R., 19, G4.
Drybridge, L.M.S., 30, E3.
•Drybrook Rd., S.V.Y., 9, E2.
•Drymen, L.N.E.R., 30, B2.
Drypool (Goods), L.N.E.R., 22, E3.
Dryslwyn, L.M.S., 13, G5.
Dubton Jc., L.M.S., 37, C3.
•Dudbridge, L.M.S., 9, E3.
Dudley, G.W.R. & L.M.S., 15, G4
Dudley Hill, L.N.E.R., 21, D2.
Dudley Port, L.M.S., 15, G4.
Duffield, L.M.S., 16, C5.
Dufftown, L.N.E.R., 36, E1.
Duirinish, L.M.S., 35, F1.
Dukeries Jc., L.N.E.R., 16, B2.
Dukinfield, L.M.S. & L.N.E.R., 21, F1.
Dullatur, L.N.E.R., 31, B1.
Dullingham, L.N.E.R., 11, C4.
Dulverton, G.W.R., 7, F5.
Dumbarton, L.M.S./ L.N.E.R., & L.M.S., 30, B2.
Dumbuck (Goods),L.N.E.R., 30, B2.
Dumfries, L.M.S., 26, B4.
Dumfries, St. Mary's (Goods), L.M.S., 26, B4.
Dumfries House, L.M.S., 30, F1.
Dumgoyne, L.N.E.R., 30, B2
Dumpton Park, S.R., 6, B1.
Dunball, G.W.R., 8, E3.
Dunbar, L.N.E.R., 32, B4.
Dunblane, L.M.S., 34, G3.
Dunbridge, S.R., 4, D4.
Dunchurch, L.M.S., 10, A2.
Dundee, D.A., L.M.S., L.N.E.R., 37, E2.
Dunfermline, L.N.E.R., 31, A3.
Dunford Bridge, L.N.E.R., 21, F2.
Dungeness, R.H.D.R. & •S.R., 6, E3.
Dunham, L.N.E.R., 18, E5.
Dunham Hill, B.J., 20, D3.
Dunham Massey, L.M.S., 20, C2.
Dunhampstead (Goods), L.M.S., 9, B3.
Dunkeld & Birnam, L.M.S., 34, D2.
Dunlop, L.M.S., 30, D2.
Dunmow, L.N.E.R., 11, E4.
Dunning, L.M.S., 34, F2.
•Dunnington, D.V.L., 21, C5.
Dunphail, L.M.S., 36, D3.
Dunragit, L.M.S., 25, C2.
Dunrobin (Private), L.M.S., 36, A4.
Duns, L.N.E.R., 32, C4.
Dunsbear Halt, S.R., 1, A5.
•Dunscore, L.M.S., 26, A4.
Dunsland Cross, S.R., 1, A5.
Dunstable, L.M.S./L.N.E.R., 10, D1.
Dunstable Town, L.N.E.R./ L.M.S., 10, D1.
Dunstall Park, G.W.R., 15, F3.
Dunster, G.W.R., 8, E5.
Dunston, *see* Nocton.
•Dunsyre, L.M.S., 31, D3.
Dunton Green, S.R., 5, C4.
•Dunure, L.M.S., 30, F3.
Dunvant, L.M.S., 7, B3.
Durham, L.N.E.R., 27, D5.
Durham Ox Jc., (Lincoln), L.N.E.R., 16, B1.
Duror, L.M.S., 33, D3.
Durrington-on-Sea, S.R., 5, F2
Dursley, L.M.S., 9, F2.
Durston, G.W.R., 8, F3.
Dyce, L.N.E.R., 38, F2.
Dyffryn-on-Sea, G.W.R., 19, G2.
Dykehead, L.N.E.R., 31, B1.
Dymchurch, R.H.D.R. 6, E3.
Dymock, G.W.R., 9, D2.
Dysart, L.N.E.R., 31, A4.
•Dyserth L.M.S., 19, C5.

E

Eaglescliffe, L.N.E.R 28, E5.
Ealing, G.W.R./L.P.T.B., & L.P.T.B., 5 A2.
Earby, L.M.S., 21, C1.
Eardington, G.W.R., 15, G2.
Eardisley, L.M.S./§G.W.R., 14, E2.
•Earith Bridge, L.N.E.R., 11, B3.
Earlestown, L.M.S., 20, C3.
Earley, S.R., 4, A2.
Earls Barton, *see* Castle Ashby.
Earls Colne, L.N.E.R., 12, E5.
Earlsfield, S.R., 5, B3.
Earlsheaton, L.N.E.R., 21 E3.
Earlston, L.N.E.R., 32, D5.
Earlswood, S.R., 5, C3.
Earlswood Lakes, G.W.R., 9, A4
Earsham, L.N.E.R., 12, A2.
Earswick, L.N.E.R., 21, C5.
Easington, L.N.E.R., 28, D5.
Easingwold, E.R., 21, B4.
Eassie, L.M.S., 37, D1.
East Anstey, G.W.R., 7, F5.
East Barkwith, L.N.E.R., 17, A2.
East Boldon, L.N.E.R., 28, C5.
Eastbourne S.R. 5, G5.
East Budleigh, S.R., 2, B2.
Eastbury G.W.R., 4, A4.
East Calder (Goods), L.N.E.R., 31, C3.
Eastchurch, S.R., 6, B4.
East Croydon, S.R., 5, C3.
Easterhouse, L.N.E.R., 30, C1.
East Farleigh, S.R., 6, C5.
East Finchley •L.N.E.R./ L.P.T.B., 5 A,3.
East Fortune, L.N.E.R., 32, B5.
East Garston G.W.R., 4, A4.
Eastgate, L.N.E.R., 27, D3.
Eastgrange, L.N.E.R., 31, A2.
East Grinstead, S.R., 5, D4.
East Halton, L.N.E.R., 22, E3.
East Haven, D.A., 37, E3.
East Horndon, L.M.S., 5, A5.
East Kilbride, L.M.S., 30, D1.
East Langton, L.M.S., 16, G3.
East Leake L.N.E.R., 16, D4.
Eastleigh, S.R./G.W.R., 4, D3.
East Linton, L.N.E.R., 32, B5.
East Malling Halt, S.R., 5, C5.
East Margate, S.R., 6, B1.
East Minster-on-Sea, S.R., 6, B4.
East Newport, L.N.E.R., 37, E2.
East Norton L.M.S./ L.N.E.R., 16, F2.
•Eastoft, A.J., 22, E5.
Easton, E.C.H., 3, G3.
Easton Court, G.W.R./ L.M.S., 9, A1.
Easton Lodge, L.N.E.R., 11, F4.
Eastriggs, L.M.S., 26, B2.
East Rudham, M.G.N., 18, E5.
Eastry, E.K.R., 6, C2.
Eastry South, E.K.R., 6, C2.
East Tilbury Halt, L.M.S., 5, B5.
East Ville, L.N.E.R., 17, C3.
East Winch, L.N.E.R, 17, E5.
Eastwood (Yorks.), L.M.S., 21, E1.
Eastwood & Langley Mill, L.N.E.R., 16, C4.
Ebberston, L.N.E.R. 22, A4.
Ebbw Vale, G.W.R. & L.M.S., 8, A4.
Ebchester, L.N.E.R., 27, C4.
Ecclefechan, L.M.S., 26, B2.
Eccles, L.M.S., 20, B1.
Ecclesfield, L.M.S. & L.N.E.R., 21, G3.
•Eccleshill, L.N.E.R., 21, D2.
Eccles Road, L.N.E.R., 12, A4.
Eccleston Park, L.M.S., 20, C3.
Eckington, L.M.S., 9, C3.
Eckington & Renishaw, L.M.S.& L.N.E.R., 16, A4.
Edale, L.M.S., 15, A5.
Edderton, L.M.S., 36, B5.
Eddleston, L.N.E.R., 31, D4.
Edenbridge, S.R., 5, D4.
Eden Park, S.R., 5, B4.
•Edgebold, S.M., 14, A1.
Edge Hill, L.M.S., 20, C4.
•Edgerley, S.M., 14, A1.
•Edgware, L.N.E.R., 5, A2.
Edinburgh, L.M.S. & L.N.E.R., 31, —.
Edington, S.D., 3, C1.
Edington & Bratton, G.W.R., 3, B4.
Edmondthorpe & Wymondham, L.M.S., 16, E2.
Edrom, L.N.E.R., 32, C3.
•Edwalton, L.M.S., 16, D3.
Edwinstowe, L.N.E.R., 16, B3.
•Edzell, L.M.S., 37, C3.
Efail Isaf, G.W.R., 8, C5.
Effingham Jc., S.R., 5, C2.
Eggesford, S.R., 2, A4.
Egginton, L.M.S./•L.N.E.R., 16, D5.
Egham, S.R., 5, B1.
Egloskerry, S.R., 1, B4.
Eglwysbach, *see* Tal-y-Cafn.
•Egremont (Cumberland), L.M.S., 26, F3.
Egton, L.N.E.R., 28, F2.
Elderslie, L.M.S., 30, C2.
Elford, L.M.S., 15, E5.
Elgin, L.N.E.R. & L.M.S., 36, C2.
§Elham, S.R., 6, D2.
Elie, L.N.E.R., 37, G2.
Elland, L.M.S., 21, E2.
Ellaston, *see* Norbury.
Ellenbrook, L.M.S., 20, B2.
Ellerby, L.N.E.R., 22, D3.
Ellerdine Halt, G.W.R., 15, E2.
Ellesmere, G.W.R., 20, F4.
Ellesmere Port, B.J., 20, D4.
Ellingham, L.N.E.R., 12, A2.
Elliot Jc., D.A., 37, D3.
Ellistown, *see* Bagworth.
Ellon, L.N.E.R., 38, E2.
•Elm Bridge, W.U.T., 17, F4.
Elmers End, S.R., 5, B4.
Elmesthorpe, L.M.S., 16, F4.
Elm Park, L.M.S./L.P.T.B., 5, A5.
Elmswell, L.N.E.R., 12, C4.
Elmton & Creswell, L.M.S., 16, A4.
See also Creswell, L.N.E.R.
•Elrington, L.N.E.R., 27, C3.
Elsecar & Hoyland, L.M.S., 21, F3.
Elsecar (Goods), L.N.E.R., 21, F4.
Elsenham, L.N.E.R., 11, E4.
Elsham, L.N.E.R., 22, F4
Elslack, L.M.S., 21, C1.
Elsted, S.R., 4, D1.
Elstree, L.M.S., 11, G2.
Elswick, L.N.E.R., 27, B5
Eltham, S.R., 5, B4.
,, Park S.R., 5, B4.
Elthorne, *see* Hanwell.
Elton (Ches.), *see* Ince.
Elton (Northants.), L.M.S., 11, A1.
Elton & Orston, L.N.E.R., 16, D2.
Elvanfoot, L.M.S, 31, F2.
•Elvet, L.N.E.R., 28, D5.
Elvington, E.K.R., 6, C2.
•Elvington, D.V.L., 20, C2.
Ely (Cambs.), L.N.E.R., 11, B4.
Ely (Glam.), G.W.R., 8, C4.
Embleton, L.M.S., 26, E2.
Embo, L.M.S., 36 A4.
Embsay, L.M.S., 21, C1.
Emneth, L.N.E.R., 17, F4.
Emsworth, S.R., 4, E2.
Enderby, L.M.S., 16, F4.
Endon, L.M.S., 15, C4.
Enfield Chase, L.N.E.R., 11, G2.
Enfield Lock, L.N.E.R., 11, G3.
Enfield Town, L.N.E.R. 11, G3.
Enthorpe, L.N.E.R., 22, C4.
Entwistle, L.M.S., 20, A2.
Epping, L.N.E.R., 11, G3.
Epsom, S.R., 5, C2.
Epsom Downs, S.R., 5, C3.
•Epworth, A.J., 22, F5.
See also Haxey, L.N.E.R.
Erdington, L.M.S., 15, F5.
Eridge, S.R., 5, D5.
Erith, S.R., 5, B4.
Errol, L.M.S., 34, E1.
Erwood, G.W.R., 14, E3.
Eryholme (Goods),L.N.E.R., 28, F5.
Escrick, L.N.E.R., 20, D5.
•Esgairgeiliog, Corris, 14, B5.
Esher, S.R., 5, C2.
Eskbank, L.N.E.R., 31, C4.
•Eskbridge, L.N.E.R., 31, C4.
Eskdale, *see* Ravenglass.
§Eskdale Green, R.E.R., 26, F2.
Eskmeals, L.M.S., 26, G3.
§Esplanade (Dundee), L.N.E.R., 37, E2.
Esplanade (Ryde, I.W.) S.R., 4, F3.
Essendine, L.N.E.R., 17, E1.
Esslemont, L.N.E.R., 38, E2.
•Eston, L.N.E.R., 28, E4.
Etchingham, S.R., 6, E5.
Etherley, L.N.E.R., 27, E5.
Eton, *see* Windsor.
Etruria, L.M.S., 15 C3.
Ettiley Heath (Goods), L.M.S., 15, B2
Ettingshall Rd. & Bilston, L.M.S., 15, F3.
See also Bilston, G.W.R.
Ettington, L.M.S., 10, C5.
•Etwall, L.N.E.R., 16, D5.
Euston, L.M.S. & L.P.T.B., 5,A3.
Euston Rd. (Morecambe), L.M.S., 24, B3.
Euxton, *see* Balshaw Lane.
Euxton Jc., L.M.S., 24. E3.
Evanton, L.M.S., 36, C5.
Evenwood, L.N.E.R., 27, E5.
Evercreech (New), S.D., 3, C3.
Evercreech Jc., S.D., 3, C3.
Everingham, L.N.E.R., 22 D5.

Evershot, G.W.R., 3, E2.
Evesham, G.W.R. & L.M.S., 9, C4.
Ewell, S.R., 5, C3.
Ewesley, L.N.E.R., 27, A4. *See also* Fontburn.
Ewood Bridge, L.M.S., 20, A1.
Exeter, G.W.R./S.R. & S.R., 2, B3.
Exhall, *see* Longford (Warwicks.).
Exminster, G.W.R., 2, B3.
Exmouth, S.R., 2, C2.
Eyarth, L.M.S., 19, E5.
Eydon Rd. Plat., L.N.E.R., 10, C4.
Eye (Hereford), *see* Berrington.
•Eye (Suffolk), L.N.E.R., 12, B4.
Eye Green, M.G.N., 17, F2.
Eyemouth, L.N.E.R., 32, C3.
Eynsford, S.R., 5, C5.
Eynsham, G.W.R., 10, E4.
Eythorne, E.K.R., 6, C2.

F

•Facit, L.M.S., 20, A1.
Failsworth, L.M.S., 20, B1.
Fairbourne, G.W.R., 13, A5.
Fairford, G.W.R., 9, F5.
Fairhaven, *see* Ansdell.
Fairlie, L.M.S., 30, D4.
Fairlie Branch, L.M.S., 30, E2.
Fairlie Pier, L.M.S., 30, D4.
•Fairlop, L.N.E.R., 5, A4.
Fakenham, L.N.E.R. & M.G.N., 18, D5.
Falahill (Goods), L.N.E.R., 31, C5.
Falkirk, L.N.E.R./L.M.S. & •L.M.S., 31, B2.
Falkirk (High), L.N.E.R. 31, B2.
Falkland Rd., L.N.E.R., 37, G1.
Fallowfield, L.N.E.R., 20, C1.
Fallside, L.M.S., 30, C1.
Falmer, S.R., 5, F3.
Falmouth, G.W.R., 1, F1.
Falstone, L.N.E.R., 27, A2.
Fambridge, L.N.E.R., 12, G5.
Fangfoss, L.N.E.R., 22, C5.
Faicet, *see* Yaxley.
Far Cotton (Goods), L.M.S., 10, B2.
Fareham, S.R., 4, E3.
Faringdon (Berks.), G.W.R., 10, F5.
Farington, L.M.S., 24, E3.
Farnborough, S.R., 4, B1.
Farncombe, S.R., 5, D1.
Farnell Rd., L.M.S. 37, C3.
Farnham, S.R., 4, C1.
Farningham Rd. & Sutton-at-Hone, S.R., 5, B5.
Farnley, L.M.S., 21, D3.
•Farnsfield, L.M.S., 16, B3.
Farnworth, C.L.C. & L.M.S., 20, C3.
Farnworth, L.M.S., 20, B2.
Farringdon (Hants.), S.R., 4, C2.
Farthinghoe, L.M.S., 10, C4.
Fauldhouse, L.M.S., 31, C2.
•Fauldhouse & Crofthead, L.N.E.R., 31, C2.
Faversham, S.R., 6, C4.
Fawkham, S.R., 5, B5.
Fawley (Hants.), S.R., 4, E3.
Fawley (Hereford), G.W.R., 9, D1.
Fay Gate, S.R., 5, D3.
Fazakerley, L.M.S., 20, B4.
Fearn, L.M.S., 36, B4.
Featherstone, L.M.S., 21, E4.
Featherstone Park, L.N.E.R., 27, C2.
Felin Fach, G.W.R., 13, E5.
Felin Foel, G.W.R., 7, B3.
Felin Fran, G.W.R., 7, B4.
Felin Hen Halt, L.M.S., 19, D2.
Felixstowe, L.N.E.R., 12, E3.
Felling, L.N.E.R., 28, C5.
Felmingham, M.G.N., 18, D3.
Felsted, L.N.E.R., 11, E5.
Feltham, S.R., 5, B2.
•Fenay Bridge & Lepton, L.M.S., 21, E2.
Fencehouses, L.N.E.R., 28, F5.
Fenchurch Street, L.M.S./•L.N.E.R., 5, B4.
Fencote, G.W.R., 9, B1.
Feniscowles, L.M.S., 24, E2.
Fenn's Bank, G.W.R., 20, F3.
Fenny Bentley (Goods), L.M.S., 15, C5.
Fenny Compton, G.W.R., 10, B4.
Fenny Compton, L.M.S., 10, B5.
Fenny Stratford, L.M.S., 10, D2.
Fenton, L.M.S., 15, C3.
Fenton Manor, L.M.S., 15, C3.
Ferndale, G.W.R., 8, D5.
Fernhill Heath, G.W.R./L.M.S. 9, B3.
Ferniegair (Goods), L.M.S., 31, D1.
Ferriby, L.N.E.R., 22, E4.
Ferry, M.G.N., 17, E3.
Ferrybridge, L.N.E.R., 21, E4.
Ferryhill, L.N.E.R., 28, D5.
Ferryhill Jc., L.M.S./L.N.E.R., 38, G2.
Ferryside, G.W.R., 7, A2.
Fersit Siding, L.N.E.R., 33, B5.
Festiniog, G.W.R., 19, F3.
Ffairfach, G.W.R., 13, G5.
•Ffridd Gate, Corris, 14, B5.
Ffrith, W.M., 20, E5.
Fidlers Ferry, L.M.S., 20, C3.
Fighting Cocks (Goods), L.N.E.R., 28, F5.
Filey, L.N.E.R., 22, A3.
Filleigh, G.W.R., 7, F4.
Fillongley, *see* Arley, L.M.S.
Filton Jc., G.W.R., 8, C1.
Fimber, *see* Sledmere.
Finchley Central, •L.N.E.R./L.P.T.B., 5, A3.
Findochty, L.N.E.R., 38, C5.
•Finedon, L.M.S., 10, A2.
Finghall Lane, L.N.E.R., 27, G5.
Finmere, L.N.E.R., 10, D3.
Finningham, L.N.E.R., 12, C4.
Finningley, L.N.E.R., 21, F5
Finsbury Park, L.N.E.R. & L.P.T.B., 5, A3.
Firsby, L.N.E.R., 17, B4.
Fishbourne Halt, S.R., 4, E1.
Fishergate Hill (Goods), L.M.S., 24, E3.
Fisherrow (Goods), L.N.E.R., 31, B4.
Fishersgate Halt, S.R., 5, F3.
Fishguard & Goodwick, G.W.R., 13, F1.
Fishguard Harbour, G.W.R., 13, F1.
Fish Ponds, L.M.S., 8, C1.
Fiskerton, L.M.S., 16, C3.
Fittleworth, S.R., 5, E1.
Five Mile House, L.N.E.R., 17, B1.
§Five Ways, L.M.S., 15, E4.
Fladbury, G.W.R., 9, C4.
Flamborough, L.N.E.R., 22, B3.
Flax Bourton, G.W.R., 8, D2.
•Flaxton, L.N.E.R., 21, B5.
Flecknoe, L.M.S., 10, B4.
Fledborough, L.N.E.R., 16 B2.
Fleet (Hants.), S.R., 4, B1.
Fleet (Lincs.), M.G.N., 17, E3.
Fleetwood, L.M.S., 24, C4.
Flemington, L.M.S., 31, C1.
Fletton (Goods), L.N.E.R., 11, A2.
Flimby, L.M.S., 26, D3.
Flint, L.M.S., 20, D5.
Flitwick, L.M.S., 10, D1.
Flixton, C.L.C., 20, C2.
Flordon, L.N.E.R., 12, A3.
Floriston, L.M.S., 26, B1.
•Flushdyke, L.N.E.R., 21, E3.
•Fochabers Town, L.M.S., 36, C1.
Fochriw, G.W.R., 8, A5.
•Fockerby, A.J., 22, E5.
Fodderty Jc., L.M.S., 35, D5.
Foggathorpe, L.N.E.R., 22, D5.
Foleshill, L.M.S., 10, A5.
Folkestone, S.R., 6, D2.
Fontburn Halt & Ewesley Goods, L.N.E.R., 27, A4.
Forcett (Goods), L.N.E.R. 27, F5.
Forcett Jc., L.N.E.R., 27, E5.
Ford (Devon), S.R., 1, D5.
,, (Sussex), S.R., 5, F1.
Ford Bridge, S.H., 9, B1.
•Ford & Crossgates (Salop), S.M., 14, A1.
Forden, G.W.R., 14, B2.
•Ford Green, L.M.S., 15, C3.
Fordham, L.N.E.R., 11, C4.
Fordingbridge, S.R., 4, E5.
Fordoun, L.M.S., 37, B4.
Foregate St. (Worcester), G.W.R., 9, B3.
Forest Gate, L.N.E.R., 5, A4.
Forest Hall, L.N.E.R., 27, B5.
•Forest Mill, L.N.E.R., 31, A2.
Forest Row, S.R., 5, D4.
Forfar, L.M.S., 37, D2.
Forgandenny, L.M.S., 34, F2.
Forge Valley, L.N.E.R. 22, A4.
Formby, L.M.S., 20, B4.
Forncett, L.N.E.R., 12, A3.
Forres, L.M.S., 36, D3.
•Forrest Field, L.N.E.R., 31, C1.
Forsinard, L.M.S., 39, E1.
§Fort Augustus, L.N.E.R., 35, G4.
Fort Brockhurst, S.R., 4, E3.
Forteviot, L.M.S., 34, F2.
•Fort George, L.M.S., 36, D4.
Forth Bridge, Forth Bridge Ry. Co., 31, B3.
Fortissat Colliery, L.N.E.R., 31, C1.
Fort Matilda, L.M.S., 30, B3.
Fortrose, L.M.S., 36, D5.
Fort William, L.N.E.R., 33, C3.
•Forty Hill, L.N.E.R., 11, G3.
•Foryd Pier (Rhyl), L.M.S., 19, C5.
Foss Cross, G.W.R., 9, E4.
Foss Islands (Goods), L.N.E.R., 21, C5.
Fotherby Halt, L.N.E.R., 22, G2.
Foulis, L.M.S., 36, C5.
Foulridge, L.M.S., 21, —
Foulsham, L.N.E.R., 18, E4.
Fountainhall Jc., L.N.E.R., 31, D5.
Four Ashes, L.M.S., 15, F3.
Four Crosses (Mont.), G.W.R., 14, A2.
Four Marks, *see* Medstead.
Four Oaks, L.M.S., 15, F5.
Fourstones, L.N.E.R., 27, B3.
Fowey, G.W.R., 1, D3.
Foxdale, I.M.R., 23, B2.
Foxfield, L.M.S., 24, A5.
Foxton, L.N.E.R., 11, D3.
Framlingham, L.N.E.R., 12, C3.
Frampton, *see* Grimstone.
Frankley, H.J., 9, A4.
Frankton, G.W.R., 20, F4.
Fransham, L.N.E.R., 18, E5.
Frant, S.R., 5, D5.
Fraserburgh, L.N.E.R., 38, C2.
Fratton, S.R., 4, E2.
Fremington, S.R., 7, F3.
French Drove & Gedney Hill, L.N.E.R., 17, F3.
Freshfield, L.M.S., 20, B4.
Freshford, G.W.R., 3, B3.
Freshwater (I.W.), S.R., 4, F4.
Friargate (Derby), L.N.E.R., 16, D5.
Friary (Plymouth), S.R., 1, D5.
Frickley, S.K., 21, F4.
Friday St. (Goods), L.M.S., 21, E2.
Friden (Goods), L.M.S., 15, B5.
•Friezland, L.M.S., 21, F1.
Frimley, S.R., 4, B1.
Frinton-on-Sea, L.N.E.R., 12, F3.
Friockheim, L.M.S., 37, D3.
Frisby, L.M.S., 16, E3.
Frittenden Rd., K.E.S.R., 6, D5.
Fritwell & Somerton, G.W.R., 10, D4.
Frizinghall, L.M.S., 21, D2.
•Frizington, L.M.S., 26, E3.
Frocester, L.M.S., 9, E3.
Frodingham, *see* Scunthorpe.
Frodsham, B.J., 20, D3.
Froghall, *see* Kingsley.
Frogmore, *see* Park Street.
Frome, G.W.R., 3, B3.
Frongoch, G.W.R., 19, F4.
Frosterley, L.N.E.R., 27, D4.
•Fryston, L.N.E.R., 21, E4.
Fulbar St. (Renfrew), L.M.S., 30, C2.
Fulbourne, L.N.E.R., 11, C4.
Fullerton, S.R., 4, C4.
Fulwell (Middx.), S.R., 5, B2.
Fulwell & Westbury (Bucks.), L.M.S., 10, D3.
Furness Abbey, L.M.S., 24, B5.
Furness Vale, L.M.S., 15, A4.
Furze Platt Halt, G.W.R., 10, G2.
•Fushiebridge, L.N.E.R., 30, C5.
Fyling Hall, L.N.E.R., 28, F1.
Fyvie, L.N.E.R., 38, E3.

G

Gadlys Jc., G.W.R., 8, B5.
Gaerwen, L.M.S., 19, D2.
Gagie, L.M.S., 37, E2.
Gailes, L.M.S., 30, E3.
Gailey, L.M.S., 15, E3.
Gainford, L.N.E.R., 27, E5.
Gainsborough, L.N.E.R., 22, G5.
§Gairlochy, L.N.E.R., 33, B4.
Gaisgill, L.N.E.R., 27, F2.
Galashiels, L.N.E.R., 31, E5.
Galligreaves St. (Goods) L.M.S., 24, E2.
•Gallions, L.N.E.R., 5, B4.
Galston, L.M.S., 30, E2.
Gamlingay, L.M.S., 11, D2.
•Ganton, L.N.E.R., 22, A4.
Gara Bridge, G.W.R., 2, D4.
Garelochhead, L.N.E.R., 31, A3.
Garforth, L.N.E.R., 21, D4.
Gargrave, L.M.S., 21, C1.
•Gargunnock, L.N.E.R., 30, A1.
•Garlieston, L.M.S., 25, D4.
Garmouth, L.N.E.R., 36, C1.
Garnant, G.W.R., 7, A4.
•Garnedd Wen, Corris, 14, A5.
Garnkirk, L.M.S., 30, C1.
Garrochburn (Goods), L.M.S., 30, E2.
Garsdale, L.M.S., 27, G2.
Garstang & Catterall, L.M.S., 24, D3.
•Garstang Town, L.M.S., 24 D3.
Garston, C.L.C. & •L.M.S., 20, C4.
Garswood, L.M.S., 20, B3.
Gartcosh, L.M.S., 30, C1.
Garth, L.M.S., 14, E4.
§*Garth & Van Road*, G.W.R., 14, C4.
Gartly, L.N.E.R., 38, F5.
Gartmore, L.N.E.R., 30, A2.
Gartness, L.N.E.R., 30, B2.
Garton, L.N.E.R., 22, C4.
§Gartsherrie, L.M.S., 30, C1.
Gartshore (Goods), L.N.E.R., 30, B1.
Garve, L.M.S., 35, D4.
Gascoigne Wood Junction, L.N.E.R., 21, D4.
Gask Siding, L.N.E.R., 31, A3.
Gaswater Branch, L.M.S., 30, F1.
Gateacre, C.L.C., 20, C4.
Gatehead, L.M.S., 30, E2.
Gatehouse-of-Fleet, L.M.S., 25, C5.
Gateshead, L.N.E.R., 27, C5.
Gateside, L.N.E.R., 34, F1.
Gathurst, L.M.S., 20, B3.
Gatwick Airport, S.R., 5, D3.
•Gatwick Racecourse, S.R., 5, D3.
Gayton Road, M.G.N., 17, E5.
Geddington, L.M.S., 16, G2.
Gedling, L.N.E.R., 16, C3.
Gedney, M.G.N., 17, E3.
Gedney Hill, *see* French Drove.
Geldeston, L.N.E.R., 12, A2.
Gelly Tarw Jc., G.W.R., 8, A5.
Georgemas Jc., L.M.S., 39, C3.
Georgetown, L.M.S., 30, C2.
•Gerrards Cross, G.W.R./L.N.E.R., 10, F1.
Gidea Park, L.N.E.R., 5, A5.
•Giffen, L.M.S., 30, D3.
Giffnock, L.M.S., 30, C2.
•Gifford, L.N.E.R., 32, C5.
Giggleswick, L.M.S., 24, B1.
Gildersome, L.N.E.R. & •L.M.S., 21, E3.
Gileston, G.W.R., 8, D5.
•Gilfach Goch, G.W.R., 8, B5.
Gilling, L.N.E.R., 21, B5.
Gillingham (Dorset), S.R., 3, D4.
Gillingham (Kent), S.R., 6, B5.
Gilmerton, L.N.E.R., 31, C4.
Gilmour Street (Paisley), L.M.S., 30, C2.
Gilnockie, L.N.E.R., 26, B1.
Gilsland, L.N.E.R., 27, B1.
Gilwern Halt, L.M.S., 8, A4.
Girvan, L.M.S., 30, G4.
Gisburn, L.M.S., 24, C1.
Glais, L.M.S., 7, B4.
Glaisdale, L.N.E.R., 28, F2.
Glamis, L.M.S., 37, D2.
Glanamman, G.W.R., 7, A4.
Glan Conway, L.M.S., 19, D4.
Glandyfi, G.W.R., 14, A5.
Glanrhyd Halt, V.T., 14, G5.
•Glanton, L.N.E.R., 32, F2.
Glan-yr-Afon Halt, G.W.R., 14, C4.
Glanyrafon, G.W.R., 20, G5.
•Glapwell, L.M.S., 16, B4.
Glasbury-on-Wye, L.M.S., 14, F2.
Glasgow, L.M.S. & L.N.E.R., 30, —.
Glassaugh, L.N.E.R., 38, C4.
Glassel, L.N.E.R., 37, A3.
§Glassford, L.M.S., 30, D1.
•Glasson Dock, L.M.S., 24, C3.
Glasterlaw, L.M.S., 37, D3.
Glastonbury & Street, S.D., 3, C2.
Glazebrook, C.L.C., 20, C2.
Glazebrook Moss Jc., C.L.C./L.N.E.R., 20, C2.
Glazebury, L.M.S., 20, B2.
Glemsford, L.N.E.R., 12, D5.
Glenbarry, L.N.E.R., 38, D4.
Glenboig, L.M.S., 31, C1.
Glenbuck, L.M.S., 31, E1.
Glenburnie Jc., L.N.E.R., 34, F1.
Glencarron Plat., L.M.S., 35, D2.
Glencarse, L.M.S., 34, F1.
Glencoe, *see* Ballachulish.
•Glencorse, L.N.E.R., 31, C4.
Glencraig Coll., L.N.E.R., 31, A3.
Glendon & Rushton, L.M.S., 10, A2.
Gleneagles, L.M.S., 34, F2.
Glenfarg, L.N.E.R., 34, F1.
•Glenfield, L.M.S., 16, F4.
Glenfinnan, L.N.E.R., 33, B2.
Glengarnock, L.M.S., 30, D3.
Gleniffer (Goods), L.M.S., 30, C2.
Glenluce, L.M.S., 25, C3.
•Glenside, L.M.S., 30, F3.
Glenwhilly, L.M.S., 25, B3.
Glogue, G.W.R., 13, F3.
Glodwick Road (Oldham), L.M.S., 21, F1.
Glossop, L.N.E.R., 21, G1.
Gloucester, G.W.R. & L.M.S., 9, E3.
Glyn Abbey, G.W.R., 7, A2.
Glyncorrwg Coll., G.W.R., 7, B5.
Glynde, S.R., 5, F4.
Glyndyfrdwy, G.W.R., 20, F5.
Glyn Neath, G.W.R., 7, A5.
Gnosall, L.M.S., 15, E3.
Goathland, L.N.E.R., 28, F2
Gobowen, G.W.R., 20, F4.
Godalming, S.R., 5, D1.
Godley, L.N.E.R., 21, G1.
Godmanchester, L.N.E.R./L.M.S., 11, B2.
Godshill (I.W.), S.R., 4, G3.
Godstone, S.R., 5, D3.
Goff's Oak, *see* Cuffley.
•Gogar, L.N.E.R., 31, B3.
Golant, G.W.R., 1, D3.
Golborne, L.M.S. & L.N.E.R., 20, B3.
Golcar, L.M.S., 21, E2.
Golden Grove, L.M.S., 13, G5.
Golden Hill, *see* Newchapel.
§Golden Hill Plat., G.W.R., 7, D2.
Goldsborough, L.N.E.R., 21, C4.
•Golfa, W.L., 14, B2.
Gollanfield Jc., L.M.S., 36, D4.
Golspie, L.M.S., 36, A4.
Gomersal, L.M.S., 21, E2.
Gomshall & Shere, S.R., 5, D2.
Goodmayes, L.N.E.R., 5, A4.
Goodwick, *see* Fishguard.
Goole, L.N.E.R./L.M.S., 22, E5.
•Goole Dks., L.M.S./L.N.E.R., 22, E5.
Goostrey, L.M.S., 15, B3.
Gordon, L.N.E.R., 32, D5.
Gordon Hill, L.N.E.R., 11, G2.
Gorebridge, L.N.E.R., 31, C5.
Goring & Streatley, G.W.R., 10, G3.
Goring-by-Sea, S.R., 5, F2.
§Gorleston North, N.S.J., 18, F1.
Gorleston-on-Sea, N.S.J., 18, F1.
Gorseinon, L.M.S., 7, B3.
Gosberton L.N.E.R., 17, D2.
•Gosford Green, L.M.S., 10, A5.
Gosport, S.R., 4, E2.
Goswick, L.N.E.R., 32, D2.
Gotham, L.N.E.R., 16, D4.
Gotherington, G.W.R., 9, D4.
Goudhurst, S.R., 6, D5.
Gourdon, L.N.E.R., 37, B4.
Gourock, L.M.S., 30, B3.
Govan, L.M.S., 30, C2.
Govilon, L.M.S., 8, A4.
Gowerton, L.M.S., 7, B3.
Goxhill, L.N.E.R., 22, E3.
Grafham, L.M.S., 11, C1.
Grafton & Burbage, G.W.R., 4, B5.
Grafton Jc., G.W.R., 4, B5.
Grahamston, L.N.E.R./L.M.S., 31, B2.
Grampound Road, G.W.R., 1, E2.
Grandtully, L.M.S., 34, D3.
Grane Rd. (Goods), L.M.S., 20, A1.
Grange, L.N.E.R., 38, D5.
Grange Court, G.W.R., 9, E2.
Grange Lane, L.N.E.R., 21, G3.
Grangemouth, L.M.S./L.N.E.R., 31, B2.
Grange-over-Sands, L.M.S., 24, B3.
Grange Road, S.R., 5, D3.
Grangetown (Durham), L.N.E.R., 28, E4.
Grantham, L.N.E.R., 16, D1.
•Granton, L.M.S. & L.N.E.R., 31, B4.
Grantown-on-Spey, L.M.S. & L.N.E.R., 36, F3.
Grantshouse, L.N.E.R., 32, C4.
•Grassington & Threshfield, L.M.S., 21, B1.
•Grassmoor, L.N.E.R., 16, B5.
Grateley, S.R., 4, C5.
Gravelly Hill, L.M.S., 15, G5.
Graveney (Goods), S.R., 6, C3.
Gravesend Central, S.R., 5, B5.
Gravesend, West Street, S.R., 5, B5.
Grayrigg, L.M.S., 27, G1.
§Great Alne, G.W.R., 9, B5.
Great Ayton, L.N.E.R., 28, F4.
Great Barr, L.M.S., 15, F4.
Great Bentley, L.N.E.R., 12, E4.
Great Bridge, G.W.R. & L.M.S., 15, F4.
Great Bridgeford, L.M.S., 15, D3.
Great Chesterford, L.N.E.R., 11, D4.
Great Coates, L.N.E.R., 22, F2.
Great Dalby, L.M.S./L.N.E.R., 16, E2.
Great Glen, L.M.S., 16, F3.
Great Grimsby, L.N.E.R., 22, F2.
Greatham, L.N.E.R., 28, E4.
Great Harwood, L.M.S., 24, D1.
•Great Haywood Halt, L.M.S., 15, E4.
Great Horton, L.N.E.R., 21, D2.
Great Linford, L.M.S., 10, C2.
Great Longstone, L.M.S., 15, B5.
Great Malvern, G.W.R./L.M.S., 9, C3.
Great Missenden, L.N.E.R. L.P.T.B., 10, F2.
Great Ormesby, M.G.N., 18, E1.
Great Ponton, L.N.E.R., 16, D1.
Great Shefford, G.W.R., 4, A4.
Greatstone, R.H.D.R. & S.R., 6, E3.
Great Yarmouth, *see* Yarmouth.
Gree (Goods), L.M.S., 30, D2.
Greenan Castle (Goods), L.M.S., 30, F3.
Green Ayre (Lancaster), L.M.S., 24, B3.
Greenfield, L.M.S., 21, F1.
Greenford, G.W.R., 5, A2.
Greengairs (Goods), L.N.E.R. 31, C1.
Greenhead, L.N.E.R., 27, B2.
Greenhill, L.M.S., 31, B1.
Greenhithe, S.R., 5, B5.
Greenlaw, L.N.E.R., 32, D4.
Greenloaning, L.M.S., 34, G3.
Greenmount, L.M.S., 20, A1
Greenock, L.M.S., 30, B3.
•Greenodd, L.M.S., 24, A4.
Green Road, L.M.S., 24, A5.
Greenside (Pudsey), L.N.E.R., 21, D2.
Green's Wharf, L.M.S., 16, F5.
Greenwich, S.R., 5, B4.
Greetland, L.M.S., 21, E2.
Greetwell Jc., L.N.E.R., 16, B1.
Grendon Underwood Jc., L.N.E.R., 10, D3.
Gresford, G.W.R., 20, E4.
Gresley, L.M.S., 16, E5.
Gretna, L.M.S. & •L.N.E.R., 26, B1.
Gretna Green, L.M.S., 26, B1.
Gretton, L.M.S., 16, F1.
•Griffith's Crossing, L.M.S., 19, D2.
Griffithstown, *see* Panteg.
Grimes Hill, G.W.R., 9, A5.
Grimethorpe Coll., L.M.S., 21, F4.
Grimoldby, L.N.E.R., 17, A3
•Grimsargh, L.M.S., 24, D2.
Grimsby, *see* Great Grimsby
Grimston, L.M.S., 16, E3.
Grimston Road, M.G.N., 17 E5.
Grimstone & Frampton G.W.R., 3, F3.
Grindleford, L.M.S., 16, A5.
•Grindley, L.N.E.R., 15, D4.
•Grinkle, L.N.E.R., 28, E3.
Gristhorpe, L.N.E.R., 22, A3
Groeslon, L.M.S., 19, E1.
Groombridge, S.R., 5, D5.
Grosmont, L.N.E.R., 28, F2
Grotton, L.M.S., 21, F1.
Grove Ferry, S.R., 6, C2.
Grove Jc., S.R., 5, D5.
Grove Park, S.R., 5, B4.
Guard Bridge, L.N.E.R., 37 F2.
Guay, L.M.S., 34, D2.
Guestwick, M.G.N., 18, E4.
Guide Bridge, L.N.E.R. L.M.S. & L.M.S., 21, F1.
Guildford, S.R., 5, C1.
Guisborough, L.N.E.R., 28, E3.
Guiseley, L.M.S. / L.N.E.R., 21, D2.
•Gullane, L.N.E.R., 31, B5.
Gunheath, G.W.R., 1, D2.
Gunhouse Wharf (Goods), L.N.E.R., 22, F5.
Gunnersbury, S.R./L.M.S./L.P.T.B., 5, B2.
Gunness & Burringham (Goods), L.N.E.R., 22, F5.
Gunnislake, S.R., 1, C5.
Gunton, L.N.E.R., 18, D3.
Gurnos (Goods), L.M.S., 7, A4.
Guthrie, L.M.S., 37, D3.
Guyhirne, L.N.E.R., 17, F3.
•Gwaun-cae-Gurwen, G.W.R., 7, A4.
Gwersyllt & Wheatsheaf, L.N.E.R., 20, E4.
Gwinear Road, G.W.R., 1, E4.
Gwyddelwern, L.M.S., 19, F5.
Gwys, L.M.S., 7, A4.

H

Habrough, L.N.E.R., 22, F3.
Hackbridge, S.R., 5, B3.
Hackney Downs, L.N.E.R., 5, A3.
Haddenham (Bucks.), G.W.R./L.N.E.R., 10, E3.
•Haddenham (Cambs.), L.N.E.R., 11, B3.
Haddington, L.N.E.R., 31, B5.
Haddiscoe, L.N.E.R., 18, F1.
Hadfield, L.N.E.R., 21, G1.
Hadham, L.N.E.R., 11, F3.
•Hadleigh, L.N.E.R., 12, D4.
Hadley, L.M.S., 15, E2.
Hadley Wood, L.N.E.R., 11, G2.
Hadlow Road, B.J., 20, D4.
Hadnall, L.M.S., 15, E1.
Hafod, see Johnstown.
Hagley, G.W.R., 9, A3.
Haigh, L.M.S., 21, F3.
Hailsham, S.R., 5, F5.
Hainton, see South Willingham.
Hairmyres, L.M.S., 30, D1.
•Halbeath, L.N.E.R., 31, A3.
Hale, C.L.C., 20, C2.
Halebank, L.M.S., 20, C3.
•Halesowen, G.W.R./L.M.S., 15, G4.
Halesowen Basin, G.W.R., 15, G4.
Halesworth, L.N.E.R., 12, B2.
Halewood, C.L.C., 20, C3.
Halifax, L.M.S. & L.N.E.R., 21, E2.
Halkirk, L.M.S., 39, C3.
Hallaton, L.M.S./L.N.E.R., 16, F2.
Hallatrow, G.W.R., 3, B2.
Hallcraig, L.M.S., 31, D1.
Hall End Coll., L.M.S., 15 F5.
Hall Green, G.W.R., 9, A4.
Halling, S.R., 5, C5.
Hallington, L.N.E.R., 17, A3.
Halliwell (Goods), L.M.S., 20, B2.
Hall Road, L.M.S., 20, B4.
•Halmer End, L.M.S., 15, C3.
•Halsall, L.M.S., 20, B4.
Halstead (Essex), L.N.E.R., 11, E5.
Halton (Ches.), B.J., 20, D3.
Halton (Lancs.), L.M.S., 24, B3.
•Halton Holgate, L.N.E.R., 17, B3.
Haltwhistle L.N.E.R., 27, B2.
Halwill, S.R., 1, B5.
Hambleton, L.N.E.R., 21, D5.
Ham Bridge Halt, S.R., 5, F2
Hamilton, L.M.S. & L.N.E.R., 30, C1.
Hamilton Sq. (Birkenhead), Mer./L.M.S., 20, C4.
Hammersmith, L.P.T.B., 5, B3.
Hammerton, L.N.E.R., 21, C4.
Hammerwich, L.M.S., 15, F4.
Hampden Park, S.R., 5, F5.
Hampole, L.N.E.R., 21, F4.
Hampstead Norris, G.W.R., 4, A3.
Hampsthwaite, L.N.E.R., 21, C3.
Hampton, S.R., 5, B2.
Hampton Court, S.R., 5, B2.
Hampton-in-Arden, L.M.S., 9, A5.
Hampton Loade, G.W.R., 15, G2.
Hampton-on-Sea, see Herne Bay.
Hampton Wick, S.R., 5, B2.
Ham Street & Orlestone, S.R., 6, D4.
Hamworthy (Goods), S.R., 3, F5.
Hamworthy Jc., S.R., 3, F3.
Handborough, G.W.R., 10, E4.
Handforth, L.M.S., 15, A3.
Handsworth, G.W.R., 15, G4.
Hanley, L.M.S., 15, C3.
Hannington, G.W.R., 9, F5.
Hanwell & Elthorne, G.W., 5, B2.
Hanwood, S.W. 14 A1.
Happendon, L.M.S., 31, E2.
Hapton, L.M.S., 24, D1.
•Harborne, L.M.S., 15, G4.
Harburn, L.M.S., 31, C3.
Harbury, see Southam Rd.
Harby, see Doddington.
Harby & Stathern, L.M.S./L.N.E.R., 16, D2.
Hardengreen (Goods), L.N.E.R., 31, C4.
Hardham Jc., S.R., 5, E1.
Hardingham, L N.E.R., 18, F4.
Hardwick Road (Goods), M.G.N., 17, E5.
Haresfield, L.M.S., 9, E3.
Hare Park, L.N.E.R., 21, E3.
Harker Parkhouse Halt, L.N.E.R., 26, C1.
Harlech, G.W.R., 19, F2.
Harleston, L.N.E.R., 12, B3.
Harling Road, L.N.E.R., 12, A4.
Harlington (Beds.), L.M.S., 10, D1.
Harlington (Middlesex), see Hayes.
Harlington (Yorks.), L.M.S., 21, F4.
Harlow, L.N.E.R., 11, F3.
Harmston, L.N.E.R., 16, B1.
Harold Wood, L.N.E.R., 5, A5.
Harpenden, L.M.S. & L.N.E.R., 11, F1.
Harperley, L.N.E.R., 27, D4.
•Harpur Hill, L.M.S., 15, B4.
Harrietsham, S.R., 6, C4.
Harrington, L.M.S., 26, E3.
Harringworth, L.M.S., 16, F1.
Harrogate, L.N.E.R., 21, C3.
Harrow & Wealdstone, L.M.S., 5, A2.
Harrow-on-the-Hill, L.N.E.R./L.P.T.B., 5, A2.
Harston, L.N.E.R., 11, D3.
Hart, L.N.E.R., 28, D4.
Hartfield, S.R., 5, D4.
Hartford, L.M.S. & C.L.C., 20, D2.
Hartington, L.M.S., 15, B5.
Hartlebury, G.W.R., 9, A3.
•Hartlepool, L.N.E.R., 28, D4.
Hartley, L.N.E.R., 28, B5.
Harton Road, G.W.R., 15, G1.
Hartwood, L.M.S., 31, C1.
Hartwood Hill, L.N.E.R., 31, C1.
Harvington, L.M.S., 9, C4.
Harwich, L.N.E.R., 12, E3.
Hasland (Goods), L.M.S., 16, B5.
Haslemere, S.R., 4, C1.
Haslingden, L.M.S., 24, E1.
•Hassall Green, L.M.S., 15, B3.
Hassendean, L.N.E.R., 32, F5.
Hassockrigg Coll., L.N.E.R., 31, C2.
Hassocks, S.R., 5, F3.
•Hassop, L.M.S., 15, B5.
Hastings, S.R., 6, F5.
Haswell, L.N.E.R., 28, D5.
Hatch, G.W.R., 8, G3.
Hatch End, L.M.S.R., 5, A2.
Hatfield (Herts.), L.N.E.R., 11, F2.
Hatfield (Yorks.), see Stainforth.
Hatfield Moor (Goods), A.J., 21, F5.
Hatfield Peverel, L.N.E.R., 11, F5.
Hatherleigh, S.R., 2, A5.
Hathern, L.M.S., 16, E4.
Hathersage, L.M.S., 15, A5.
•Hatton (Aberdeen), L.N.E.R., 38, E1.
Hatton (Warwick), G.W.R., 9, B5.
Haughley, L.N.E.R., 12, C4.
Haughton, L.M.S., 15, E3.
Havant, S.R., 4, E2.
Havenhouse, L.N.E.R., 17, B4.
Haven Street (I.W.), S.R., 4, F3.
Haverfordwest, G.W.R., 7, C2.
Haverhill, L.N.E.R., 11, D5.
•Haverthwaite, L.M.S., 24, A4.
Haverton Hill, L.N.E.R., 28, E4.
Hawarden, L.N.E.R., 20, D4.
Hawarden Bridge, L.N.E.R., 20, D4.
Hawes, L.M.S./L.N.E.R., 27, G3.
Hawick, L.N.E.R., 32, F5.
Hawkesbury Lane, L.M.S., 16, G5.
Hawkhurst, S.R., 6, E5.
Haworth, L.M.S., 21 D1.
Hawkser, L.N.E.R., 28, F2.
Hawthornden, see Rosewell.
Haxby, L.N.E.R., 21, C5.
•Haxey, A.J., 22, F5.
Haxey & Epworth, L.N.E.R., 22, G5.
•Haxey Jc., A.J., 22, F5.
•Haxey Town, A.J., 22, F5.
Hay, L.M.S./G.W.R., 14, F2.
Hayburn Wyke, L.N.E.R., 28, G1.
Haydock, L.N.E.R., 20, B3.
Haydon Bridge, L.N.E.R., 27, B3.
Hayes (Kent), S.R., 5, C4.
Hayes & Harlington (Middx), G.W.R., 5. B2.
Hayfield, L.M.S./L.N.E.R., 15, A4.
Hayle, G.W.R., 1, E4.
Hayling Island, S.R., 4, E2.
Haymarket (Edinburgh), L.N.E.R., 31, B4.
Haywards Heath. S.R., 5, E3.
Haywood, L.M.S., 31, C2.
Hazel Grove, L.M.S., 15, A3.
•Hazelwell, L.M.S., 9, A4.
•Hazelwood, L.M.S., 16, C5.
Hazlehead Bridge, L.N.E.R., 21, F2.
Heacham, L.N.E.R., 17, D5.
Headcorn, S.R./K.E.S.R., 6, D5.
Headingley, L.N.E.R., 21, D3.
Heads Nook, L.N.E.R., 27, C1.
•Heads of Ayr, L.M.S., 30, F3.
Headstone Lane, L.M.S., 5, A2.
Healey House, L.M.S., 21, F2.
Healing, L.N.E.R., 22, F2.
•Heanor, L.M.S. & L.N.E.R., 16, C4.
Heap Bridge (Goods), L.M.S., 20, B1.
Heapey, L.M.S., 24, E2.
Heath, L.N.E.R., 16, B4.
•Heather & Ibstock, L.M.S., 16, E5.
Heathfield (Devon), G.W.R. 2, C4.
Heathfield (Sussex), S.R., 5, E5.
Heath Jc., G.W.R., 8, C4.
Heathway, L.M.S./L.P.T.B., 5, A4.
Heatley & Warburton, L.M.S., 20, C2.
Heaton, L.N.E.R., 27, B5.
Heaton Chapel, L.M.S., 20, C1.
Heaton Lodge Jc., L.M.S., 21, E2.
Heaton Mersey, L.M.S., 20, C1.
Heaton Norris, L.M.S., 20, C1.
Heaton Park, L.M.S., 20, B1.
Hebburn, L.N.E.R., 28, B5.
Hebden Bridge, L.M.S., 21, E1.
Heck, L.N.E.R., 21, E5.
Heckington, L.N.E.R., 17, C2.
Heckmondwike, L.M.S., 21, E2.
Heddon-on-the-Wall, L.N.E.R., 27, B5.
•Hedgeley, L.N.E.R., 32, F2.
Hednesford, L.M.S., 15, E4.
Hedon, L.N.E.R., 22, E3.
Heeley, L.M.S., 16, A5.
Heighington (Durham), L.N.E.R., 27, E5.
Heighington (Lincs.), see Branston.
Hele & Bradninch, G.W.R., 2, A3.
Helensburgh, L.N.E.R., 30, B3.
Hellaby (Goods), L.M.S./L.N.E.R., 21, G4.
Hellesdon, M.G.N., 18, F3.
Hellifield, L.M.S., 24, C1.
Hellingly, S.R., 5, F5.
Helmdon, L.N.E.R., 10, C3.
„ L.N.E.R., 10, C4.
Helmsdale, L.M.S., 39, F2.
Helmshore, L.M.S., 20, A1.
Helmsley, L.N.E.R., 21, A5.
Helpringham, L.N.E.R., 17, D1.
Helpston, L.M.S., 17, F1.
Helsby B.J. & •C.L.C., 20, D3.
Helston, G.W.R., 1, F5.
•Hemel Hempsted, L.M.S., 10, E5.
Hemel Hempsted & Boxmoor, L.M.S., 10, E5.
Hemingborough, L.N.E.R., 21, D5.
Hemsby, M.G.N., 18, E1.
Hemsworth, L.N.E.R., 21, F4.
Hemyock, G.W.R., 2, A2.
Henbury, G.W.R., 8, C2.
Hendford (Goods), G.W.R., 3, D2.
Hendon, L.M.S., 5, A3.
Henfield, S.R., 5, F2.
Hengoed, G.W.R., 8, B4.
Henham Halt, L.N.E.R., 11, E4.
•Heniarth, W.L., 14, B3.
Henley-in-Arden, G.W.R., 9, B5.
Henley-on-Thames, G.W.R., 10, G2.
Henllan, G.W.R., 13, F4.
Henlow, see Arlesey.
Henlow Camp, L.M.S., 11, E1.
Hensall, L.M.S./L.N.E.R., 21, E5.
Hensall Jc., L.M.S./L.N.E.R., 21, E5.
Henstridge, S.D., 3, D3.
Henwick (Worcs.), G.W.R., 9, B3.
Hepscott, L.N.E.R., 27, A5.
Hereford, S.H., 9, C1.
Heriot, L.N.E.R., 31, C5.
Hermitage, G.W.R., 4, A3.
Herne Bay & Hampton-on-Sea, S.R., 6, B3.
Herne Hill, S.R., 5, B3.
Hersham, S.R., 5, C2.
Hertford, L.N.E.R., 11, F2.
Hertingfordbury, L.N.E.R., 11, F2.
Hesketh Bank, L.M.S., 24, E3.
Hesketh Park, L.M.S., 20, A4.
Hesleden, L.N.E.R., 28, D4.
Heslerton, L.N.E.R., 22, B4.
Hessay, L.N.E.R., 21, C4.
Hessle, L.N.E.R., 22, E4.
Hest Bank, L.M.S., 24, B3.
Heswall, B.J., 20, C5.
Heswall Hills, L.N.E.R., 20, C4.
Hethersett, L.N.E.R., 18, F3.
Hetton (Durham), L.N.E.R., 28, D5.
Hever, S.R., 5, D4.
Heversham, L.M.S., 24, A3.
Hexham, L.N.E.R., 27, B3.
Heybridge, see Maldon East.
Heyford, G.W.R., 10, D4.
Heysham, L.M.S., 24, C3.
Heytesbury, G.W.R., 3, C4.
Heywood, L.M.S., 20, B1.
Hibaldstow, see Scawby.
Hibel Road (Macclesfield), L.M.S., 15, A3.
Hibel Road Jc., L.M.S./L.N.E.R., 15, A3.
•Hickleton, L.N.E.R., 21, F4.
Higham (Kent), S.R., 6, B5.
Higham (Suffolk), L.N.E.R., 11, C5.
Higham Ferrers, L.M.S., 10, A1.
Highams Park, L.N.E.R., 5, A4.
High Barnet, •L.N.E.R./L.P.T.B., 11, G2.
•High Blantyre, L.M.S., 30, C1.
Highbridge, G.W. & S.D., 8, E3.
High Brooms, S.R., 5, D5.
Highclere, G.W.R., 4, B3.
Higher Buxton, L.M.S., 15, A4.
Higher Poynton, L.M.S./L.N.E.R., 15, A4.
High Field, L.N.E.R., 22, D5.
Highgate, •L.N.E.R./L.P.T.B., 5, A3.
High Halden Road, K.E.S.R., 6, D4.
•High Harrington, L.M.S., 26, E3.
Highlandman, L.M.S., 34, F3.
High Lane, L.M.S./L.N.E.R., 15, A4.
Highley, G.W.R., 9, A2.
High Shields, L.N.E.R., 28, B5.
High Peak Jc., L.M.S., 16, C5.
Hightown, L.M.S., 20, B4.
Highworth, L.M.S., 9, F5.
High Wycombe, G.W.R./L.N.E.R., 10, F2.
Hildenborough, S.R., 5, C5.
Hilgay, L.N.E.R., 11, A4.
Hill End, L.N.E.R., 11, F2.
Hillfoot, L.N.E.R., 30, B1.
Hillhouse (Lancs.), see Altcar.
Hillhouse (Yorks.), Goods, L.M.S., 21, E2.
Hillhouse Jc., L.M.S./C.L.C., 20, B4.
Hillington, M.G.N., 17, E5.
•Hillside (Kincard.), L.N.E.R., 37, C4.
Hillside (Southport), L.M.S., 20, A4.
Hills Road (Goods), L.M.S., 11, C3.
Hilton Jc., L.M.S./L.N.E.R., 34, F1.
Hilton House, L.M.S., 20, B2.
•Himley, G.W.R., 15, G3.
Hincaster Jc., L.M.S., 24, A3.
Hindpool, L.M.S., 24, B5.
Hinckley, L.M.S., 16, F4.
Hinderwell, L.N.E.R., 28, E2.
Hindley, L.M.S. & L.N.E.R., 20, B2.
Hindley Green, L.M.S., 20, B2.
Hindlow, L.M.S., 15 B5.
Hindolvestone, M.G.N., 18, D4.
Hinton (Glos.), L.M.S., 9, C4.
Hinton (Northants.), see Woodford.
Hinton Admiral, S.R., 4, F5.
Hipperholme, L.M.S., 21, E2.
Hirwaun, G.W.R., 8, A5.
Histon, L.N.E.R./L.M.S., 11, C3.
Hitchin, L.N.E.R./L.M.S. & •L.M.S., 11, E2.
§Hixon Halt, L.M.S., 15, D4.
Hockham, see Wretham.
Hockley (Birmingham), G.W.R., 15, G4.
Hockley (Essex), L.N.E.R., 6, A5.
Hodbarrow Siding, L.M.S., 24, A5.
Hoddesdon, see Broxbourne.
Hoddlesden (Goods), L.M.S., 24, E1.
Hodnet, G.W.R., 15, D2.
Hoghton, L.M.S., 24, E2.
Holbeach, M.G.N., 17, E3.
Holbeck, L.N.E.R./L.M.S. & L.M.S., 21, D3.
Holborn Viaduct, S.R., 5, B3.
Holbrook Colls., L.M.S. & L.N.E.R., 16, A4.
Holcombe Brook, L.M.S., 20, A1.
Hole, S.R., 1, A5.
Holehouse Jc., L.M.S., 30, F2.
Holgate Jc., L.N.E.R., 21, C5.
Holkham, L.N.E.R., 18, C5.
Holland Arms, L.M.S., 19, D1.
Holland-on-Sea, see Clacton.
Holland Road, S.R., 5, F3.
Hollingbourne, S.R., 6, C5.
•Hollin Well, L.N.E.R., 16, C4.
Hollins (Goods), L.M.S., 24, E2.
Hollinwood, L.M.S., 20, B1.
Hollinswood (Goods), G.W.R., 15, E2.
Hollybush (Ayr), L.M.S., 30, F2.
Holly Bush (Mon.), L.M.S., 8, A4.
Holme (Hunts.), L.N.E.R., 11, A2.
•Holme (Lancs)., L.M.S., 24, E1.
Holme (West'd.), see Burton.
Holme Hale, L.N.E.R., 18, F5.
Holme Lacy, G.W.R., 9, C1.
Holme Moor, L.N.E.R., 22, D5.
Holmes, L.M.S., 21, G4.
Holmes Chapel, L.M.S., 15, B3.
Holmfield, L.M.S./L.N.E.R., 21, E2.
Holmfirth, L.M.S., 21, F2.
Holmsley, S.R., 4, E5.
Holmwood, S.R., 5, D2.
Holsworthy, S.R., 1, A4.
Holt (Norfolk), M.G.N., 18, D4.
•Holtby, L.N.E.R., 21, C5.
Holt Jc., G.W.R., 3, B4.
Holton Heath, S.R., 3, F4.
Holton-le-Clay, L.N.E.R., 22, F2.
Holton-le-Moor, L.N.E.R., 22, F3.
Holton Village Halt, L.N.E.R., 22, F2.
Holwell (Goods), L.M.S., 16, E3.
Holygate (Goods), L.N.E.R., 31, B3.
Holyhead, L.M.S., 19, B2.
Holytown, L.M.S., 31, C1.
Holywell (North'd.) Goods, L.N.E.R., 28, B5.
Holywell Jc., L.M.S., 20, D5.
Holywell Town, L.M.S., 20, D5.
Holywood, L.M.S., 26, A4.
Homersfield, L.N.E.R., 12, A3.
Honeybourne, G.W.R., 9, C5
Honing, M.G.N., 18, D2.
Honington, L.N.E.R., 16 C1.
Honiton, S.R., 2, A2.
Honley, L.M.S., 21, F2.
Hook, S.R., 4, B2.
•Hookagate, S.M., 15, E1.
Hook Norton, G.W.R., 10, D5.
Hoole, L.M.S., 24, E3.
Hooton, B.J., 20, D4.
Hope (Derbys), L.M.S., 15, A5.
Hope (Flint), L.M.S. & L.N.E.R., 20, E4.
Hope Village, L.N.E.R., 20, E4.
•Hopeman, L.M.S., 36, C2.
Hopperton, L.N.E.R., 21, C4.
Hopton Heath, L.M.S., 14, C1.
Hopton-on-Sea, N.S.J., 18, F1.
Horam, see Waldron.
Horbling, see Billingboro'.
Horbury & Ossett, L.M.S., 21, E3.
Horbury, Millfield Road, L.M.S., 21, E3.
See also Ossett, L.N.E.R.
Horden, L.N.E.R., 28, D4.
•Horeb, G.W.R., 7, A3.
Horham, L.N.E.R., 12, B3.
Horley, S.R., 5, D3.
Hornby, L.M.S., 24, B2.
Horncastle, L.N.E.R., 17, B2.
Hornchurch, L.M.S./L.P.T.B., 5, A5.
Horninglow, L.M.S./•L.N.E.R., 15, D5.
Horninglow (Goods), L.N.E.R., 16, E5.
Hornsea, L.N.E.R., 22, C2.
Hornsea Bridge, L.N.E.R. 22, C3.
Horrabridge, G.W.R., 1, C5.
Horringford (I.W.), S.R., 4, F3.
Horrocksford, L.M.S., 24, D1.
Horsebridge, S.R., 4, D4.
Horsehay, G.W.R., 15, F2.
Horsforth, L.N.E.R., 21, D3.
Horsham, S.R., 5, E2.
Horsley, S.R., 5, C2.
Horsmonden, S.R., 5, D5.
Horsted Keynes, S.R., 5, E4.
Horton-in-Ribblesdale, L.M.S., 24, B1.
Horton Park, L.N.E.R., 21, D2.
Horwich, L.M.S., 20, B2.
Hoscar, L.M.S., 20, B3.
Hose, see Long Clawson.
Hothfield, S.R., 6, D4.
Hougham, L.N.E.R., 16, C2
Hough Green, C.L.C., 20, C3.
Hounslow, L.P.T.B. & S.R., 5, B2.
Houston & Crosslee, L.M.S., 30, C2.
Hove, S.R., 5, F3.
•Hovingham Spa, L.N.E R., 21, B5.
Howden Clough, L.N.E.R., 21, E3.
Howdon-on-Tyne, L.N.E.R., 28, B5.
Howe Bridge, L.M.S., 20, B2.
How Mill, L.N.E.R., 27, C1.
Howsham, L.N.E.R., 22, F3.
Howwood, L.M.S., 30, C2.
Hoy Halt, L.M.S., 39, C3.
Hoylake, L.M.S., 20, C5.
Hoyland, see Elsecar.
Hoyland Common, see Wentworth.
Hubbert's Bridge, L.N.E.R., 17, D2.
Hucknall, L.M.S. & L.N.E.R. 16, C4.
Hucknall Coll., L.N.E.R., 16, B4.
Huddersfield, L.M.S., 21, E2.
•Hugglescote, L.M.S., 16, E4.
Hull, L.N.E.R., 22, E3.
Hullavington, G.W.R., 9, G3.
Humber Rd. Jc., L.N.E.R., 22, E3.
Humberstone, L.N.E.R., 16, F3.
Humberstone Road, L.M.S., 16, F3.
•Humbie, L.N.E.R., 31, C5.
Humshaugh, L.N.E.R., 27, B3.
Huncoat, L.M.S., 24, D1.
Hundred End, L.M.S., 24, E3.
Hungerford, G.W.R., 4, A4.
Hunmanby, L.N.E.R., 22, B3.
•Hunnington, H.J., 9, A4.
Hunslet, L.M.S.& •L.N.E.R. 21, D3.
Hunstanton, L.N.E.R., 17, D5.
Huntingdon East, L.N.E.R., L.M.S., 11, B2.
Huntingdon Nth., L.N.E.R., 11, B2.
Huntly, L.N.E.R., 38, E5.
Hunt's Cross, C.L.C., 20, C4.
Hunwick, L.N.E.R., 27, D5.
Hurdlow, L.M.S., 15, B5.
Hurlford, L.M.S., 30, E2.
Hurstbourne, S.R., 4, B4.
Hurst Green Jc., S.R., 5, C4.
•Hurworth Burn, L.N.E.R., 28, D5.
•Huskisson (L'pool), C.L.C., 20, C4.
Husthwaite Gate, L.N.E.R., 21, B4.
Hutton (Essex), see Shenfield.
Hutton (Lancs.), see New Longton.
Hutton Cranswick, L.N.E.R., 22, C4.
Hutton Gate, L.N.E.R., 28, F3.
•Huttons Ambo, L.N.E.R 22, B5.
Huyton, L.M.S., 20, C4.
Huyton Quarry, L.M.S., 20, C3.
Hyde, L.M.S./L.N.E.R., 21, G1.
Hyde Jc., L.M.S./L.N.E.R., 21, G1.
Hykeham, L.M.S., 16, B2.
Hylton, L.N.E.R., 28, C5.
Hythe (Essex), L.N.E.R., 12, E4.
Hythe (Hants.), S.R., 4, E4.
Hythe (Kent), S.R. & R.H.D.R., 6, D3.

I

Ibrox, L.M.S., 30, C2.
Ibstock, see Heather.
Ickenham, see West Ruislip.
Ide, G.W.R., 2, B3.
•Idle, L.N.E.R., 21, D2.
•Idridgehay, L.M.S., 16, C5.
Ifield, S.R., 5, D3.
•Ilderton, L.N.E.R., 32, E2.
Ilford, L.N.E.R., 5, A4.
Ilfracombe, S.R., 7, E3.
Ilkeston, L.M.S. & L.N.E.R., 16, C4.
Ilkley, O.J., 20, C2.
Ilminster, G.W.R., 8 G3.
Immingham, L.N.E.R., 22, E3.
Immingham Dock, L.N.E.R. 22, E2.
Ince (Lancs.), L.M.S., 20, B3.
See also Lower Ince.
Ince & Elton, B.J., 20, D3.
Inchcoonans (Goods), L.M.S., 34, E1.
Inches, L.M.S., 31, E1.
•Inchgreen, L.M.S., 30, B3.
Inchture, L.M.S., 37, E1.
Ingarsby, L.N.E.R., 16, F3.
Ingatestone, L.N.E.R., 11, G4.

INGESTRE—LLANSAMLET

•Ingestre, L.N.E.R., 15, D4
See also Weston, L.M.S
Ingham, L.N.E.R., 12, B5
Ingleby, L.N.E.R., 28, F4.
Ingleton, L.M.S., 24, B2.
Ingliston (Goods), L.M.S., 31, B1.
Ingrow, L.M.S. & L.N.E.R., 21, D1.
Innerleithen, L.N.E.R., 31, E4.
Innerpeffray, L.M.S., 34, F3.
Innerwick, L.N.E.R., 32, B4.
Insch, L.N.E.R., 38, E4.
Instow, S.R., 7, F3.
Inveramsay, L.N.E.R., 38, E3.
•Inverbervie, L.N.E.R., 37, B4.
Inveresk, L.N.E.R., 31, B4.
§Invergarry, L.N.E.R., 30, A4.
§Invergloy, L.N.E.R., 33, B4.
Invergordon, L.M.S., 36, C5.
Invergowrie, L.M.S., 37, E1.
Inverkeilor, L.N.E.R., 37, D3.
Inverkeithing, L.N.E.R., 31, B3.
Inverkip, L.M.S., 30, C4.
Inverness, L.M.S., 36, E5.
Invershin, L.M.S., 35, A5.
Invertiel Jc., L.N.E.R., 31, A4.
Inverugie, L.N.E.R., 38, D1.
Inverurie, L.N.E.R., 38, F3.
Inworth, L.N.E.R., 12, F5.
•Ipstones, L.M.S., 15, C4.
Ipswich, L.N.E.R., 12, D3.
Irchester, L.M.S., 10, B1.
Irlam, C.L.C., 20, C2.
•Iron Acton, L.M.S., 9, G2.
Iron Bridge & Broseley, G.W.R., 15, F2.
•Irongray, L.M.S., 26, A4.
Ironville, *see* Codnor Park, L.M.S.
Irthlingborough, L.M.S., 10, A1.
§Irton Rd., R.E.R., 26, F3.
Irvine, L.M.S., 30, E3.
Isfield, S.R., 5, E4.
Isleham, L.N.E.R., 11, B4.
Isleworth, S.R., 5, B2.
Islip, L.M.S., 10, E4.
Itchen Abbas, S.R., 4, C3.
Itchingfield Jc., S.R., 5, E2.
Iver, G.W.R., 5, B1.
Ivybridge, G.W.R., 2, D5.

J

•Jamestown, L.N.E.R., 30, B2.
Jarrow, L.N.E.R., 28, B5.
Jarvis Brook, *see* Crowborough.
Jedburgh, L.N.E.R., 32, F5.
Jedfoot, L.N.E.R., 32, E4.
Jervaulx, L.N.E.R., 27, G5.
Jesmond, L.N.E.R., 27, B5.
•Jersey Marine, G.W.R., 7, B4.
John o' Gaunt, L.N.E.R./L.M.S., 16, E2.
Johnshaven, L.N.E.R., 37, C4.
Johnston, G.W.R., 7, C1.
Johnstone, L.M.S., 30, C2.
Johnstown & Hafod, G.W.R., 20, F4.
Jones' Drove (Goods), L.N.E.R., 11, A3.
Joppa, L.N.E.R., 31, B4.
Jordanstone, L.M.S., 37, D1.
Junction Road, K.E.S.R., 6, E5.
•Juniper Green, L.M.S., 31, C5.
Justinhaugh, L.M.S., 37, C2.

K

Keadby (Goods), L.N.E.R., 22, F5.
Kearsley, L.M.S., 20, B2.
Kearsney, S.R., 6, D2.
Keele, L.M.S., 15, C3.
Kegworth, L.M.S., 16, D4.
Keighley, **L.M.S.**/L.N.E.R. & •L.N.E.R., 21, D1.
Keinton Mandeville, G.W.R., 3, C2.
Keith, L.M.S./L.N.E.R. & L.N.E.R., 38, D5.
Kelmarsh, L.M.S., 10, A3.
Kelmscott & Langford, G.W.R., 10, F5.
Kelso, L.N.E.R., 32, E4.
Kelston, L.M.S., 8, D1.
•Kelty, L.N.E.R., 31, A3.
Kelvedon, L.N.E.R., 12, F5.
Kemble Jc., G.W.R., 9, F4.
Kemnay, L.N.E.R., 38, F3.
•Kemp Town, S.R., 5, F3.
Kemsing, S.R., 5, C5.
Kendal, L.M.S., 27, G1.
Kenfig Hill, G.W.R., 7, C5.
Kenilworth, L.M.S., 10, A5.
Kenley, S.R., 5, C3.
Kennethmont, L.N.E.R., 38, E5.
Kennett, L.N.E.R., 11, C5.
Kennington Jc. (Oxon.), G.W.R., 10, F4.
Kennishead, L.M.S., 30, C2.
Kennoway (Goods), L.N.E.R., 37, G2.
•Kensington (Olympia), G.W.R./L.M.S./S.R., 5, B3.
Kensington Road (Southport) Goods, L.M.S., 20, A4.
Kentallen, L.M.S., 33, D3.
Kentish Town, L.M.S., 5, A3.
Kenton (Suffolk), L.N.E.R., 12, C3.
•Kenton Bank, L.N.E.R., 27, B5
Kents Bank, L.M.S., 24, B3.
Kenyon Jc., L.M.S., 20, C2.
Kerne Bridge, G.W.R., 9, D1.
•Kerry, G.W.R., 14, C2.
Kershope Foot, L.N.E.R., 27, A1.
Keswick, L.M.S., 26, E2.
Ketley, G.W.R., 15, E2.
Kettering, L.M.S., 10, A2.
Kettleness, L.N.E.R., 28, E2.
Ketton & Collyweston, L.M.S., 16, F1.
Kew Bridge, S.R. & •L.M.S., 5, B2.
•Kew Gardens (Lancs.), L.M.S., 20, A4.
Keyham, (Devonport), G.W.R., 1, D5.
Keyingham, L.N.E.R., 22, E2.
Keynsham & Somerdale, G.W.R., 8, D1.
Kibworth, L.M.S., 16, F3.
Kidbrooke, S.R., 5, B4.
Kidderminster, G.W.R., 9, A3.
Kidlington, G.W.R., 10, E4.
Kidsgrove, L.M.S., 15, C3.
Kidwelly, G.W.R., 7, A2.
Kielder, L.N.E.R., 27, A2.
•Kilbagie, L.N.E.R., 31, A2.
Kilbarchan, L.M.S., 30, C2.
Kilbirnie, L.M.S., 30, D3.
Kilbowie, L.M.S., 30, C2.
Kilconquhar, L.N.E.R., 37, G2.
Kildale, L.N.E.R., 28, F3.
Kildary, L.M.S., 36, C4.
Kildonan, L.M.S., 39, F1.
Kildwick & Crosshills, L.M.S., 21, C1.
Kilgerran, G.W.R., 13, F3.
Kilgetty, G.W.R., 7, D3.
Kilkerran, L.M.S., 30, G3.
Kilknowe Jc., L.N.E.R., 30, D5.
Killamarsh, L.M.S. & **L.N.E.R.**/•L.M.S., 16, A4.
Killay, L.M.S., 7, B3.
Killearn, L.N.E.R., 30, B2.
Killiecrankie, L.M.S., 34, C3.
Killin, L.M.S., 34, E5.
Killin Jc., L.M.S., 34, E5.
Killingholme, L.N.E.R., 22, E3.
Killingworth, L.N.E.R., 27, B5.
Killochan, L.M.S., 30, G3.
Killywhan, L.M.S., 26, B4.
Kilmacolm, L.M.S., 30, C3.
Kilmany, L.N.E.R., 37, F2.
Kilmarnock, L.M.S., 30, E2.
Kilmaurs, L.M.S., 30, D2.
Kilnhurst, L.M.S. & L.N.E.R., 21, G4.
Kilnwick Gate (Goods), L.N.E.R., 22, C4.
Kilpatrick, L.N.E.R., 30, B2
Kilsby & Crick, L.M.S., 10, A4.
Kilsyth, L.N.E.R., 30, B1.
Kilwinning, L.M.S., 30, D3.
Kilworth, *see* Welford.
Kimberley, L.N.E.R. & •L.M.S., 16, C4.
Kimberley Park, L.N.E.R., 18, F4.
Kimbolton, L.M.S., 11, B1.
Kimbridge Jc., S.R., 4, D4.
Kinaldie, L.N.E.R., 38, F3.
Kinbrace, L.M.S., 39, E1.
Kinbuck, L.M.S., 34, G3.
•Kincardine, L.N.E.R., 30, A2.
Kincraig, L.M.S., 36, G4.
Kineton, L.M.S., 10, C5.
Kinfauns, L.M.S., 34, F1.
King Edward, L.N.E.R., 38, C3.
Kingennie L.M.S., 37, E2.
King George Dock, L.N.E.R., 22, E3.
Kingham, G.W.R., 10, D5.
Kinghorn, L.N.E.R., 30, A4.
Kinglassie Coll., L.N.E.R., 31, A4.
•Kingsbarns, L.N.E.R., 37, F3.
Kingsbridge, G.W.R., 2, E4.
Kingsbury (Som.), *see* Thorney.
Kingsbury (Warwicks.), L.M.S., 15, F5.
Kingscliffe, L.M.S., 16, F1.
Kingscote, S.R., 5, D4.
King's Cross, L.N.E.R. & L.P.T.B., 5, A3.
•King's Heath, L.M.S., 9, A4.
Kingshouse, L.M.S., 34, F5.
Kingskerswell, G.W.R., 2, D3.
Kingskettle, L.N.E.R., 37, F1.
Kingsknowe, L.M.S., 31, C4.
Kingsland, G.W.R., 14, D1.
King's Langley & Abbot's Langley, L.M.S., 11, G1.
Kingsley & Froghall, L.M.S., 15, C4.
King's Lynn, **L.N.E.R.**/M.G.N., 17, E4.
Kingsmuir, L.M.S., 37, D2.
King's Norton, L.M.S., 9, A4.
King's Sutton, G.W.R., 10, C4.
Kingston (Cambs.), *see* Toft.
Kingston (Surrey), S.R., 5 B2.
Kingston Wharf (Goods), S.R., 5, F2
Kingswear, G.W.R., 2, E3.
Kingswood & Burgh Heath, S.R., 5, C3.
King's Worthy, G.W.R., 4, C3.
Kingthorpe, L.N.E.R., 17, B2.
Kington, G.W.R., 14, E2.
Kingussie, L.M.S., 34, A4.
Kinloss, L.M.S., 36, C2.
Kinnaber Jc., L.M.S. L.N.E.R., 37, C4.
•Kinneil, L.N.E.R., 31, B2.
•Kinnerley Jc., S.M., 14, A1.
Kinnersley, L.M.S., 14, E1.
Kinnerton, L.M.S., 20, E4.
Kinross, L.N.E.R., 34, G1.
Kintbury, G.W.R., 4, A4.
Kintore, L.N.E.R., 38, F3.
Kipling Cotes, L.N.E.R., 22, D4.
Kippax, L.N.E.R., 21, D4.
Kippen, L.N.E.R., 30, A1.
Kirby Cross, L.N.E.R., 12, F3.
Kirby Moorside, L.N.E.R., 21, A5.
Kirby Muxloe, L.M.S., 16, F4.
Kirby Park, B.J., 20, C5.
Kirkandrews, L.N.E.R., 26, C1.
Kirkbank, L.N.E.R., 32, E4.
Kirkbride, L.N.E.R., 26, C2.
Kirkbuddo, L.M.S., 37, D2.
•Kirkburton, L.M.S., 21, F2.
Kirkby (Lancs.), L.M.S., 20, B4.
Kirkby Bentinck, L.N.E.R., 16, C4.
Kirkby-in-Ashfield, L.M.S., & L.N.E.R., 16, C4.
Kirkby-in-Furness, L.M.S., 24, A4.
Kirkby Lonsdale, L.M.S., 24, B2.
Kirkby Stephen, L.M.S. & L.N.E.R., 27, F2.
Kirkby Thore, L.N.E.R., 27 E2.
Kirkcaldy, L.N.E.R., 31, A4.
Kirkconnel, L.M.S., 31, F1.
Kirkcowan, L.M.S., 25, C3.
Kirkcudbright, L.M.S., 26, C5.
Kirk Ella, *see* Willerby.
Kirkgate (Wakefield), **L.M.S.**/L.N.E.R., 21, E3.
Kirkgunzeon, L.M.S., 26, B4.
•Kirkham Abbey, L.N.E.R., 22, B5.
Kirkham & Wesham, L.M.S., 24, D3.
•Kirkheaton, L.M.S., 21, E2.
Kirkinner, L.M.S., 25, C4.
Kirkintilloch, L.N.E.R., 30, B1.
•Kirkland, L.M.S., 26, A5.
Kirkley (Goods), L.N.E.R., 18, G1.
•Kirklington, L.M.S., 16, B3.
•Kirkliston, L.N.E.R., 31, B3.
Kirk Michael, I.M.R., 23, B2.
•Kirknewton, L.N.E.R., 32, E3.
Kirkoswald, *see* Lazonby.
Kirkpatrick, L.M.S., 26, B2.
Kirk Sandall Jc., L.N.E.R./S.Y., 21, F5.
•Kirk Smeaton, L.N.E.R., 21, E4.
Kirkstall, L.M.S., 21, D3.
Kirkstall Forge (Goods), L.M.S., 21, D3.
Kirriemuir, L.M.S., 37, D2.
Kirtlebridge, L.M.S., 26, B2.
Kirton, L.N.E.R., 17, D3.
Kirton Lindsey, L.N.E.R., 22, F4.
Kittybrewster, L.N.E.R., 38, F2.
Kiveton Bridge, L.N.E.R., 16, A4.
Kiveton Park, L.N.E.R., 16, A4.
Kiveton Colls., L.M.S., 16, A4.
•Knapton (Yorks.), L.N.E.R., 22, B4.
Knapton (Norfolk), *see* Paston.
Knaresborough, L.N.E.R., 21, C3.
Knebworth, L.N.E.R., 11, F2.
Knighton, L.M.S., 14, D2.
Knighton Jc., L.M.S., 16, F3.
Knightwick, G.W.R., 9, B2.
•Knitsley, L.N.E.R., 27, C4.
Knock, L.N.E.R., 38, D5.
Knockando, L.N.E.R., 36, E2.
Knockholt, S.R., 5, C4.
•Knott End-on-Sea, L.M.S., 24, C4.
Knottingley, L.M.S./L.N.E.R., 21, E4.
Knotty Ash, C.L.C., 20, C4.
Knowesgate, L.N.E.R., 27, A4.
•Knoweside, L.M.S., 30, F3.
Knowle & Dorridge, G.W.R., 9, A5.
Knowlton, E.K.R., 6, C2.
Knucklas, L.M.S., 14, D2.
Knutsford, C.L.C., 20, D2.
Kyle of Lochalsh, L.M.S., 35, F1.

L

Lade Halt, R.H.D.R., 6, E3.
Ladmanlow (Goods), L.M.S. 15, B4.
Ladock, *see* Probus.
Ladybank, L.N.E.R., 37, F1.
Lady Helen Coll., L.N.E.R., 31, A4.
Ladysbridge, L.N.E.R., 38, C4.
Laindon, L.M.S., 5, A5.
Lairg, L.M.S., 35, A5.
Laisterdyke, **L.N.E.R.**/L.M.S., 21, D2
Lakenheath, L.N.E.R., 11, A5.
Lake Side, *see* Windermere.
Lambley, L.N.E.R., 27, C2.
Lambourn, G.W.R., 10, G5.
Lamington, L.M.S., 31, E2.
Lampeter, G.W.R., 13, E5.
Lamphey, G.W.R., 7, D2.
•Lamplugh, L.M.S., 26, E3.
Lamport, L.M.S., 10, A2.
Lanark, L.M.S., 31, D2.
Lancaster, L.M.S., 24, C3.
•Lanchester, L.N.E.R., 27, D5.
Lancing, S.R., 5, F2.
Landore, G.W.R., 7, B4.
Langbank, L.M.S., 30, B3.
Langford (Oxon), *see* Kelmscott.
Langford (Beds.), Goods, L.N.E.R., 11, D2.
•Langford (Som.), G.W.R., 8, D2.
Langford & Ulting, L.N.E.R., 12, F5.
Langho, L.M.S., 24, D2.
Langholm, L.N.E.R., 26, A1.
Langley (Bucks.), G.W.R., 5, B1.
Langley Green, *see* Oldbury.
Langley Jc., L.N.E.R., 11, E2.
Langley Mill, L.M.S., 16, C4.
See also Eastwood, L.N.E.
•Langley-on-Tyne, L.N.E.R., 27, C3.
Langloan, L.M.S., 31, C1.
Langport, G.W.R., 3, D1.
Langrick, L.N.E.R., 17, C2.
Langston, S.R., 4, E2.
Langwathby, L.M.S., 27, D1.
Langwith, L.M.S., 16, B4.
Langwith Coll. L.N.E.R., 16, B4.
Langworth, L.N.E.R., 17, A1.
Lansdown (Cheltenham), **L.M.S.**/G.W.R., 9, D3.
Lapford, S.R., 2, A4.
Lapworth, G.W.R., 9, A5.
Larbert, **L.M.S.**/L.N.E.R., 31, B1.
Largo, L.N.E.R., 37, G2.
Largoward (Goods), L.N.E.R., 37, F2.
Largs, L.M.S., 30, C4.
Larkhall, L.M.S., 31, D1.
Lartington, L.N.E.R., 27, E4.
Lasswade, L.N.E.R., 31, C4.
Latchford, L.M.S., 20, C2.
Latchley Halt, S.R., 1, C5.
Latimer, *see* Chalfont.
•Lauder, L.N.E.R., 32, D5.
Laughton, *see* Dinnington.
Launceston, G.W.R. & S.R., 1, C4.
Launton, L.M.S., 10, D3.
Laurencekirk, **L.M.S.**/L.N.E.R., 37, B4.
Lauriston, L.N.E.R., 37, C4.
•Lavant, S.R., 4, E1.
Lavenham, L.N.E.R., 12, D5.
Lavernock, G.W.R., 8, D4.
Lavington, G.W.R., 3, B5.
Law Jc., L.M.S., 31, D1.
Lawley Bank, G.W.R., 15, E2.
Lawrence Hill, G.W.R., 8, C1.
•Lawton, L.M.S., 15, B3.
Laxey, M.E., 23, B3.
Laxfield, L.N.E.R., 12, B3.
Layton (Lancs.), L.M.S., 24, D4.
Lazonby & Kirkoswald, L.M.S., 27, D1.
Lea, L.N.E.R., 16, A2.
Lea Bridge, L.N.E.R., 5, A4.
Leadburn, L.N.E.R., 31, C4.
Leadenham, L.N.E.R., 16, C1.
Leadgate, L.N.E.R., 27, C5.
Lea End Weighs, L.N.E.R., 31, C1.
Leagrave, L.M.S., 10, D1.
Lea Green, L.M.S., 20, C3.
Lea Hall, L.M.S., 15, G5.
Lealholm, L.N.E.R., 28, F3.
Leamington Spa, G.W.R. & L.M.S., 10, B5.
Leamside, L.N.E.R., 28, D5.
Lea Road (Gainsborough), L.N.E.R., 22, G5.
Leasingthorne (Goods), L.N.E.R., 27, E5.
Leasowe, L.M.S., 20, C5.
Leatherhead, S.R., 5, C2.
Leaton, G.W.R., 15, E1.
Lechlade, G.W.R., 9, F5.
Leckhampton, *see* Cheltenham South.
Ledbury, G.W.R., 9, C2.
Ledsham, B.J., 20, D4.
Ledston, L.N.E.R., 21, E4.
Lee (Kent), S.R., 5, B4.
Leebotwood, S.H., 15, F1.
Leeds, L.M.S. & L.N.E.R., 21, —.
Leegate, L.M.S., 26, D2.
Leek, L.M.S., 15, C4.
Leeming Bar, L.N.E.R., 28, G5.
Lees, L.M.S., 21, F1.
•Legacy, G.W.R., 20, E4.
Legbourne Road, L.N.E.R., 17, A3.
Leicester, L.M.S. & L.N.E.R. 16, —.
Leigh (Lancs.), L.M.S., 20, B2.
Leigh (Staffs.), L.M.S., 15, D4.
Leigh Court, G.W.R., 9, B2.
Leigh-on-Sea, L.M.S., 6, A5.
Leigh's Wood, L.M.S., 15, F4.
Leighton Buzzard, L.M.S., 10, D2.
Leiston, L.N.E.R., 12, C2.
Leith, L.M.S. & L.N.E.R., 31, B4.
Lelant, G.W.R., 1, E4.
Lemington, L.N.E.R., 27, B5.
Lenham, S.R., 6, C4.
Lennoxtown, L.N.E.R., 30, B1.
Lenton (Goods), L.M.S., 16, D4.
Lentran, L.M.S., 36, E5.
Lenwade, M.G.N., 18, E4.
Lenzie Jc., L.N.E.R., 30, B1.
Leominster, S.H., 9, B1.
Lepton, *see* Fenay Bridge.
•Leslie, L.N.E.R., 37, G1.
Lesmahagow, L.M.S., 31, D1.
Letchworth, L.N.E.R., 11, E2.
•Letham Grange, L.N.E.R., 37, D3.
•Lethenty, L.N.E.R., 38, E3.
•Letterston, G.W.R., 13, F1.
Leuchars Jc., L.N.E.R., 37, F2.
Leven, L.N.E.R., 37, G2.
Levenshulme, L.M.S., 20, C1.
Leverton, L.N.E.R., 16, A2.
Levisham, L.N.E.R., 28, G2.
Lewes, S.R., 5, F4.
•Lewes Road, S.R., 5, F3.
Lewisham, S.R., 5, B4.
Leyburn, L.N.E.R., 27, G5.
•Leycett, L.M.S., 15, C3.
Leyland, L.M.S., 24, E2.
Leysdown, S.R., 6, B3.
Leysmill, L.M.S., 37, D3.
Leyton, **•L.N.E.R.**/L.P.T.B., 5, A4.
Leytonstone, **•L.N.E.R.**/L.P.T.B., 5, A4.
Lezayre, I.M.R., 23, A3.
Lhanbryde, L.M.S., 36, C1.
Lichfield, L.M.S., 15, E5.
Lidlington, L.M.S., 10, C1.
Liff, L.M.S., 37, E1.
•Lifford, L.M.S., 9, A4.
Lifton, G.W.R., 1, B5.
Lightcliffe, L.M.S., 21, E2.
Lightmoor Plat., G.W.R., 15, F2.
Lilbourne, L.M.S., 10, A4.
Lilliehill Jc., L.N.E.R., 31, A3.
Limbury Rd., L.M.S., 11, E1.
Lime St. (L'pool.) L.M.S., 20, C4.
Limpley Stoke, G.W.R., 3, B3.
Linby, L.M.S., 16, C4.
Lincoln, L.N.E.R. & L.M.S., 16, B1.
Lindal, L.M.S., 24, B4.
Lindean, L.N.E.R., 31, E5.
Lindores, L.N.E.R., 37, F1.
Lingdale Mines, L.N.E.R., 28, E3.
Lingfield, S.R., 5, D4.
Lingwood, L.N.E.R., 18, F2.
Linley, G.W.R., 15, F2.
Linlithgow, L.N.E.R., 31, B2.
Linthwaite (Goods), L.M.S., 21, E2.
Linton, L.N.E.R., 11, D4.
Lintz Green, L.N.E.R., 27, C5.
Linwood (Goods), L.M.S., 30, C2.
Liphook, S.R., 4, D1.
Liscard, **L.M.S.**/L.N.E.R., 20, C4.
Liskeard, G.W.R., 1, D4.
Liss, S.R., 4, D1.
Lissens (Goods), L.M.S., 30, D3.
Litchfield (Hants.), G.W.R., 4, B3.
Littleborough, L.M.S., 21, E1.
Little Bytham, L.N.E.R., 17, E1.
•Little Eaton, L.M.S., 16, C5.
Littleham, S.R., 2, C2.
Littlehampton, S.R., 5, F1.
Little Hulton, L.M.S., 20, B2
Little Kimble, G.W.R./L.N.E.R., 10, E2.
Little Mill, L.N.E.R., 32, F1.
Little Mill Jc., G.W.R., 8, B3.
Littlemore, G.W.R., 10, F4.
Littleport, L.N.E.R., 11, A4.
Little Salkeld, L.M.S., 27, D1.
Little Somerford, G.W.R., 9, G4.
Little Steeping, L.N.E.R., 17, B3.
Littlestone-on-Sea, *see* New Romney.
Little Sutton, B.J., 20, D4.
Littleton & Badsey, G.W.R., 9, C4.
Little Weighton, L.N.E.R., 22, D4.
Littleworth, L.N.E.R., 17, E2.
Liverpool, C.L.C., L.M.S., Mer., & •L.N.E.R., 20, —.
Liverpool Rd. (Chester), L.N.E.R., 20, D4.
Liverpool Rd. (Kidsgrove), L.M.S., 15, C3.
Liverpool St., L.N.E.R. & L.P.T.B., 5, B3.
Liversedge, L.M.S., 21, E2.
Livingston, L.N.E.R., 31, C3.
Llanarthney, L.M.S., 13, G5.
Llanbedr & Pensarn, G.W.R., 19, G2.
Llanberis, S.M.R. & •L.M.S., 19, E2.
Llanbister Rd., L.M.S., 14, D2.
Llanbradach, G.W.R., 8, B4.
Llanbrynmair, G.W.R., 14, B4.
Llandaff, G.W.R., 8, C4.
Llandderfel, G.W.R., 19, F5.
Llandebie, G.W.R., 7, A4.
Llandenny, G.W.R., 8, B3.
Llandilo, **G.W.R.**/L.M.S., 13, G5.
Llandilo Bridge, L.M.S., 13, G5.
Llandinam, G.W.R., 14, C3.
Llandovery, V.T., 14, F5.
Llandre, G.W.R., 13, C5.
Llandrillo, G.W.R., 19, F5.
Llandrindod Wells, L.M.S., 14, D3.
•Llandrinio Road, S.M., 14, A2.
Llandudno, L.M.S., 19, C3.
Llandudno Jc., L.M.S., 19, D3.
Llandulas, L.M.S., 19, D4.
Llandyssul, G.W.R., 13, F4.
Llanelly, G.W.R., 7, B3.
Llanerch Siding, G.W.R., 8, B4.
Llanerchymedd, L.M.S., 19, C1.
Llanfair, L.M.S., 19, D2.
•Llanfair Caereinion, W.L., 14, B3.
Llanfairfechan, L.M.S., 19, D3.
Llanfalteg, G.W.R., 13, G2.
Llanfechain, G.W.R., 14, A2.
Llanfyllin, G.W.R., 14, A3.
Llanfynydd, W.M./L.M.S., 20, E5.
Llanfyrnach, G.W.R., 13, F3
Llangadock, V.T., 14, F5.
Llangammarch Wells, L.M.S., 14, E4.
Llangedwyn, G.W.R., 20, G5.
Llangefni, L.M.S., 19, D1.
Llangeinor, G.W.R., 7, B5.
Llangennech, G.W.R., 7, B3.
Llanglydwen, G.W.R., 13, G2.
Llangollen, G.W.R., 20, F5.
Llangunllo, L.M.S., 14, D2.
Llangwyllog, L.M.S., 19, C1.
Llangybi (Caer'n.), L.M.S., 19, F1.
Llangybi (Card'n.), G.W.R., 13, E5.
•Llangyfelach, G.W.R., 7, B4.
Llangynog, G.W.R., 19, G5.
Llangynwyd, G.W.R., 7, B5.
Llanharan, G.W.R., 8, C5.
Llanharry, G.W.R., 8, C5.
Llanhilleth, G.W.R., 8, B4.
Llanidloes, G.W.R., 14, C4.
Llanilar, G.W.R., 13, D5.
Llanishen, G.W.R., 8, C4.
•Llanmorlais, L.M.S., 7, B3.
Llanpumpsaint, G.W.R., 13, F4.
Llanrhaiadr, L.M.S., 19, D5.
Llanrhaiadr Mochnant, G.W.R., 20, G5.
Llanrhystyd Road, G.W.R., 13, C5.
Llanrwst & Trefriw, L.M.S., 19, D4.
Llansamlet, G.W.R., 7, B4.

Llansantffraid, G.W.R., 14, A2.
Llansilin Road, G.W.R., 20, G5.
Llantarnam, G.W.R., 8, B3.
Llantrisant, G.W.R., 8, C5.
Llantwit Fardre, G.W.R., 8, C5.
Llantwit Major, G.W.R., 8, D5.
Llanuwychllyn, G.W.R., 19, G4.
Llanvihangel (Mon.), G.W.R., 14, G2.
Llanwern, G.W.R., 8, C3.
Llanwnda, L.M.S., 19, E1.
Llanwrda, V.T., 14, F5.
Llanwrtyd Wells, L.M.S., 14, E4.
Llanyblodwell, G.W.R., 20, G5.
Llanybyther. G.W.R.,13, E5.
•Llan-y-Cefn, G.W.R., 13, G2.
Llanymynech, G.W.R., 14, A2.
•Lletty Brongu, G.W.R., 7, B5.
Llong, L.M.S., 20, E5.
Llwydcoed, G.W.R., 8, A5.
•Llwyngwern, Corris, 14, B5.
Llwyngwril, G.W.R., 13, A5.
Llwynypia, G.W.R., 8, B5.
Llynclys, G.W.R., 20, G4.
Llyswen, *see* Boughrood.
•Loanhead, L.N.E.R., 31, C4.
Lochailort, L.N.E.R., 33, B1.
§Lochanhead, L.M.S., 26, B4.
Locharbriggs, L.M.S., 26, A3.
Loch Awe, L.M.S., 33, F4.
Lochearnhead, L.M.S., 34, F5.
Lochee, L.M.S., 37, E2.
•Lochee West, L.M.S., 37, E2.
Locheilside, L.N.E.R., 33, B3.
Lochgelly, L.N.E.R., 31, A3.
Loch Leven (Goods), L.N.E.R., 34. G1.
Lochluichart, L.M.S., 35, C4.
Lochmaben, L.M.S., 26, A3.
Lochmill (Goods). L.N.E.R., 31, B2.
Lochside, L.M.S., 30, C3.
Loch Tay, L.M.S., 34 ,E5.
•Lochty, L.N.E.R., 37, F2.
Lochwinnoch, L.M.S., 30, C3.
Lockerbie, L.M.S., 26, A3.
Lockington, L.N.E.R., 22, C4.
Lockwood, L.M.S., 21, E2.
Loddington Sdg., L.M.S., 10, A2.
Loddiswell, G.W.R., 2, E4.
Lode, *see* Bottisham.
Lodge Hil, G.W.R., 3, B2.
Lofthouse, L.N.E.R., 21, E3.
Loftus, L.N.E.R., 28, E3.
Logierieve, L.N.E.R., 38, E2.
Login, G.W.R., 13, G2.
Londesborough, L.N.E.R., 22, D5.
London Bridge, S.R., 5, B3.
London Road (Brighton), S.R., 5, F3.
London Road (Guildford), S.R., 5, C1.
London Road (Manchester), L.M.S./L.N.E.R. & M.S.J.A., 20, B1.
London Road (Wellingborough), L.M.S., 10, B2.
Long Ashton Plat., G.W.R., 8, D2.
•Longbridge (Rubery), H.J., 9, A4.
Long Buckby, L.M.S., 10, B3.
Long Clawson & Hose, L.M.S./L.N.E.R., 16, D2.
Longcliffe (Goods), L.M.S., 15, C5.
Longcross Halt, S.R., 5, B1.
Longdown, G.W.R., 2, B3.
Long Eaton, L.M.S., 16, D4.
Longford & Exhall (Warwicks.), L.M.S., 16, G5.
Longforgan, L.M.S., 37, E1.
§Longhaven, L.N.E.R., 38, D1.
Longhirst, L.N.E.R., 27, A5.
Longhope, G.W.R., 9, D2.
Longhoughton, L.N.E.R., 32, F1.
Long Itchington, *see* Southam.
Long Marston, G.W.R., 9, C5.
Long Marton, L.M.S., 27, E2.
Long Melford, L.N.E.R., 12, D5.
Longmorn, L.N.E.R., 36, D1.
Longniddry, L.N.E.R., 31, B5.
•Longparish, S.R., 4, C4.
Longport, L.M.S. 15, C3.
Long Preston, L.M.S., 24, C1.
•Longridge, L.M.S., 24, D2.
•Longriggend, L.N.E.R., 31, C1.
Longside, L.N.E.R., 38, D2.
Longsight, L.M.S., 20 C1.
Long Stanton, **L.N.E.R.**/L.M.S., 11, C3
Long Stow (Goods), L.M.S., 11, C1.
Long Sutton (Lincs.), M.G.N., 17, E3.
Long Sutton & Pitney (Som.). G.W.R., 3, D1.
Longton, L.M.S., 15, C3.
Longton Bridge, L.M.S., **24**, E3.
Longtown, L.N.E.R., 26, B1.
Longville, G.W.R., 15, F1.
Longwitton, L.N.E.R., 27, A4.
Longwoo! & Milnsbridge, L.M.S., 21, E2.
Lonmay, L.N.E.R., 38, C2.
Looe, G.W.R., 1, D4.
Lord's Bridge, L.M.S., 11, C3.
Lord Street (Southport), C.L.C., 20, A4.
Lossiemouth, L.N.E.R., 36, C1.
Lostock Gralam, C.L.C. 20, D2.
Lostock Hall, L.M.S., 24, E2.
Lostock (Jc.), L.M.S., 20, B2.
Lostwithiel, G.W.R., 1, D3.
Loth. L.M.S., 39, G2.
Loudwater, G.W.R., 9, F2.
Loughborough, L.M.S. & L.N.E.R., 16, E4.
Loughor, G.W.R., 7, B3.
Loughton, L.N.E.R., 11, G3.
Louth, L.N.E.R., 17, A3.
Low Bentham (Goods), L.M.S., 24, B2.
Lowdham, L.M.S., 16, C3.
Lower Darwen, L.M.S., 24, E2.
Lower Edmonton, L.N.E.R., 5, A3.
Lower Ince, L.N.E.R., 20, B3. *See also* Ince (Lancs.).
Lower Penarth, G.W.R. 8, D4.
Lower Pontnewydd, G.W.R., 8, B3.
Lowesby, L.N.E.R., 16, F2.
Lowestoft, **L.N.E.R.**/N.S.J., 18, G1.
Lowestoft North, N.S.J., 18, F1.
Low Fell, L.N.E.R., 27, C5.
Lowfield Siding, L.N.E.R., 16, C2.
Low Gill, L.M.S., 27, G1.
Low Moor, L.M.S., 21, E2.
Low Row, L.N.E.R., 27, C1.
Low Street, L.M.S., 5, B5.
Lowther, *see* Clifton.
Lowthorpe, L.N.E.R., 22, C3.
Lowton, L.M.S., 20, C2.
Lowton St. Mary's, L.N.E.R., 20, B2.
Lowtown (Pudsey), L.N.E.R., 21, D3.
Lubenham, L.M.S., 16, G3.
Lucker, L.N.E.R., 32, E2.
Luckett, S.R., 1, C5.
Ludborough, L.N.E.R., 22, E4.
Luddendenfoot, L.M.S., 21, E1.
•Luddington, A.J., 22, E5.
Ludgershall (Bucks.), *see* Brill.
Ludgershall (Wilts.), G.W.R., 4, B5.
Ludlow, S.H., 9, A1.
Luffenham, L.M.S., 16, F1.
Lugar, L.M.S., 30, F1.
Lugton, L.M.S., 30, D2.
Luib, L.M.S., 34, E5.
Lullingstone, S.R., 5, B5.
Lumphanan, L.N.E.R., 38, G4.
•Lunan Bay, L.N.E.R., 37, D4.
Luncarty, L.M.S., 34, E2.
Lundin Links, L.N.E.R., 37, G2.
Lustleigh, G.W.R., 2, C4.
Luthrie, L.N.E.R., 37, F1.
Luton, L.M.S. & L.N.E.R., 11, E1.
Luton Hoo, L.N.E.R., 11, F1.
Lutterworth, L.N.E.R., 16, G4.
Luxulyan G.W.R., 1 D3.
•Lybster, L.M.S., 39, E3.
Lydbrook Jc., G.W.R./•S.V.Y., 9, E1.
Lydden, *see* Stonehall Halt.
Lydd-on-Sea, S.R., 6, E3.
Lydd Town, S.R., 6, E3.
Lydford, G.W.R. & S.R., 1, C5.
Lydiate, C.L.C., 20, B4.
Lydney, G.W.R. & S.V.Y., 9, F2.
Lydstep Halt, G.W.R. 7, D2.
Lye, G.W.R., **15**, G3.
Lyme Regis, S.R., 3, F1.
§Lyminge, S.R., 6, D3.
Lymington Pier, S.R., 4, F4.
,, Town, S.R., 4, F4.
Lymm, L.M.S., 20 C2.
Lympstone, S.R., 2, C3.
Lyndhurst Rd., S.R., 4, E4.
Lyne, L.M.S., 31, D4.
Lynedoch, L.M.S., 30, B3.
•Lyneside, L.N.E.R., 26, B1.
§Lyonshall, G.W.R., 14, E1.
Lytham, L.M.S., 24, E4.

M

Mablethorpe, L.N.E.R., 17, A4.
Macclesfield Central, **L.M.S.**/L.N.E.R., 15 A3.
Macclesfield, Hibel Road, L.M.S., 15, A3.
Macduff, L.N.E.R., 38, C4.
Machen, G.W.R., 8, B4.
Machynlleth, G.W.R. & •Corris, 14, B5.
Macmerry (Goods), L.N.E.R., 31, B5.
Madderty, L.M.S., 34, F2.
•Madeley (Salop), G.W.R., 15, F2.
Madeley (Staffs.), L.M.S., 15, C3.
Madeley Market, L.M.S., 15, F2.
•Maenclochog, G.W.R., 13, F2.
Maentwrog Road, G.W.R., 19, F3.
Maerdy, G.W.R., 8, B5.
•Maesbrook, S.M., 14, A2.
Maesaraul Jc., G.W.R., 8, C5.
Maesteg, G.W.R., 7, B5.
Maesycrugiau, G.W.R., 13, F4.
Maesycwmmer, G.W.R., 8, B4.
Magdalen Green (Dundee), L.M.S., 37, E2.
Magdalen Road, L.N.E.R., 17, F4.
Maghull, L.M.S., 20, B4.
Magor, G.W.R., 8, C3.
Maidenhead, G.W.R., 10, G2.
Maiden Newton, G.W.R., 3, F2.
•Maidens, L.M.S., 30, G3.
Maidstone, S.R., 6, C5.
Malden, S.R., 5, B3.
Maldon East & Heybridge, L.N.E.R., 12, F5.
•Maldon West, L.N.E.R., 12, F5.
Malins Lee, L.M.S., 15, E2.
Mallaig, L.N.E.R., 33, A1.
Malling, S.R., 5, C5.
Malmesbury, G.W.R., 9, F3.
Malpas, L.M.S., 15, C1.
•Maltby, S.Y., 21, G5.
Malton, L.N.E.R., 22, B5.
Malvern, *see* Great Malvern.
Malvern Link, G.W.R., 9, C3.
Malvern Rd. (Cheltenham), G.W.R., 9, D4.
Malvern Wells, G.W.R. & L.M.S., 9, C3.
Manchester, C.L.C., L.M.S., L.N.E.R., M.S.J.A., 20.—
Manchester Road (Burnley), L.M.S., 24, D1.
Manchester Rd. (Bradford), Goods, L.N.E.R., 21, D2.
Manea, L.N.E.R., 11, A3.
Mangotsfield, L.M.S., 8, C1.
•Manley, C.L.C., 20, D3.
Manningham, L.M.S., 21, D2.
Manningtree, L.N.E.R., 12, E4.
Manod, G.W.R., 19, F3.
Manorbier, G.W.R., 7, D2.
Manor Park, L.N.E.R., 5, A4.
Manor Road, L.M.S., 20, C5.
Manors, L.N.E.R., 27, B5.
Mansfield, L.M.S. & L.N.E.R., 16, B4.
Mansfield Woodhouse, **L.M.S.**/L.N.E.R., 16, B4.
Manton, L.M.S., 16, F2.
Manuel, L.N.E.R., 31, B2.
Manvers St. (Nottingham) Goods, L.M.S., 16, D3.
Marazion, G.W.R., 1, F4.
March, L.N.E.R., 11, A3.
Marchington, **L.M.S.**/•L.N.E.R., 15, D5.
Marchmont, L.N.E.R. 32, D4.
Marchwiel, G.W.R., 20, E4.
Marchwood, S.R., 4, E4.
Marden, S.R., 6, D5.
Mardock, L.N.E.R., 11, F3.
Marefield Jc., L.M.S./L.N.E.R., 16, F2.
Marfleet, L.N.E.R., 22, D3.
Margam Jc., G.W.R., 7, C4.
Margate, S.R., 6, B2.
Marishes Road, L.N.E.R., 22. E5.
Mark Cross, *see* Rotherfield.
•Market Bosworth, L.M.S., 16, F5.
Market Drayton, **G.W.R.**/L.M.S., 15, D2.
Market Harborough, L.M.S., 16, G2.
Market Weighton, L.N.E.R., 22, D4.
Markham Coll., L.M.S. & L.N.E.R., 16, B4.
Markham (Mon.), L.M.S., 8, B4.
Markinch, L.N.E.R., 37, G1.
Mark's Tey, L.N.E.R., 12, E5.
Marlborough, G.W.R., 4, A5.
Marlesford, L.N.E.R., 12, C2.
Marlow, G.W.R., 10, G2.
Marple, L.M.S./L.N.E.R., 21, G1.
Marron Jc., L.M.S., 26, E3.
Marsden (Durham), S.S.M.W., 28, B5.
Marsden (Yorks.), L.M.S., 21, F1.
Marsden Cottage Halt, S.S.M.W., 28, B5.
•Marsh Brook, S.H., 14, C1.
Marsh Farm Jc., S.H./G.W.R., 14, C1.
Marshfield, G.W.R., 8, C3.
Marsh Gate (Goods), L.N.E.R., 21, F5.
Marsh Gibbon & Poundon, L.M.S., 10, D3.
Marshland Jc., L.N.E.R./A.J., 22, E5.
Marsh Lane, L.N.E.R., 21, D3.
Marsh Mills, G.W.R., 2, D5.
Marske, L.N.E.R. 28, E3.
Marston Gate, L.M.S., 10, E2.
Marston Green, L.M.S., 15, G5.
Marston Magna, G.W.R., 3, D2.
Marston Moor, L.N.E.R., 21, C4.
Martham, M.G.N., 18, E1.
Martin Mill, S.R., 6, D2.
Martock, G.W.R., 3, D1.
Marton, L.M.S., 10, B5.
•Maryfield (Dundee) L.M.S., 37, E2.
Maryhill, L.N.E.R. & L.M.S., 30, C1.
Marykirk, L.M.S., 37, C3.
Marylebone, L.N.E.R. & L.P.T.B., 5, A3.
Maryport, L.M.S., 26, D3.
Mary Tavy & Blackdown, G.W.R., 1, C5.
Masborough (Rotherham), L.M.S., 21, G4. *See also* Rotherham.
Masbury, S.D., 3, C2.
•Masham, L.N.E.R., 21, A3.
Massingham, M.G.N., 18, E5.
Mathry Road, G.W.R., 13, F1.
Matlock, L.M.S., 16, B5.
Matlock Bath, L.M.S., 16, B5.
Mauchline, L.M.S., 30, E2.
Maud, L.N.E.R., 38, D2.
Maud's Bridge (Goods), L.N.E.R., 22. F5.
Mawcarse, L.N.E.R., 34, G1.
Maxton, L.N.E.R., 32, E5.
•Maxwelltown, L.M.S., 26, B4.
Maybole, L.M.S., 30, F3.
Mayfield, S.R., 5, E5.
May Hill (Monmouth), G.W.R., 8, A1.
Meadow Hall, L.N.E.R., 21, G3.
•Mealsgate, L.M.S., 26, D2.
•Measham, L.M.S., 16, E5.
Medge Hall, L.N.E.R., 22, F5.
Medstead & Four Marks, S.R., 4, C2.
Meeth, S.R., 2, A5.
Meigle, L.M.S., 37, D1.
•Meikle Earnock, L.M.S., 30, D1.
Meir, L.M.S., 15, C4.
•Melangoose Mill, G.W.R., **1**, D2.
Melbourn, *see* Meldreth.
•Melbourne, L.M.S., 16, D5.
Melcombe Regis, G.W.R./S.R., 3, G3.
Meldon, L.N.E.R., 27, A5.
Meldon Jc., S.R., 2, B5.
Meldreth & Melbourn, L.N.E.R., 11, D3.
•Meledor Mill, G.W.R., 1, D2.
•Meliden, L.M.S., 19, C5.
Melksham, G.W.R., 3, A4.
Melling, L.M.S., 24, B2.
Mellis, L.N.E.R., 12, B4.
Mells Road, G.W.R., 3, B3.
Melmerby, L.N.E.R., 21, B3.
Melrose, L.N.E.R., 32, E5.
Meltham, L.M.S., 21, F2.
Melton, L.N.E.R., 12, D3.
Melton Constable, M.G.N., 18, D4.
Melton Mowbray, L.M.S. & L.M.S./L.N.E.R., 16, E2.
•Melverley, S.M., 14, A2.
Menai Bridge, L.M.S., 19, D2.
Mendlesham, L.N.E.R., 12, C4.
Menheniot, G.W.R., 1, D4.
Menston, L.M.S., 21, D2.
Menstrie, L.N.E.R., 31, A1.
Menthorpe Gate, L.N.E.R., 21, D5.
•Meole Brace, S.M., 15, E1.
Meols, L.M.S., 20, C5.
Meols Cop, L.M.S., 20, A4.
Meopham, S.R., 5, B5.
Merchiston, L.M.S., 31, B4.
Merrybent Jc., L.N.E.R., 27, E5.
Mersey Road, C.L.C., 20, C4.
Merstham, S.R., 5, C3.
Merstone (I.W.), S.R., 4, F3.
Merthyr, **G.W.R.**/L.M.S., 8, A5.
Merthyr Vale, G.W.R., 8, B5.
Merton Park, S.R., 5, B3.
Metheringham, *see* Blankney.
Methil, L.N.E.R., 37, G2.
Methley, L.M.S. & M.J., 21, E4.
•Methven, L.M.S., 34, E2.
Methven Jc., L.M.S., 34, E2.
Mexborough, **L.N.E.R.**/•L.M.S., 21, F4.
Micheldever, S.R., 4, C3.
Micklefield, L.N.E.R., 21, D4.
Micklehurst (Goods), L.M.S., 21, F1.
•Mickleover, L.N.E.R., 16, D5.
Mickleton, L.N.E.R., 27, E4.
Mickle Trafford, B.J. & C.L.C., 20, D4.
Midcalder, L.M.S., 31, C3.
§Mid-Clyth, L.M.S., 39, E4.
Middle Drove, L.N.E.R., 17, F4.
Middlesbrough, L.N.E.R., 28, E4.
Middleton (Lancs.), L.M.S., 20, B1.
Middleton (Salop), S.H., 9, A1.
Middleton-in-Teesdale, L.N.E.R., 27, E3.
Middleton Jc., L.M.S., 20, B1.
Middleton North, L.N.E.R., 27, A4.
•Middleton-on-Lune, L.M.S., 24, A2.
Middleton-on-the-Wolds, L.N.E.R., 22, C4.
Middleton Rd. (Heysham) Goods, L.M.S., 24, C3.
Middleton Towers, L.N.E.R., 17, E5.
Middlewich, L.M.S., 20, D2.
Middlewood, L.M.S./L.N.E.R., 15, A4.
Midford, S.D., 3, B3.
Midge Hall, L.M.S., 24, E3.
Midgham, G.W.R., 4, A3.
Midhurst, S.R., 4, D1.
Midsomer Norton & Welton, G.W.R. & S.D., 3, B3.
Midville, L.N.E.R., 17, C3.
Milborne Port, S.R., 3, D3.
Milcote, G.W.R., 9, C5.
Mildenhall, L.N.E.R., 11, B5.
Miles Platting, L.M.S., 20, B1.
Milford (Surrey), S.R., 5, D1.
Milford & Brocton, L.M.S., 15, E4.
Milford Haven, G.W.R., 7, D1.
Milford Jc., L.N.E.R., 21, D4.
•Milkwall, S.V.Y., 9, E1.
•Millbay (Plymouth), G.W.R., 1, D5.
Millbrook (Beds.), L.M.S., 10, C1.
Millbrook (Hants.), S.R., 4, E4.
Millbrook (Lancs.), *see* Staley.
Millerhill, L.N.E.R., 31, C4.
Miller's Dale, L.M.S., 15, A5.
Millfield, L.N.E.R., 28, C5.
Mill Hill (I.W.), S.R., 4, F3.
Mill Hill (Lancs.), L.M.S., 24, E2.
•Mill Hill (Middx.), L.M.S. & L.N.E.R., 5. A3.
Mill Hill East, •**L.N.E.R.**/L.P.T.B., 5, A3.
Millhouses, L.M.S., 16, A5.
Milliken Park, L.M.S., 30, C2.
Millisle, L.M.S., 25, D4.
Mill Lane Platform, G.W.R., 3, A4.
Millom, L.M.S., 24, A5.
Mill Rd. (Cambridge Goods), L.M.S., 11, C3.
Mill St. (Newport) Goods, G.W.R., 8, B3.
Milnathort, L.N.E.R., 34, G1.
Milner Wood Jc., L.M.S./O.I., 21, C2.
Milngavie, L.N.E.R., 30, B1.
Milnrow, L.M.S., 21, E1.
Milnsbridge, *see* Longwood.
Milnthorpe, L.M.S., 24, A3.
Milton (Staffs.), L.M.S., 15, C3.
Milton of Campsie, L.N.E.R., 30, B1.
Milton Regis, *see* Sittingbourne.
Milverton (Som.), G.W.R., 8, F4.
Milverton (Warwick), L.M.S., 10, B5.
•Mindrum, L.N.E.R., 32, E3.
Minehead, G.W.R., 8, E5.
Minera Lime Works, G.W.R., 20, E5.
Minety & Ashton Keynes, G.W.R., 9, F4.
Minffordd, G.W.R., 19, F2.
Minster (Thanet), S.R., 6, C2.
Minster (Sheppey), S.R., 6, B4.
Minsterley, S.W., 14, B1.
Mintlaw, L.N.E.R., 38, D2.
Mirfield, L.M.S., 21, E2.
Mislingford (Goods), S.R., 4, E3.
Misson (Goods), L.N.E.R., 21, G5.
Misterton, L.N.E.R., 22, G5.
Mistley, L.N.E.R., 12, E4.
Mitcham, S.R., 5, B3.
Mitcham Jc., S.R., 5. B3.
Mitcheldean Road, G.W.R., 9, D2.
Moat Lane Jc., G.W.R. 14, C3.
Mobberley C.L.C. 20, C1.
Moffat, L.M.S, 31, G3
Moira, L.M.S., 16, E5
Mold. L.M.S., 20, E5.
Molland, *see* Bishop's Nympton.
Mollington, B.J., 20, D4.
•Moniaive, L.M.S., 26, A5.
Monifieth, D.A., 37, E2.
Monikie, L.M.S., 37, D2.
Monk Fryston, L.N.E.R., 21, D4.
Monkhill (Pontefract), L.M.S., 21, E4.
Monkseaton, L.N.E.R., 28, B5.
•Monkton, L.M.S., 30, E3.
•Monkton Combe, G.W.R., 3, B3.
Monkwearmouth, L.N.E.R., 28, C5.
Monmore Green (Goods), L.M.S., 15, F3.
Monmouth, G.W.R., 8, A1.
Monsal Dale, L.M.S., 15, B5.
Montacute, G.W.R., 3, D2.
Montgomerie Pier (Ardrossan), L.M.S., 30, D3.
Montgomery, G.W.R., 14 B2.
Montgreenan, L.M.S., 30, D3.
Monton Green, L.M.S., 20, B2.
Montpelier, G.W.R./L.M.S., 8, C2.
Montrave (Goods), L.N.E.R., 37, G2.
Montrose, L.N.E.R./L.M.S. & •L.M.S., 37, C4.
Monument Lane, L.M.S., 15, G4.
Monymusk, L.N.E.R., 38, F4.
Moorbridge Jc., L.N.E.R., 16, C4.
§Moore, L.M.S., 20, C3.
Moorfields (Hereford) Goods, L.M.S., 9, C1.
Moorhampton, L.M.S., 14, E1.
•Moorhouse, L.N.E.R., 21, F4.
•Moor Park, L.M.S., 30, D3.
Moor Park & Sandy Lodge, L.N.E.R./L.P.T.B., 5, A2.
•Moor Row, L.M.S., 26, F3.
Moorside, L.M.S., 20, B2.
•Moor St. (Burton-on-T.), L.M.S., 15, E5.
•Moorswater, G.W.R., 1, D4.
Moorthorpe & S. Kirkby, S.K., 21, F4.
Moortown, L.N.E.R., 22, F3.
Morar, L.N.E.R., 33, B1.
Morchard Road, S.R., 2, A4.
Morcott, L.M.S., 16, F1.
Morden (Cambs.), *see* Ashwell.
Morden Halt (Surrey), S.R., 5, B3.
Morebath, G.W.R., 8, F5.
Morecambe, L.M.S., 24, B3.
•Moresby Parks, L.M.S., 26, E3.
Moreton (Ches.), L.M.S., 20, C5.
Moreton (Dorset), S.R., 3, F3.
Moretonhampstead, G.W.R., 2, B4.
Moreton-in-Marsh, G.W.R., 9, D5.
Moreton-on-Lugg, S.H., 9, C1.
Morlais Jc., G.W.R./L.M.S. 8, A5.
Morley, L.M.S. & L.N.E.R., 21, E3.
Mormond Halt, L.N.E.R. 38, C2.
•Morningside, L.M.S. & L.N.E.R., 31, D1.
Morpeth, L.N.E.R., 27, A5.
Morris Cowley, G.W.R., 10 E4.
Morriston, G.W.R. & L.M.S. 7, B4.
Morteboe, S.R., 7, E3.
Mortimer, G.W.R., 4, A2.
Mortlake, S.R., 5, B2.
Morton Pinkney, L.M.S., 10, C4.
•Morton Road, L.N.E.R., 17, E1.
Moses Gate, L.M.S., 20, B2.
Moss (Denbigh), •G.W.R. & §L.N.E.R., 20, E4.
Moss (Yorks.), L.N.E.R., 21, E5.
Moss Bank, L.M.S., 20, B3.
Moss Bay Iron & Steel Works, L.M.S., 26, E3.
Mossend, L.M.S., 31, C1.
Mossley, L.M.S., 21, F1.
Mossley Hill, L.M.S., 20, C4.
Moss Side, L.M.S., 24, D4.
Mosstowie, L.M.S., 36, C2.
Moston, L.M.S., 20, B1.
Mostyn, L.M.S., 20, C5.
Motherwell, L.M.S., 31, C1
Mottingham, S.R., 5, B4.
Mottisfont, S.R., 4, D4.
Mottram & Broadbottom, L.N.E.R., 21, G1.
Mouldsworth, C.L.C., 20, D3.
Moulsford, *see* Cholsey.
Moulton (Lincs.), M.G.N., 17, E3.
Moulton (Yorks.), L.N.E.R. 27, F5.
Mound, *see* The Mound.

MOUNTAIN ASH—PINCHBECK

Mountain Ash, G.W.R., 8, B5.
•Mount Melville, L.N.E.R., 37, F2.
Mountsorrel Jc. & Quarries, L.M.S., 16, E3.
Mount Vernon, L.N.E.R. & •L.M.S., 30, C1.
Mow Cop, L.M.S., 15, B3.
Moy, L.M.S., 36, E4.
Muchalls, L.M.S., 37, A5.
Much Wenlock, G.W.R., 15, F2.
Muiredge Colliery, L.N.E.R., 37, G1.
Muirend, L.M.S., 30, C1.
Muirkirk, L.M.S., 30, E1.
Muir of Ord Jc., L.M.S., 35, D5.
Mulben, L.M.S., 36, D1.
Mumbles Mum. R., 7, B3.
Mumbles Road, L.M.S., 7, B3.
Mumby Road L.N.E.R., 17, B4.
Mumps (Oldham), L.M.S., 21, F1.
Mundesley-on-Sea, N.S.J., 18, D2.
Munlochy, L.M.S., 36, D5.
Murrow, L.N.E.R. & M.G.N., 17, F3.
Murthly, L.M.S., 34, E2.
Murton, L.N.E.R., 28, D5.
•Murton Lane, D.V.L., 21, C5.
Musgrave, L.N.E.R., 27, F2.
Musselburgh, L.N.E.R., 31, B4.
Muswell Hill, L.N.E.R., 5, A3.
Muthill, L.M.S., 34, F3.
Mynydd-y-Garreg (Goods), G.W.R., 7, A2.
Mytholmroyd, L.M.S., 21, E1.

N

Naburn, L.N.E.R., 21, C5.
Nafferton, L.N.E.R., 22, C3.
Nailsea & Backwell, G.W.R., 8, D2.
•Nailsworth, L.M.S., 9, F3.
Nairn, L.M.S., 36, D4.
Nancegollan, G.W.R., 1, F5.
Nannerch, L.M.S., 20, D5.
Nantclwyd, L.M.S., 19, E5.
Nantgaredig, L.M.S., 13, G4.
•Nantlle, L.M.S., 19, E2.
•Nantmawr, G.W.R., 20, G5.
Nantwich, **L.M.S.**/G.W.R., 15, C2.
Nantybwch, L.M.S., 8, A4.
Nantyderry, G.W.R., 8, A3.
Nantyffyllon, G.W.R., 7, B5.
Nantyglo, **G.W.R.**/L.M.S., 8, A4.
Nantymoel, G.W.R., 7, B5.
•Nantyronen, V.R., 13, C5.
Napsbury, L.M.S., 11, G2.
Napton & Stockton, L.M.S., 10, B4.
Narberth, G.W.R., 7, C3.
Narborough (Leics.), L.M.S., 16, F4.
Narborough & Pentney, L.N.E.R., 17, E5.
Nassington, L.M.S., 11, A1.
•Nateby, L.M.S., 24, D3.
Navenby, L.N.E.R., 16, B1.
Naworth, L.N.E.R., 27, C1.
Nawton, L.N.E.R., 21, A5.
Neasden, L.P.T.B., 5, A2.
Neath, G.W.R., 7, B4.
•Neath Abbey, G.W.R., 7, B4.
Needham, L.N.E.R., 12, C4.
Needingworth Jc., L.N.E.R., 11, B3.
Neen Sollars, G.W.R., 9, A2.
§Neepsend, L.N.E.R., 21, G3.
Neilston, L.M.S., 30, C2.
Nelson (Glam.), G.W.R., 8, B4.
Nelson (Lancs.), L.M.S., 24, D1.
Neptune Street (Goods), L.N.E.R., 22, E3.
Nesfield Branch, L.M.S., 16, A5.
•Nesscliff & Pentre, S.M., 14, A1.
Neston, B.J. & L.N.E.R., 20, D4.
Netherburn, L.M.S., 31, D1.
Nethercleugh, L.M.S., 26, A3.
Netherfield, L.M.S., 16, D3. *See also* Carlton, L.N.E.R.
Netherseal Coll., L.M.S., 16, E5.
Netherton (Renfrew) Goods, L.M.S., 30, C2.
Netherton (Yorks.), L.M.S., 21, E2.
Nethertown, L.M.S., 26, F3.
Nethy Bridge, L.N.E.R., 36, F3.
Netley, S.R., 4, E3.
Newarthill (Goods), L.M.S., 31, C1.
Newark, L.M.S. & L.N.E.R., 16, C2.
New Barnet, L.N.E.R. 11, G2.
New Basford, L.N.E.R., 16, C4.
New Biggin, L.M.S., 27, E2.
Newbiggin - by - the - Sea, L.N.E.R., 28 A5.
•Newbigging, L.M.S., 31, D3.
New Bolingbroke, L.N.E.R., 17, C3.
Newbridge (Mon.), G.W.R., 8, B4.
•New Bridge St. (Newcastle), L.N.E.R., 27, B5.
Newbridge-on-Wye, G.W.R., 14, E3.
New Brighton, L.M.S., 20, C4.
Newburgh, L.N.E.R., 37, F1.
Newburn, L.N.E.R., 27, B5.
Newbury, G.W.R., 4, A3.
•Newbury Racecourse, G.W.R. 4, A3.
•Newby Wiske, L.N.E.R., 21, A3.
Newcastle Emlyn, G.W.R., 13, F3.
Newcastle-on-Tyne, L.N.E.R., 27, —.
Newcastleton, L.N.E.R., 26, A1.
Newcastle - under- Lyme, L.M.S., 15, C3.
Newchapel & Goldenhill, L.M.S., 15, C3.
Newchurch (I.W.), S.R., 4, F3.
New Clee, L.N.E.R., 22, F2.
New Cumnock, L.M.S., 30, F1.
New Eltham, S.R., 5, B4.
Newent, G.W.R., 9, D2.
New Ferry, see Bebington.
Newfields (Goods), L.M.S., 15, C3.
New Galloway, L.M.S., 25, B5.
Newhailes, L.N.E.R., 31, B4.
Newham (Truro) Goods, G.W.R., 1, E1.
Newham (Northumberland), L.N.E.R., 32, E1.
Newhaven Harbour, S.R., 5, F4.
Newhaven Town, S.R., 5, F4.
New Hey, L.M.S., 21, F1.
New Holland, L.N.E.R., 22, E3.
•Newhouse, L.M.S., 31, C1.
New Hythe, S.R., 6, C5.
Newick & Chailey, S.R., 5, E4.
Newington, S.R., 6, C5.
New Lane, L.M.S., 20, A4.
Newlay, L.M.S., 21, D3.
New Longton & Hutton, L.M.S., 24, E3.
New Luce, L.M.S., 25, B3.
Newmachar, L.N.E.R., 38, F2.
•Newmains, L.M.S. 31, C1.
Newmarket, L.N.E.R., 11, C5.
New Mills (Derbys.), L.M.S./L.N.E.R., 15, A4.
Newmilns, L.M.S., 30, E2.
New Milton, S.R., 4, F5.
Newnham, G.W.R., 9, E2.
Newnham Bridge, G.W.R., 9, A2.
Newpark, L.M.S., 31, C3.
Newport (Essex), L.N.E.R., 11, E4.
Newport (I.W.), S.R., 4, F3.
Newport (Mon.), **G.W.R.**/L.M.S., 8, B3.
Newport (Salop), L.M.S., 15, E2.
Newport Pagnell, L.M.S., 10, C2.
Newport Rd., G.W.R., 8, C4.
Newquay, G.W.R., 1, D1.
New Radnor, G.W.R., 14, D2.
New Romney & Littlestone-on-Sea, R.H.D.R. & S.R., 6, E3.
Newseat Halt, L.N.E.R., 38, D1.
Newsham, L.N.E.R., 28, A5.
Newsholme, L.M.S., 24, C1.
New Southgate, L.N.E.R., 5, A3.
New Street (Birmingham), L.M.S., 15, G4.
Newstead, L.M.S. & •L.N.E.R., 16, C4.
Newstead Lane Jc., M.G.N./N.S.J., 18, D3.
Newthorpe, L.N.E.R., 16, C4.
Newton (Ches.), L.N.E.R., 21, G1.
Newton (Lanarks.), L.M.S., 30, C1.
Newton Abbot, G.W.R., 2, C3.
•Newtonairds, L.M.S., 26, A4.
Newtongrange, L.N.E.R., 31, C4.
Newton Heath, L.M.S., 20, B1.
Newtonhill, L.M.S., 37, A1.
Newton Kyme, L.N.E.R., 21, D4.
Newton-le-Willows, L.M.S., 20, C3.
Newtonmore, L.M.S., 34, A4.
Newton-on-Ayr, L.M.S., 30, F3.
Newton Poppleford, S.R., 2, B2.
Newton St. Cyres, S.R., 2, B3.
Newton Stewart, L.M.S., 25, B4.
Newton Tony, S.R., 4, C5.
Newtown (Derbys.), L.M.S., 15, A4.
Newtown (Mont.), G.W.R., 14, C3.
New Tredegar, G.W.R., 8, A4.
Newtyle, L.M.S., 37, D1.
Neyland, G.W.R., 7, D2.
Nidd Bridge, L.N.E.R., 21, C3.
Nigg, L.M.S., 36, B4.
Nine Mile Point, L.M.S. 8, B4.
Ningwood (I.W.), S.R., 4, F4.
Nisbet, L.N.E.R., 32, E5.
Nitshill, L.M.S., 30, C2.
Nocton & Dunston, L.N.E.R., 17, B1.
Norbiton, S.R., 5, B2.
Norbury & Ellaston, L.M.S., 15, C5.
Norham, L.N.E.R., 32, D3.
Normacot, L.M.S., 15, C4.
Normanby Park (Goods), L.N.E.R., 22, E4.
Norman's Bay Halt, S.R., 5, F5.
Normanton (Derby), see Pear Tree.
Normanton (Yorks.), **L.M.S.**/L.N.E.R., 21, E4.
Northallerton, L.N.E.R., 28, G5.
Northam (Hants.), **S.R.**/G.W.R., 4, E4.
Northampton, L.M.S., 10, B2.
North Berwick, L.N.E.R., 32, B5.
North Bridge (Halifax), L.M.S./L.N.E.R., 21, E2.
North Camp, S.R., 4, B1.
North Cave, L.N.E.R., 22, D4.
North Connel, L.M.S., 33, E2.
North Drove, M.G.N., 17, E2.
North Eastrington Halt, L.N.E.R., 22, D5.
North Elmham, L.N.E.R., 18, E4.
Northenden, **C.L.C.**/L.M.S., 20, C1.
Northfield, L.M.S., 9, A4.
North Filton Plat., G.W.R., 8, C1.
Northfleet S.R., 5, B5.
Northgate (Chester), **C.L.C.**/L.N.E.R., 20, D4.
North Grimston, L.N.E.R., 22, B5.
North Harrow L.N.E.R./L.P.T.B., 5, A2.
North Hayling, S.R., 4, E2.
North Howden, L.N.E.R., 22, D5.
Northiam, K.E.S.R., 6, E5.
North Johnstone, L.M.S., 30, C2.
North Kelsey, L.N.E.R., 22, F3.
•North Mersey, L.M.S., 20, C4.
Northolt Junction, G.W.R./L.N.E.R., 5, A2.
Northorpe (Lincs.), L.N.E.R., 22, G4.
Northorpe (Yorks.), L.M.S., 21, E2.
North Queensferry, L.N.E.R., 31, B3.
North Road (Darlington), L.N.E.R., 28, E5.
North Road (Plymouth), G.W.R./S.R., 1, D5.
North Rode, L.M.S., 15, B3.
North Seaton, L.N.E.R., 27, A5.
North Shields, L.N.E.R., 28, B5.
North Skelton, L.N.E.R., 28, E3.
North Sunderland, N.S.L.R., 32, E1.
North Tawton, S.R., 2, B5.
North Thoresby, L.N.E.R., 22, F2.
Northumberland Park, L.N.E.R., 5, A3.
North Walsham, L.N.E.R. & M.G.N., 18, D2.
North Water Bridge, L.N.E.R., 37, C4.
North Weald, L.N.E.R., 11, G4.
Northwich, **C.L.C.**/L.M.S., 20, D2.
Northwood (Staffs.), *see* Bucknall.
Northwood (Middlesex), L.N.E.R./L.P.T.B., 5, A2.
Northwood Hills, L.N.E.R./L.P.T.B., 5, A2.
North Wootton, L.N.E.R., 17, E5.
North Wylam, L.N.E.R., 27, B4.
Norton (Ches.), B.J., 20, C3.
•Norton (Yorks.), L.M.S., 21, E5.
Norton Bridge, L.M.S., 15, D3.
Norton Fitzwarren, G.W.R., 8, F4.
Norton-in-Hales, L.M.S., 15, D2.
Norton Jc., G.W.R., 10, C3.
Norton-on-Tees, L.N.E.R., 28, E5.
Norwich, L.N.E.R. & M.G.N., 18, F3.
Norwood Jc., S.R., 5, B3.
Nostell, L.N.E.R., 21, E4.
Notgrove, G.W.R., 9, D4.
Nottingham, L.M.S. & L.N.E.R., 16, D3.
Nottingham Road, L.M.S., 16, D5.
•Notton & Royston, L.N.E.R., 21, F3. *See also* Royston, L.M.S.
Nunburnholme, L.N.E.R., 22, C5.
Nuneaton, L.M.S., 16, G5.
Nunnington, L.N.E.R., 21, A5.
Nunthorpe, L.N.E.R., 28, F4.
Nursling, S.R., 4, D4.
Nutbourne Halt, S.R., 4, E1.
Nutfield, S.R., 5, D3.

O

Oakamoor, L.M.S., 15, C4.
Oakengates, L.M.S. & G.W.R., 15, E2.
•Oakenshaw, L.M.S., 21, E3.
Oakes (Goods), see Staveley, L.N.E.R.
Oakham, L.M.S., 16, E2.
Oakington, **L.N.E.R.**/L.M.S., 11, C3.
Oakleigh Park, L.N.E.R., 11, G2.
Oakle Street, G.W.R., 9, E2.
Oakley (Beds.), L.M.S., 10, B1.
Oakley (Fife), L.N.E.R. 31, A2.
Oakley Coll. (Fife), L.N.E.R., 31, A2.
Oakley (Hants.), S.R., 4, B3.
Oakworth, L.M.S., 21, D1.
Oban, L.M.S., 33, E2.
•Occumster, L.M.S., 39, E4.
Ochiltree, L.M.S., 30, F2.
Ockendon, L.M.S., 5, A5.
Ockley, S.R., 5, D2.
Offord & Buckden, L.N.E.R., 11, C2.
Ogbourne, G.W.R., 4, A5.
Ogmore Vale, G.W.R., 7, B5.
Okehampton, S.R., 2, B5.
Oldbury, L.M.S., 15, G4.
Oldbury & Langley Green, G.W.R., 15, G4.
Old Colwyn, L.M.S., 19, C4.
Old Cumnock, L.M.S., 30, F1.
Old Dalby, L.M.S., 16, E3.
Oldfield Park Platform, G.W.R., 3, A3.
Oldham, L.M.S., L.N.E.R., O.A.G.B., 20, B1.
Old Hill, G.W.R., 15, G4.
Oldland Common, L.M.S., 8, C1.
Old Leake, L.N.E.R., 17, C3.
•Old Meldrum, L.N.E.R., 38, E3.
Old North Road, L.M.S., 11, C2.
Old Roan, L.M.S., 20, B4.
Old Trafford, M.S.J.A., 20, C1.
Old Woods, G.W.R., 15, E1.
Ollerton, L.N.E.R., 16, B3.
Olney, L.M.S., 10, B2.
Olton, G.W.R., 9, A5.
Olympia, see Kensington.
Omoa (now Cleland), L.M.S., 31, C1.
Ongar, L.N.E.R., 11, G4.
Onibury, S.H., 9, A1.
Onllwyn, G.W.R., 7, A5.
Orbliston, L.M.S., 36, D1.
Ordens Platform, L.N.E.R., 38, C4.
Ordsall Lane, L.M.S., 20, B1.
Ore, S.R., 6, F5.
Oreston, S.R., 1, D5.
Orlestone, see Ham Street.
Ormesby, L.N.E.R., 28, E4.
Ormiston, L.N.E.R., 31, C5.
Ormside, L.M.S. 27, E2.
Ormskirk, L.M.S., 20, B4.
Orpington, S.R., 5, B4.
Orrell, L.M.S., 20, B3.
Orston, see Elton, L.N.E.R.
Orton, L.M.S., 36, D1.
•Orton Waterville, L.M.S., 11, A1.
Orwell, L.N.E.R., 12, D3.
•Osbaldwick, D.V.L., 21, C5.
Ossett, L.N.E.R., 21, E3. *See also* Horbury.
Osterley, L.P.T.B., 5, B2.
Oswaldtwistle, see Church.
Oswestry, G.W.R., 20, G4.
Otford, S.R., 5, C5.
Otley, O.I., 21, D2.
Otterham, S.R., 1, B3.
Otterington, L.N.E.R., 21, A4.
Otterspool, C.L.C., 20, C4
Ottery St. Mary S.R., 2 B 2·
Ottringham, L.N.E.R., 22, E2.
Oughty Bridge, L.N.E.R., 21, G3.
Oulton Broad North, L.N.E.R., 18, G1.
Oulton Broad South, L.N.E.R., 18, G1.
Oundle, L.M.S., 11, A1.
•Outwell Basin, W.U.T., 17, F4.
•Outwell Village, W.U.T., 17, F4.
Ovenden, L.M.S./L.N.E.R., 21, E2.
•Over & Wharton, L.M.S., 20, D2. *See also* Winsford, C.L.C.
Over Jc., G.W.R., 9, D3.
Overstrand, N.S.J., 18, D3.
Overton, S.R., 4, B3.
Overton-on-Dee, G.W.R., 20, F4.
§Overtown, L.M.S., 31, D1.
Oxendon, *see* Clipston.
Oxenholme, L.M.S., 24, A3.
Oxenhope, L.M.S., 21, D5.
Oxford, G.W.R. & L.M.S., 10, E4.
Oxford Rd. (Manchester), M.S.J.A., 20, B1.
Oxford Rd. Jc. (Oxford), L.M.S., 10, E4.
Oxhey, *see* Bushey.
•Oxheys (Cattle), L.M.S., 24, D3.
Oxshott, S.R., 5, C2.
Oxted, S.R., 5, C4.
•Oxton, L.N.E.R., 31, C5.
Oyne, L.N.E.R., 38, E4.

P

Padbury, L.M.S., 10, D5.
Paddington, G.W.R. & L.P.T.B., 5, A3.
Paddock Wood, S.R., 5, D5.
Padeswood, L.M.S., 20, E5.
Padgate, C.L.C., 20, C2.
Padiham, L.M.S., 24, D1.
Padstow, S.R., 1, C2.
Paignton, G.W.R., 2, D3.
Paisley, L.M.S., 30, C2.
Palace Gates, L.N.E.R., 5, A3.
Pallion, L.N.E.R., 28, C5.
Palmers Green, L.N.E.R., 5, A3.
Palnure, L.M.S., 25, B4.
Pampisford, L.N.E.R., 11, D4.
Pandy, G.W.R., 14, G1.
Pangbourne, G.W.R., 4, A2.
Pannal, L.N.E.R., 21, C3.
Pant (Glam.), G.W.R., 8, A5.
Pant (Salop), G.W.R., 20, G4.
Panteg & Griffithstown, G.W.R., 8, B3.
Pant Glas, L.M.S., 19, E1.
Pantydwr, G.W.R., 14, D4.
Pantyffynnon, **G.W.R.**/L.M.S., 7, A3.
Par, G.W.R., 1, D3.
Paragon (Hull), L.N.E.R., 22, E3.
Parbold, L.M.S., 20, B3.
Parham, L.N.E.R., 12, C3.
Park (Birkenhead), L.M.S., 20, C4.
Park (Kincard.), L.N.E.R., 37, A4.
Park (Lancs.), Goods, L.M.S., 24, B5.
Park Bridge, O.A.G.B., 21, F1.
Park Drain, L.N.E.R., 22, F5.
•Parkend, S.V.Y., 9, E1.
Parkeston Quay, L.N.E.R., 12, F3.
Parkgate (Ches.), B.J., 20, D5.
Parkgate (Yorks.), L.M.S., 21, G4.
Parkgate & Aldwarke, L.N.E.R., 21, G4.
Parkhill, L.N.E.R., 38, F2.
Parkstone, **S.R.**/S.D., 3, F5.
Park Street & Frogmore, L.M.S., 11, G1.
Parsley Hay, L.M.S., 15, B5.
Partington, C.L.C., 20, C2.
Parton (Cumb.), L.M.S., 26, E4.
Parton (Kirkcud.), L.M.S., 26, B5.
Partridge Green, S.R., 5, E2.
Paston & Knapton, N.S.J., 18, D2.
Patchway, G.W.R., 8, C1.
Pateley Bridge, L.N.E.R., 21, B2.
Patna, L.M.S., 30, F2.
Patney & Chirton, G.W.R., 3, B5.
Patricroft, L.M.S., 20, B2.
Patrington, L.N.E.R., 22, E2.
Patterton, L.M.S., 30, C2.
Peak Forest, L.M.S., 15, A5.
Peakirk, L.N.E.R., 17, F2.
Pear Tree & Normanton, L.M.S., 16, D5.
Peasmarsh Jc., S.R., 5, D1.
Peckham Rye, S.R., 5, B3.
Pedair Ffordd, G.W.R., 19, G5.
Peebles, L.M.S. & L.N.E.R., 31, D4.
Peel, I.M.R., 23, B2.
Peel Road, I.M.R., 23, B2.
Pegswood, L.N.E.R., 27, A5.
Pelaw, L.N.E.R., 28, C5.
•Pellon, L.M.S./L.N.E.R., 21, E2.
Pelsall, L.M.S., 15, F4.
Pelton, L.N.E.R., 27, C5.
Pemberton, L.M.S., 20, B3.
Pembrey Halt, G.W.R., 7, B2.
Pembrey & Burry Port, G.W.R., 7, B2.
Pembridge, G.W.R., 14, E1.
Pembroke, G.W.R., 7, D2.
Penallta Jc., G.W.R., 8, B4.
Penally, G.W.R., 7, D3.
Penarth, G.W.R., 8, C4.
Penarth Curve Jcs., G.W.R., 8, C4.
Penarth Dock, G.W.R., 8, C4.
•Pencader, G.W.R., 13, F4.
Pencaitland, L.N.E.R., 31, C5.
•Penclawdd, L.M.S., 7, B3.
Pencoed, G.W.R., 8, C5.
Penda's Way, L.N.E.R., 21, D3.
Pendlebury, L.M.S., 20, B1.
Pendleton, L.M.S., 20, B1.
•Pendre, Tal., 13, B5.
Pengam (Glam.), G.W.R., 8, B4.
Pengam (Mon.), G.W.R., 8, B4.
Penicuik, L.N.E.R., 31, C4.
Penicuik Gas Wks., L.N.E.R. 31, C4.
Penistone, L.N.E.R./L.M.S. 21, F3.
Penkridge, L.M.S., 15, E3.
Penmaenmawr, L.M.S., 19, D3.
Penmaenpool, G.W.R., 14, A5.
Penmere Platform, G.W.R. 1, F1.
Pen Mill (Yeovil), G.W.R., 3, D2.
Pennington, L.M.S., 20, B2.
Penns, L.M.S., 15, F5.
Penpergwm, G.W.R., 8, A3.
Penrhiwceiber, G.W.R., 8, B5.
Penrhyndeudraeth, G.W.R., 19, F2.
Penrith, **L.M.S.**/L.N.E.R., 27, E1.
Penruddock, L.M.S., 26, E1.
Penryn, G.W.R., 1, F1.
Pensarn, *see* Llanbedr.
Pensford, G.W.R., 8, D1.
Penshaw, L.N.E.R., 28, C5.
Penshurst, S.R., 5, D4.
Pentir Rhiw, G.W.R., 14, G3.
Pentney, *see* Narborough.
Penton, L.N.E.R., 26, B1.
•Pentraeth, L.M.S., 19, D2.
Pentre, *see* Nesscliff.
Pentrebach, G.W.R., 8, B5.
Pentrecourt Plat., G.W.R., 13, F4.
Pentrefelin, G.W.R., 20, G5.
Penwithers Jc., G.W.R., 1, E1.
Penwyllt, *see* Craig-y-nos.
Penybont, L.M.S., 14, D3.
Penybontfawr, G.W.R. 19, G5.
Penychain (Halt), G.W.R., 19, F1.
Pen-y-ffordd, L.N.E.R., 20, E4.
Pen-y-graig, G.W.R., 8, B5.
Penygroes, L.M.S., 19, E1.
Penyrheol, G.W.R., 8, B4.
Penzance, G.W.R., 1, F4.
Peplow, G.W.R., 15, D2.
Percy Main, L.N.E.R., 28 B5.
Perranporth, G.W.R., 1, D1.
Perranwell, G.W.R., 1, E1.
Perry Barr, L.M.S., 15, F5.
Pershore, G.W.R., 9, C4.
Perth, **L.M.S.**/L.N.E.R., •L.M.S., •L.N.E.R., 34, F1.
Peterborough (East), **L.N.E.R.**/L.M.S., 11, A2.
Peterborough (North), **L.N.E.R.**/L.M.S., 17, F2.
•Peterchurch, G.W.R., 14, F1.
Peterhead, L.N.E.R., 38, D1.
Petersfield, S.R., 4, D2.
Peterston, G.W.R., 8, C5.
Petrockstow, S.R., 2, A5.
Petteril Jc. (Carlisle), L.M.S./L.N.E.R., 26, C1.
Pettycur, L.N.E.R., 31, A4.
Petworth, S.R., 5, E1.
Pevensey & Westham, S.R. 5, F5.
Pevensey Bay Halt, S.R., 5, F5.
Pewsey, G.W.R., 4, B5.
Philorth Halt, L.N.E.R., 38, C2.
Philpstoun, L.N.E.R., 31, B3.
•Pickburn, L.N.E.R., 21, F4.
Pickering, L.N.E.R., 22, A5.
Pickhill, L.N.E.R., 21, A3.
Picton, L.N.E.R., 28, F5.
Piddington, L.M.S., 10, B2.
Piercebridge, L.N.E.R., 27, E5.
Pier Head (Ryde, I.W.), S.R., 4, F3.
Piershill, L.N.E.R., 31, B4.
Pill, G.W.R., 8, C2.
Pilley (Goods), *see* Birdwell.
•Pilling, L.M.S., 24, C3.
Pilmoor, L.N.E.R., 21, B4.
Pilning, G.W.R., 8, C2.
Pilot Halt, R.H.D.R., 6, E3.
Pilsley, L.N.E.R., 16, B4.
Pinchbeck, L.N.E.R. 17, E2.

SALFORD—STRETHAM

Salford, L.M.S., 20, B1.
Salford Priors, L.M.S., 9, C4.
Salfords, S.R., 5, D3.
Salhouse, L.N.E.R., 18, E2.
Salisbury, S.R./G.W.R., & *G.W.R., 4, C5.
*Salsburgh, L.M.S., 31, C1.
Saltaire, L.M.S., 21, D2.
Saltash, G.W.R., 1, D5.
Saltburn, L.N.E.R., 28, E3.
Saltcoats, L.M.S., 30, D3.
Saltfleetby, L.N.E.R., 17, A3.
Saltford, G.W.R., 8, D1.
Saltley, L.M.S., 15, G5.
Saltmarshe, L.N.E.R., 22, E5.
Saltney, G.W.R., 20, D4.
Saltney Ferry, L.M.S., 20, D4.
*Saltoun, L.N.E.R., 31, C5.
Salwick, L.M.S., 24, D3.
Sampford Courtenay, S.R., 2, B5.
Sampford Peverell, G.W.R., 2, A2.
Sandal, L.M.S. & L.N.E.R., 21, E3.
Sandbach, L.M.S., 15, B2.
Sanderstead, S.R., 5, C3.
Sandford & Banwell, G.W.R., 8, D3.
Sandhills, L.M.S., 20, C4.
Sandholme, L.N.E.R., 22, D5.
Sandhurst Halt, S.R., 4, B1.
Sandiacre, see Stapleford.
Sandilands, L.M.S., 31, D2.
Sandling Jc., S.R., 6, D3.
Sandon, L.M.S., 15, D4.
Sandown (I.W.), S.R., 4, F3.
Sandplace, G.W.R., 1, D4.
Sandsend, L.N.E.R., 28, F2.
*Sandside, L.M.S., 24, A3.
Sandtoft (Goods), A.J., 22, F5.
Sandwich, S.R., 6, C2.
*Sandwich Rd., E.K.R., 6, C2.
Sandy, L.N.E.R. & L.M.S., 11, D2.
Sandycroft, L.M.S., 20, D4.
Sandy Jc., G.W.R., 7, B3.
Sandy Lodge, see Moor Park.
Sankey, C.L.C., 20, C3.
Sankey Bridges, L.M.S., 20, C3.
Sanquhar, L.M.S., 31, F1.
Santon, I.M.R., 23, C2.
Sarnau, G.W.R., 13, G3.
Sarsden Halt, G.W.R., 10, D5.
*Sauchie, L.N.E.R., 31, A2.
Saughall, L.N.E.R., 20, D4.
Saughton, L.N.E.R., 31, B4.
*Saughtree, L.N.E.R., 32, G5.
Saundersfoot, G.W.R., 7, D3.
Saunderton, G.W.R./L.N.E.R., 10, F2.
Savernake, G.W.R., 4, A5.
Sawbridgeworth, L.N.E.R., 11, F4.
Sawdon, L.N.E.R., 22, A4.
*Sawley, L.M.S., 16, D4.
Sawley Jc., L.M.S., 16, D4.
Saxby, L.M.S., 16, E2.
Saxham & Risby, L.N.E.R., 11, C5.
Saxilby, L.N.E.R., 16, A1.
Saxmundham, L.N.E.R., 12, C2.
Saxondale Jc., L.N.E.R./L.M.S., 16, C3.
Saxthorpe, see Corpusty.
Scalby, L.N.E.R., 28, G1.
Scalford, L.M.S./L.N.E.R., 16, E2.
Scarborough, L.N.E.R., 22, A3.
Scarcliffe, L.N.E.R., 16, B4.
Scawby & Hibaldstow, L.N.E.R., 22, F4.
Scholes, L.N.E.R., 21, D4.
Scopwick & Timberland L.N.E.R., 17, C1.
Scorrier, G.W.R., 1, E1.
Scorton, L.N.E.R., 27, F5.
Scotby, L.N.E.R., 26, C1.
Scotch Dyke, L.N.E.R., 26, B1.
Scotscalder, L.M.S., 39, D2.
Scotsgap, L.N.E.R., 27, A4.
Scotswood, L.N.E.R., 27, B5.
Scraptoft, see Thurnby.
Scremerston, L.N.E.R., 32, D2.
Scruton, L.N.E.R., 28, G5.
*Sculcoates, L.N.E.R., 22, D3.
Scunthorpe & Frodingham, L.N.E.R., 22, F4.
Seaburn, L.N.E.R., 28, C5.
Seacombe, L.M.S./L.N.E.R., 20, C4.
Seacroft, L.N.E.R., 17, B4.
Seaford, S.R., 5, G4.
Seaforth, L.M.S. & L.O.R., 20, B4.
Seaham, L.N.E.R., 28, C5.
Seahouses, N.S.L.R., 32, E1.
Sealand, L.N.E.R., 20, D4.
Seamer, L.N.E.R., 22, A3.
Sea Mills, G.W.R./L.M.S., 8, C2.
Seascale, L.M.S., 26, F3.
*Seaton (Cumb.), L.M.S., 26, D3.
Seaton (Devon), S.R., 2, B1.
Seaton (Durham), L.N.E.R., 28, C5.
Seaton (Rutland), L.M.S., 16, F1.
Seaton Carew, L.N.E.R., 28, E4.
Seaton Delaval, L.N.E.R., 28, B5.
Seaton Jc. (Devon), S.R., 2, B1.
*Seaton-on-Tees, L.N.E.R., 28, E4.
Sebastopol, G.W.R., 8, B3.
Sedbergh, L.M.S., 27, G2.
Sedgebrook, L.N.E.R., 16, D2.
Sedgefield, L.N.E.R., 28, E5.
Sedgeford, L.N.E.R., 17, D5.
Seend, G.W.R., 3, B4.
Seer Green, G.W.R./L.N.E.R., 10, F1.
Sefton, C.L.C., 20, B4.
Seghill, L.N.E.R., 28, B5.
Selby, L.N.E.R., 21, D5.
Selham, S.R., 5, E1.
Selkirk, L.N.E.R., 31, E5.
Sellafield, L.M.S., 26, F3.
Selling, S.R., 6, C3.
Selly Oak, L.M.S., 9, A4.
Selsdon, S.R., 5, C3.
Semley, S.R., 3, D4.
Senghenydd, G.W.R., 8, B4.
Sennybridge, see Devynock.
Sessay, L.N.E.R., 21, B4.
Settle, L.M.S., 24, B1.
Settrington, L.N.E.R., 22, B5.
Seven Kings, L.N.E.R., 5, A4.
Sevenoaks, S.R., 5, C4.
Seven Sisters (Glam.), G.W.R., 7, A5.
Seven Sisters (Middx.), L.N.E.R., 5, A3.
Severn Beach, G.W.R., 8, C2.
Severn Bridge, S.V.Y., 9, E2.
Severn Tunnel Jc., G.W.R., 8, B2.
Sexhow, L.N.E.R., 28, F4.
*Shackerstone, L.M.S., 16, F5.
Shaftholme Jc., L.N.E.R., 21, F5.
Shafton Jc., L.M.S./L.N.E.R., 21, F3.
Shalfleet, see Calbourne.
Shalford, S.R., 5, D1.
Shandon, L.N.E.R., 30, B3.
Shankend, L.N.E.R., 32, F5.
Shanklin (I.W.), S.R., 4, G3.
Shap, L.M.S., 27, F1.
Shapwick, S.D., 3, C1.
Shardlow, see Castle Donington.
Sharlston, L.M.S., 21, E4.
Sharnal Street, S.R., 6, B5.
Sharnbrook, L.M.S., 10, B1.
Sharpness, S.V.Y., 9, F2.
Shaugh Bridge Platform, G.W.R., 2, D5.
Shaw & Crompton, L.M.S., 21, F1.
*Shawclough, L.M.S., 20, A1.
Shawford, S.R./G.W.R., 4, D3.
*Shawforth, L.M.S., 20, A1.
*Shawhill, L.M.S., 26, B2.
Sheepbridge, L.M.S. & L.N.E.R., 16, A5.
Sheerness East, S.R., 6, B4.
Sheerness-on-Sea, S.R., 6, B4.
Sheffield, L.M.S. & L.N.E.R., 16,—.
Sheffield Park, S.R., 5, E4.
Shefford, L.M.S., 11, D1.
Shelford, L.N.E.R., 11, D3.
Shelwick Jc., S.H./G.W.R., 9, C1.
Shenfield & Hutton, L.N.E.R., 5, A5.
Shenstone, L.M.S., 15, F5.
*Shenton, L.M.S., 16, F5.
Shepherds, G.W.R., 1, D1.
Shepherd's Well, S.R. & E.K.R., 6, D2.
Shepley, L.M.S., 21, F2.
Shepperton, S.R., 5, B2.
Shepreth, L.N.E.R., 11, D3.
*Shepshed, L.M.S., 16, E4.
Shepton Mallet, G.W.R. & S.D., 3, C2.
Sherborne, S.R., 3, D3.
Sherburn Coll., L.N.E.R., 28, D5.
*Sherburn House, L.N.E.R., 28, D5.
Sherburn-in-Elmet, L.N.E.R., 21, D4.
Shere, see Gomshall.
Sheringham, M.G.N., 18, D3.
*Sherwood, L.N.E.R., 16, C3.
Shettleston, L.N.E.R., 30, C1.
Shide (I.W.), S.R., 4, F3.
Shieldhill, L.M.S., 26, A3.
Shieldhill Colliery, L.N.E.R., 31, B2.
Shifnal, G.W.R., 15, E2.
Shildon, L.N.E.R., 27, E5.
Shillingstone, S.D., 3, E4.
Shilton, L.M.S., 16, G4.
*Shincliffe, L.N.E.R., 28, D5.
Shiplake, G.W.R., 10, G2.
Shipley, L.M.S./L.N.E.R. & *L.N.E.R., 21, D2.
Shipley Gate, L.M.S., 16, C4.
Shippea Hill, L.N.E.R., 11, B4.
*Shipston-on-Stour, G.W.R., 10, C5.
Shipton, G.W.R., 10, E5.
*Shirdley Hill, L.M.S., 20, A4.
Shirebrook, L.M.S. & L.N.E.R., 16, B4.
Shirehampton, G.W.R./L.M.S., 8, C2.
Shireoaks, L.N.E.R./L.M.S., 16, A4.
Shirley, G.W.R., 9, A5.
Shobnal Jc., L.M.S., 15, E5.
Shoeburyness, L.M.S., 6, A4.
Sholing, S.R., 4, E3.
Shoreham (Kent), S.R., 5, C5.
§Shoreham Airport (Sussex), S.R., 5, F3.
Shoreham-by-Sea, S.R., 5, F3.
Shore Rd. Goods (Stirling), L.N.E.R., 31, A1.
Shorncliffe, S.R., 6, D2.
*Short Heath, L.M.S./G.W.R., 15, F4.
Shortlands, S.R., 5, B4.
Shoscombe & Single Hill Halt, S.D., 3, B3.
Shotley Bridge, L.N.E.R., 27, C4.
*Shottle, L.M.S., 16, C5.
Shotton, L.M.S., 20, D4.
See also Connah's Quay.
Shotton Bridge, L.N.E.R., 28, D5.
Shotts, L.M.S. & *L.N.E.R., 31, C2.
*Shrawardine, S.M., 14, A1.
Shrewsbury, L.M.S./G.W.R. & *S.M., 15, E1.
Shrivenham, G.W.R., 9, F5.
Shrub Hill (Worcester), G.W.R./L.M.S., 9, B3.
Shustoke, L.M.S., 16, G5.
Sible & Castle Hedingham, L.N.E.R., 11, E5.
Sibley's, L.N.E.R., 11, E4.
Sibsey, L.N.E.R., 17, C3.
Sidcup, S.R., 5, B4.
Siddick Jc., L.M.S., 26, D3.
Sidley, S.R., 6, F5.
Sidmouth, S.R., 2, B2.
Sidmouth Jc., S.R., 2, B2.
Sigglesthorne, L.N.E.R., 22, D3.
Sileby, L.M.S., 16, E3.
Silecroft, L.M.S., 24, A5.
Silian Halt, G.W.R., 13, E5.
Silkstone, L.N.E.R., 21, F3.
Silkstone Colliery, L.M.S., 21, F3.
Silloth, L.N.E.R., 26, C3.
Silsden, see Steeton.
Silverdale (Lancs.), L.M.S., 24, B3.
Silverdale (Staffs.), L.M.S., 15, C3.
Silverton, G.W.R., 2, A3.
Simonstone, L.M.S., 24, D1.
Sincil Jc., L.N.E.R., 16, B1.
Sinclairtown, L.N.E.R., 31, A4.
Sinderby, L.N.E.R., 21, A3.
Singer, L.N.E.R., 30, C2.
Single Hill, see Shoscombe.
§Singleton (Lancs.), L.M.S., 24, D4.
*Singleton (Sussex), S.R., 4, E1.
Sinnington, L.N.E.R., 22, A5.
Sirhowy, L.M.S., 8, A4.
Sittingbourne & Milton Regis, S.R., 6, C4.
Six Mile Bottom, L.N.E.R., 11, C4.
Skares, L.M.S., 30, F2.
*Skegby, L.N.E.R., 16, B4.
Skegness, L.N.E.R., 17, B4.
Skelbo, L.M.S., 36, A4.
Skellingthorpe, L.N.E.R., 16, B1.
Skelmanthorpe, L.M.S., 21, F3.
Skelmersdale, L.M.S., 20, B3.
Skewen, G.W.R., 7, B4.
Skinningrove, L.N.E.R., 28, E3.
Skipton, L.M.S., 21, C1.
*Skipwith, D.V.L., 21, D5.
Skirlaugh, L.N.E.R., 22, D3.
Slades Green, S.R., 5, B4.
Slaggyford, L.N.E.R., 27, C2.
Slaithwaite, L.M.S., 21, E2.
*Slamannan, L.N.E.R., 31, B1.
Slateford, L.M.S., 31, B4.
Sleaford, L.N.E.R., 17, C1.
Sledmere & Fimber, L.N.E.R., 22, B4.
Sleights, L.N.E.R., 28, F2.
Slinfold, S.R., 5, E2.
*Slingsby, L.N.E.R., 21, B5.
Slough, G.W.R., 5, B1.
Smallford, L.N.E.R., 11, F2.
Small Heath, L.M.S., 15, G5.
Smardale, L.N.E.R., 27, F2.
Smeaton, L.N.E.R., 31, B5.
Smeeth, S.R., 6, D3.
Smeeth Road, L.N.E.R., 17, F4.
Smethwick, L.M.S., 15, G4.
Smethwick Jc., G.W.R., 15, G4.
Smitham, S.R., 5, C3.
Smithy Bridge, L.M.S., 21, E1.
Snae Fell, M.E., 23, B3.
Snailbeach Mine, S.B.H., 14, B1.
Snailwell Jc., L.N.E.R., 11, C4.
Snainton, L.N.E.R., 22, A4.
Snaith, L.M.S., 21, E5.
*Snaith & Pollington, L.N.E.R., 21, E5.
Snape Jc. & Goods, L.N.E.R., 12, C2.
Snaresbrook, L.N.E.R., 5, A4.
*Snarestone, L.M.S., 16, E5.
Snelland, L.N.E.R., 17, A1.
Snettisham, L.N.E.R., 17, D5.
Snodland, S.R., 6, C5.
Snowdon, S.M.R., 19, E2.
Snow Hill (Birmingham), G.W.R., 15, G5.
Soham, L.N.E.R., 11, B4.
Soho, G.W.R. & L.M.S., 15, G4.
Sole Street, S.R., 5, B5.
Solihull, G.W.R., 9, A5.
Somercotes, see Pye Hill.
Somerdale, see Keynsham.
Somerleyton, L.N.E.R., 18, F1.
Somersham, L.N.E.R., 11, B3.
Somerton (Oxon.) See Fritwell.
Somerton (Som.), G.W.R., 3, D2.
Sorbie, L.M.S., 25, C4.
Southall, G.W.R., 5, B2.
Southam & Long Itchington, L.M.S., 10, B5.
Southampton (Central), S.R., 4, E4.
Southampton (Town), S.R./G.W.R., 4, E4.
Southam Road & Harbury, G.W.R., 10, B5.
South Bank, L.N.E.R., 28, E4.
South Beach (Ardrossan), L.M.S., 30, D3.
Southbourne Halt, S.R., 4, E1.
Southburn, L.N.E.R., 22, C4.
§South Canterbury, S.R., 6, C3.
South Cave, L.N.E.R., 22, D4.
South Cerney, G.W.R., 9, F4.
Southcoates, L.N.E.R., 22, D3.
Southcote Jc., G.W.R., 4, A2.
South Croydon, S.R., 5, C3.
Southease & Rodmell Halt, S.R., 5, F4.
South Eastrington, L.N.E.R., 22, E5.
South Elmsall, L.N.E.R., 21, F4.
Southend East, L.M.S., 6, A4.
Southend-on-Sea, L.M.S. & L.N.E.R., 6, A4.
Southerham Jc., S.R., 5, F4.
Southerndown Road, G.W.R., 7, C5.
Southfleet, S.R., 5, B5.
South Gosforth, L.N.E.R., 27, B5.
South Harrow, L.P.T.B., 5, A2.
South Hetton, L.N.E.R., 28, D5.
South Howden, L.N.E.R., 22, E5.
Southill, L.M.S., 11, D1.
South Kirkby, see Moorthorpe.
South Leigh, G.W.R., 10, E5.
South Lynn, M.G.N., 17, E4.
South Medomsley Coll., L.N.E.R., 27, C5.
South Milford, L.N.E.R., 21, D4.
Southminster, L.N.E.R., 12, G5.
South Molton, G.W.R., 7, F4.
South Molton Road, S.R., 7, G4.
Southport, L.M.S. & C.L.C., 20, A4.
South Queensferry (Goods), L.N.E.R., 31, B3.
South Renfrew, L.M.S., 30, C2.
Southrey, L.N.E.R., 17, B2.
South Rhondda (Goods), G.W.R., 8, C5.
Southsea, see Portsmouth.
South Shields, L.N.E.R. & S.S.M.W., 28, B5.
South Shore (B'pool.), Goods, L.M.S., 24, D4.
South Town (Gt. Yarmouth), L.N.E.R., 18, F1.
Southwaite, L.M.S., 26, D1.
Southwater, S.R., 5, E2.
Southwell, L.M.S., 16, C3.
Southwick (Durham), Goods, L.N.E.R., 28, C5.
Southwick (Kircud.), L.M.S., 26, C4.
Southwick (Sussex), S.R., 5, F3.
South Willingham & Hainton, L.N.E.R., 17, A2.
South Witham, L.M.S., 16, E1.
South Woodford, L.N.E.R., 5, A4.
Sowerby Bridge, L.M.S., 21, E1.
Spalding, L.N.E.R./M.G.N. & *L.M.S., 17, E2.
Sparkford, G.W.R., 3, D2.
Spean Bridge, L.N.E.R., 33, B4.
*Speech House Rd., S.V.Y., 9, E1.
Speen, G.W.R., 4, A3.
Speeton, L.N.E.R., 22, B3.
Spennithorne, L.N.E.R., 27, G5.
Spennymoor, L.N.E.R., 27, D5.
Spetchley (Goods), L.M.S., 9, B3.
Spetisbury Halt, S.D., 3, E4.
Spey Bay, L.N.E.R., 36, C1.
§Spiersbridge (Goods), L.M.S., 30, C2.
*Spilsby, L.N.E.R., 17, B3.
Spital, B.J., 20, C4.
Spofforth, L.N.E.R., 21, C3.
Spondon, L.M.S., 16, D5.
Spon Lane, L.M.S., 15, G4.
Spooner Row, L.N.E.R., 18, F4.
Spratton, L.M.S., 10, A3.
Springfield, L.N.E.R., 37, F2.
Springside, L.M.S., 30, E3.
Spring Vale, L.M.S., 24, F2.
*Sprotborough, L.N.E.R., 21, F4.
Sprouston, L.N.E.R., 32, E4.
Squires Gate, L.M.S., 24, D4.
Stacksteads (Lancs.), L.M.S., 20, A1.
Staddlethorpe, L.N.E.R., 22, E5.
Stafford, L.M.S./*L.N.E.R., 15, E3.
*Stafford Common, L.N.E.R., 15, D3.
*Stainby, L.N.E.R., 16, E1.
Staincliffe, L.M.S., 21, E3.
*Staincross, L.N.E.R., 21, F3.
Staines, S.R. & G.W.R., 5, B1.
Stainforth & Hatfield, L.N.E.R., 21, F5.
*Stainland, L.M.S., 21, E2.
Stainton, L.M.S., 24, B4.
Stainton Dale, L.N.E.R., 28, G1.
Stairfoot, L.N.E.R., 21, F4.
Staithes, L.N.E.R., 28, E2.
Stalbridge, S.D., 3, D3.
Staley & Millbrook (Goods), L.M.S., 21, F1.
Stalham, M.G.N., 18, E2.
Stallingborough, L.N.E.R., 22, F3.
Stalybridge, L.M.S./L.N.E.R., 21, F1.
Stamford, L.M.S. & L.N.E.R., 17, F1.
Stammerham Jc., S.R., 5, E2.
Stamford Bridge (Yorks.), L.N.E.R., 22, C5.
Stanbridgeford, L.M.S., 10 D1.
Standish (Lancs.), L.M.S., 20, B3.
Standish Jc. (Glos.), G.W.R./L.M.S., 9, E3.
Standon, L.N.E.R., 11, E3.
Standon Bridge, L.M.S., 15, D3.
Stanford-le-hope, L.M.S., 5, A5.
Stanford Park, see Yelvertoft.
Stanhoe, L.N.E.R., 18, D5.
Stanhope, L.N.E.R., 27, D4.
Stanley (Perth), L.M.S., 34, E1.
Stanley (Yorks.), M.J., 21, E3.
Stanley Siding, L.M.S., 16, G5.
Stanlow & Thornton, B.J., 20, D4.
Stanmore, L.M.S. & L.P.T.B., 5, A2.
Stanner, G.W.R., 14, E2.
Stannergate (Goods), D.A., 37, E2.
Stanningley, L.N.E.R./L.M.S., 21, D2.
Stannington, L.N.E.R., 27, A5.
§Stansfield Hall, L.M.S., 21, E1.
Stansted, L.N.E.R., 11, E4.
Stanton, G.W.R., 9, F5.
Stanton Gate, L.M.S. 16, D4.
Staple, E.K.R., 6, C2.
§Stapleford (Herts.), L.N.E.R., 11, F2.
Stapleford & Sandiacre (Notts.), L.M.S., 16, D4.
Staple Hill, L.M.S., 8, C1.
Staplehurst, S.R., 6, D5.
Stapleton Rd., G.W.R., 8, C1.
Starbeck, L.N.E.R., 21, C3.
Starcross, G.W.R., 2, C3.
Stathern, see Harby.
Staveley (Westmorland), L.M.S., 27, G1.
Staveley & Oakes (Goods), L.N.E.R., 16, A5.
Staveley Town (Derby.), L.M.S. & L.N.E.R., 16, A4.
Staveley Works, L.N.E.R., 16, A4.
See also Barrow Hill.
Staverton, G.W.R., 2, D4.
*Staward, L.N.E.R., 27, C3.
Stechford, L.M.S., 15, G5.
§Steelend (Goods), L.N.E.R. 31, A3.
Steele Rd., L.N.E.R., 27, A1
Steens Bridge, G.W.R., 9 B1.
Steeplehouse (Goods), L.M.S. 16, C5.
*Steer Point, G.W.R., 2, E5.
Steeton & Silsden, L.M.S. 21, D1.
*Stepford, L.M.S., 26, A4.
Stepney (Yorks.), L.N.E.R. 22, D3.
Stepps, L.M.S., 30, C1.
Stevenage, L.N.E.R., 11, E2
Stevenston, L.M.S., 30, D3.
Steventon, G.W.R., 10, F4.
Steyning, S.R., 5, F2.
Stickney, L.N.E.R., 17, C3.
Stillington, L.N.E.R., 28, E5
Stirchley, see Dawley.
Stirling, L.M.S. & L.N.E.R. 31, A1.
Stixwould, L.N.E.R., 17, B2
Stobo, L.M.S., 31, E3.
Stobs, L.N.E.R., 32, F5.
Stockbridge, S.R., 4, C4.
Stockcross & Bagnor, G.W.R. 4, A4.
Stockingford, L.M.S., 16, F5
Stockport, L.M.S. & C.L.C. 20, C1.
Stocksfield, L.N.E.R., 27, C4
Stocksmoor, L.M.S., 21, F2.
Stockton (Durham) L.N.E.R., 28, E5.
Stockton (Warwicks.), see Napton.
Stockton Brook, L.M.S., 15, C3.
Stogumber, G.W.R., 8, F4.
Stoke (Suffolk), L.N.E.R. 11, D5.
Stoke Bruern (Goods) L.M.S., 10, C3.
Stoke Canon, G.W.R., 2, B3
Stoke Edith, G.W.R., 9, C2.
*Stoke Ferry, L.N.E.R., 17 F5.
*Stoke Golding, L.M.S., 16 F5.
Stoke Mandeville, L.N.E.R. L.P.T.B., 10, E2.
Stoke-on-Trent, L.M.S., 15 C3.
Stoke Prior, G.W.R., 9, B3.
Stoke Prior Jc., L.M.S. G.W.R., 9, B4.
Stoke Works, L.M.S./G.W.R & *L.M.S. 9, B4.
Stokesay, see Craven Arms.
Stokesley, L.N.E.R., 28, F4
Stone, L.M.S., 15, D3.
Stonea, L.N.E.R., 11, A3.
Stone Cross Jc., S.R., 5, F5.
Stoneferry (Goods), L.N.E.R. 22, D3.
Stonegate, S.R., 5, E5.
Stonehall & Lydden Halt S.R., 6, D2.
Stonehaven, L.M.S./L.N.E.R. 37, B5.
Stonehouse (Glos.), G.W.R & L.M.S., 9, E3.
Stonehouse (Lanarks), L.M.S. 31, D1.
Stoneleigh, S.R., 5, C3.
Stoneywood (Goods), L.M.S. 31, B1.
Storeton, L.N.E.R., 20, C5.
§Stottesdon, G.W.R., 9, A2.
Stoulton, G.W.R., 9, C4.
Stourbridge, G.W.R., 9, A3.
Stourport-on-Severn, G.W.R. 9, A3.
Stourton Jc., L.M.S., 21, D3
Stow, L.N.E.R., 31, D5.
Stow Bardolph, L.N.E.R. 17, F4.
Stow Bedon, L.N.E.R., 18 F5.
Stowe, see Chartley.
Stowmarket, L.N.E.R., 12 C4.
Stow-on-the-Wold, G.W.R. 9, D5.
Stow Park, L.N.E.R., 16, A2
*Stracathro, L.M.S., 37, C3.
Stradbroke, L.N.E.R., 12 B3.
Stranraer, L.M.S., 25, C2.
Strata Florida, G.W.R., 14 D5.
Stratford, L.N.E.R. & L.P.T.B., 5, A4.
Stratford-on-Avon, G.W.R & L.M.S., 9, B5.
Strathaven, L.M.S., 30, D1.
Strathblane, L.N.E.R., 30 B1.
Strathbungo, L.M.S., 30, C1
Strathcarron, L.M.S., 35, E2
Strathmiglo, L.N.E.R., 34 F1.
*Strathord, L.M.S., 34, E2.
*Strathpeffer, L.M.S., 35, D
Strathyre, L.M.S., 34, F5.
Stratton (Wilts.), G.W.R., 9 F5.
*Stravithie, L.N.E.R., 37, F3
Strawberry Hill, S.R., 5, B2
Streatley, see Goring.
Street see Glastonbury.
Streetly, L.M.S., 15, F4.
*Strensall, L.N.E.R., 21, C5.
Stretford, M.S.J.A., 20, C1.
*Stretham, L.N.E.R., 11 B4.

Stretton (Derbys.), L.M.S., 16, B5.
Stretton & Clay Mills (Staffs.), L.M.S., 16, D5.
Stretton Jc., L.M.S., 16, D5.
Strichen, L.N.E.R., 38, C2.
Strines, L.M.S./L.N.E.R., 15, A4.
Strome Ferry, L.M.S., 35, E1.
Strood, S.R., 6, B5.
Stroud, G.W.R. & §L.M.S., 9, E3.
Struan, L.M.S., 34, C3.
Stubbins, L.M.S., 20, A1.
Studley & Astwood Bank, L.M.S., 9, B4.
Sturmer, L.N.E.R., 11, D5.
Sturminster Newton, S.D., 3, E3.
Sturry, S.R., 6, C3.
Sturton, L.N.E.R., 16, A2.
Stutton (Goods), L.N.E.R., 21, D4.
Styal, L.M.S., 15, A3.
Suckley, G.W.R., 9, B2.
Sudbury (Middlesex), *see* Wembley.
Sudbury (Staffs.), **L.M.S.**/•L.N.E.R., 15, D5.
Sudbury (Suffolk), L.N.E.R., 12, D5.
Sulby Bridge, I.M.R., 23, A3.
Sulby Glen, I.M.R., 23, A3.
Sully, G.W.R., 8, D4.
Summer Lane, L.N.E.R., 21, F3.
Summerseat, L.M.S., 20, A1.
Summerston, L.N.E.R., 30, B1.
Summit (Beattock) Goods, L.M.S., 31, F2.
Sunbury, S.R., 5, B2.
Sunderland, L.N.E.R., 28, C5.
Sundridge Park, S.R., 5, B4.
Sunilaws, L.N.E.R., 32, D4.
Sunningdale, S.R., 5, B1.
Sunnymeads, S.R., 5, B1.
Sunnyside (Coatbridge), L.N.E.R., 31, C1.
Surbiton, S.R., 5, B2.
Surfleet, L.N.E.R., 17, D2.
•Sutton (Cambs.), L.N.E.R., 11, B3.
Sutton (Notts.), *see* Barnby Moor.
Sutton (Surrey), S.R., 5, C3.
Sutton-at-Hone, *see* Farningham Road.
Sutton Bingham, S.R., 3, E2.
Sutton Bridge, M.G.N., 17, E4.
Sutton Coldfield, L.M.S., 15, F5.
Sutton-in-Ashfield, L.M.S. & L.N.E.R., 16, B4.
Sutton Jc., L.M.S., 16, B4.
Sutton Oak, L.M.S., 20, C3.
Sutton-on-Hull, L.N.E.R., 22, D3.
Sutton-on-Sea, L.N.E.R., 17, A4.
Sutton Park, L.M.S., 15, F5.
Sutton Scotney, G.W.R., 4, C3.
•Swadlincote, L.M.S., 16, E5.
Swaffham, L.N.E.R., 18, F5.
Swaffhamprior, L.N.E.R., 11, C4.
Swainsthorpe, L.N.E.R., 18, F3.
Swalecliffe, *see* Chestfield Halt.
Swalwell, L.N.E.R., 27, C5.
Swanage, S.R., 3, G5.
Swanbourne, L.M.S., 10, D2.
Swanley, S.R., 5, B4.
Swannington, L.M.S., 16, E5.
Swansea, G.W.R., L.M.S. & Mum. R., 7, B4.
Swansea Bay, L.M.S., 7, B4.
Swan Village, G.W.R., 15, F4.
Swanwick, S.R., 4, E3.
Swarkestone, *see* Chellaston.
Swavesey, **L.N.E.R.**/L.M.S., 11, C3.
Sway, S.R., 4, F4.
Swaythling, **S.R.**/G.W.R., 4, D4.
Swimbridge, G.W.R., 7, F4.
Swinderby, L.M.S., 16, B2.
Swindon, G.W.R., 9, G5.
Swine, L.N.E.R., 22, D3.
Swineshead, L.N.E.R., 17, D2.
Swinlees Branch, L.M.S., 30, D3.
Swinton (Lancs.), L.M.S., 20, B1.
Swinton (Yorks.), L.M.S. & L.N.E.R., 21, F4.
Swithland Siding, L.N.E.R., 16, E4.
•Sykehouse, L.N.E.R., 21, E5.
Sykes Jc., L.N.E.R., 16, A2.
•Sylfaen, W.L., 14, B2.
Symington, L.M.S., 31, E2.
Symonds Yat, G.W.R., 9, E1.
Syston, L.M.S., 16, E3.

T

Tadcaster, L.N.E.R., 21, D4.
Tadworth & Walton-on-Hill, S.R., 5, C3.
Taffs Well, G.W.R., 8, C4.
Tain, L.M.S., 36, B4.
Takeley, L.N.E.R., 11, F4.
Talacre, L.M.S., 19, C5.
Talerddig, G.W.R., 14, B4.
Talgarth, **G.W.R.**/L.M.S., 14, F3.
Talley Road, V.T., 13, G5.
Tallington, L.N.E.R., 17, F1.
Talsarn Plat., G.W.R., 13, E5.
Talsarnau, G.W.R., 19, F2.
Talybont-on-Usk, G.W.R., 14, G3.
Tal-y-Cafn & Eglwysbach, L.M.S., 19, D3.
Talyllyn Jc., **G.W.R.**/L.M.S., 14, G3.
Talywain, *see* Abersychan.
Tamerton Foliot, S.R., 1, D5.
Tamworth, L.M.S., 15, F5.
•Tanfield, L.N.E.R., 21, A3.
†Tanhouse Lane, L.N.E.R./L.M.S., 20, C3.
Tankerton, *see* Whitstable.
Tannadice, L.M.S., 37, C2.
Tanshelf, L.M.S., 21, E4.
Taplow, G.W.R., 5, B1.
Tarbet, *see* Arrochar.
•Tarbolton, L.M.S., 30, E2.
Tarff, L.M.S., 26, C5.
Tarset, L.N.E.R., 27, A3.
Tattenhall, L.M.S., 20, E3.
Tattenhall Road, L.M.S., 20, E3.
Tattenham Corner, S.R., 5, C3.
Tattershall, L.N.E.R., 17, C2.
Taunton, G.W.R., 8, F4.
Tavistock, G.W.R. & S.R., 1, C5.
Tay Bridge (Dundee) L.N.E.R., 37, E2.
Taynuilt, L.M.S., 33, E3.
Tayport, L.N.E.R., 35, E4.
Tean, L.M.S., 15, D4.
Tebay, **L.M.S.**/L.N.E.R., 27, F1.
Teddington, S.R., 5, B2.
Teigngrace, G.W.R., 2, C4.
Teignmouth, G.W.R., 2, C3.
Templecombe, S.R./S.D. & S.D., 3, D3.
Temple Hirst, L.N.E.R., 21, E5.
Temple Meads (Bristol), G.W.R./L.M.S., 8, C2.
Temple Sowerby, L.N.E.R., 27, E1.
Templeton, G.W.R., 7, C3.
Tempsford, L.N.E.R., 11, C2.
Tenbury Wells, G.W.R./L.M.S., 9, A1.
Tenby, G.W.R., 7, D3.
Tenterden St. Michael's Halt, K.E.S.R., 6, D4.
Tenterden Town, K.E.S.R., 6, E4.
Tern Hill, G.W.R., 15, D2.
Terrington, M.G.N., 17, E4.
Teston Crossing Halt, S.R., 6, C5.
Tetbury, G.W.R., 9, F3.
•Tettenhall, G.W.R., 15, F3.
•Teversall, L.M.S. & L.N.E.R., 16, B4.
Tewkesbury, L.M.S., 9, D3.
Teynham, S.R., 6, C4.
Thame, G.W.R., 10, E3.
Thames Ditton, S.R., 5, B2.
•Thames Haven, L.M.S., 6, B5.
Thames Haven Jc., L.M.S., 5, B5.
Thankerton, L.M.S., 31, E2.
Thatcham, G.W.R., 4, A3.
Thatto Heath, L.M.S., 20, C3.
Thaxted, L.N.E.R., 11, E4.
Thealby, *see* Winterton.
Theale, G.W.R., 4, A2.
Theddingworth, L.M.S., 16, G3.
Theddlethorpe, L.N.E.R., 17, A4.
Thelwall, L.M.S., 20, C2.
The Mound Jc., L.M.S., 36, A4.
The Oaks, L.M.S., 20, B2.
•Theobalds Grove, L.N.E.R., 11, G3.
Thetford, L.N.E.R., 12, B5.
Thetford Bridge, L.N.E.R., 12, B5.
Theydon Bois, L.N.E.R., 8, G3.
Thingley Jc., G.W.R., 3, A4.
Thirsk, L.N.E.R., 21, A4.
Thongs Bridge, L.M.S., 21, F2.
•Thorganby, D.V.L., 21, D5.
Thorington, L.N.E.R., 12, E4.
Thornaby, L.N.E.R., 28, E4.
•Thornbury, L.M.S., 9, F2.
Thorndon, *see* Aspall.
Thorne, L.N.E.R., 21, E5.
Thorner, L.N.E.R., 21, D4.
Thorney, M.G.N., 17, F2.
Thorney & Kingsbury Halt, G.W.R., 3, D1.
Thorneyburn, L.N.E.R., 27, A2.
•Thorneywood, L.N.E.R., 16, C3.
Thornfalcon, G.W.R., 8, F3.
Thornhill (Dumfries), L.M.S., 31, G2.
Thornhill (Yorks.), L.M.S., 21, E3.
Thornielee, L.N.E.R., 31, E5.
Thornley, L.N.E.R., 28, D4.
Thornley Coll., L.N.E.R., 28, D5.
Thornliebank, L.M.S., 30, C1.
Thornton (Ches.), *see* Stanlow.
Thornton (Lancs.), L.M.S., 24, D4.
Thornton (Yorks.), L.N.E.R., 21, D2.
Thornton Abbey, L.N.E.R., 22, E3.
Thornton Dale, L.N.E.R., 22, A5.
Thorntonhall, L.M.S., 30, D1.
Thornton-in-Craven, L.M.S., 21, C1.
Thornton Jc., L.N.E.R., 31, A4.
Thorp Arch, L.N.E.R., 21, C4.
Thorpe (Northants.), L.M.S., 11, B1.
Thorpe (Norwich), L.N.E.R., 18, F3.
Thorpe Bay, L.M.S., 6, A4.
Thorpe Cloud, L.M.S., 15, C5.
Thorpe Culvert, L.N.E.R., 17, B4.
Thorpe Gates (Goods), L.N.E.R., 21, D5.
•Thorpe-in-Balne, L.N.E.R., 21, F5.
Thorpe-le-Soken, L.N.E.R., 12, F3.
Thorpeness, L.N.E.R., 12, C2.
Thorpe-on-the-Hill, L.M.S., 16, B1.
•Thorpe Thewles, L.N.E.R., 28, E5.
Thorverton, G.W.R., 2, A3.
Thrapston, L.M.S., 10, A1.
Three Bridges, S.R., 5, D3.
Three Cocks Jc., **G.W.R.**/L.M.S., 14, F2.
Three Counties, L.N.E.R., 11, E2.
Three Horse Shoes Siding (Cambs.), L.N.E.R., 11, A3.
Threlkeld, L.M.S., 26, E1.
Threshfield, *see* Grassington.
Throsk, L.M.S., 31, A1.
•Thrumster, L.M.S., 39, D4.
Thrumpton (Goods), L.N.E.R., 16, A3.
Thurcroft (Goods), L.M.S./L.N.E.R., 21, G4.
Thurgarton, L.M.S., 16, C3.
Thurgoland, L.N.E.R., 21, F3.
Thurlby, L.N.E.R., 17, E1.
Thurnby & Scraptoft, L.N.E.R., 16, F3.
Thurnham, *see* Bearsted.
Thursford, M.G.N., 18, D4.
Thurso, L.M.S., 39, C3.
Thurstaston, L.M.S., 20, C5.
Thurston, L.N.E.R., 12, C5.
Thuxton, L.N.E.R., 18, F4.
Tibbermuir, L.M.S., 34, E2.
Tibshelf, L.N.E.R. & •L.M.S., 16, B4.
•Tickhill & Wadworth, S.Y., 21, G5.
Tiddington, G.W.R., 10, E3.
Tidenham, G.W.R., 8, B2.
Tidworth, G.W.R., 4, B5.
Tilbury, L.M.S., 5, B5.
Tile Hill, L.M.S., 10, A5.
Tilehurst, G.W.R., 4, A2.
Tillicoultry L.N.E.R., 31, A2.
Tillietudlem, L.M.S., 31, D1.
Tillyfourie, L.N.E.R., 38, F4.
Tillynaught, L.N.E.R., 38, C4.
Tilton, L.M.S./L.N.E.R., 16, F2.
Timberland, *see* Scopwick.
Timperley, M.S.J.A., 20, C1.
Tingley, L.N.E.R., 21, E3.
Tinsley, L.N.E.R., 21, G4.
Tintern, G.W.R., 8, B2.
Tipton, G.W.R. & L.M.S., 15, F4.
Tipton St. John's, S.R., 2, B2.
Tiptree, L.N.E.R., 12, F5.
Tir Pentwys Coll., G.W.R., 8, B4.
Tir Phil, G.W.R., 8, A4.
Tirydail, **G.W.R.**/L.M.S., 7, A4.
Tisbury, S.R., 3, D4.
Tissington, L.M.S., 15, C5.
Tisted, S.R., 4, C2.
Titley, G.W.R., 14, E2.
Tiverton, G.W.R., 2, A3.
Tiverton Jc., G.W.R., 2, A2.
Tivetshall, L.N.E.R., 12, A3.
Tochieneal, L.N.E.R., 38, C5.
Toddington, G.W.R., 9, D4.
Todmorden, L.M.S., 21, E1.
•Tod Point, L.N.E.R., 28, E4.
Toft & Kingston (Goods), L.M.S., 11, C3.
Tolcarn Jc., G.W.R., 1, D1.
Toller, G.W.R., 3, E2.
Tollerton, L.N.E.R., 21, B4.
Tollesbury, L.N.E.R., 12, F5.
Tolleshunt D'Arcy, L.N.E.R., 12, F5.
Tomatin, L.M.S., 36, E4.
Tonbridge, S.R., 5, D5.
Tondu, G.W.R., 7, C5.
Tonfanau, G.W.R., 13, B5.
•Tonge & Bredon, L.M.S., 16, E5.
•Tongham, S.R., 4, B1.
Tonyrefail, G.W.R., 8, B5.
Tooting, S.R., 5, B3.
Topcliffe, L.N.E.R., 21, A4.
Topsham, S.R., 2, B3.
Torksey, L.N.E.R., 16, A2.
Torpantau, G.W.R., 8, A5.
Torphins, L.N.E.R., 38, G4.
Torquay, G.W.R., 2, D3.
Torrance, L.N.E.R., 30, B1.
Torre, G.W.R., 2, D3.
Torrington, S.R., 7, G3.
•Torryburn, L.N.E.R., 30, B2.
Torver, L.M.S., 26, G2.
Totley, *see* Dore.
Totnes, G.W.R., 2, D4.
Tottenham, L.N.E.R., 5, A3.
Totteridge, •**L.N.E.R.**/L.P.T.B., 5, A3.
Tottington, L.M.S., 20, A1.
Totton, S.R., 4, E4.
Towcester, L.M.S., 10, C3.
Tower Hill, S.R., 1, B5.
Towiemore Halt, L.N.E.R., 38, D5.
Tow Law, L.N.E.R., 27, D4.
Towneley, L.M.S., 24, D1.
Town Green, L.M.S., 20, B4.
Townhill Jc., L.N.E.R., 31, A3.
Towyn, G.W.R. & Tal., 13, B5.
Trabboch, L.M.S., 30, F2.
Trafford Park, C.L.C., 20, C1.
Tram Inn, G.W.R., 9, D1.
•Tranent, L.N.E.R., 31, B5.
Trawscoed, G.W.R., 13, D5.
Trawsfynydd, G.W.R., 19, F3.
Treborth, L.M.S., 19, D2.
Tredegar, L.M.S., 8, A4.
Treeton, L.M.S., 21, G4.
Trefeglwys, *see* Pwllglas.
Trefeinon, **G.W.R.**/L.M.S., 14, F3.
Trefnant, L.M.S., 19, D5.
Treforest, G.W.R., 8, B5.
Trefriw, *see* Llanrwst.
Tregaron, G.W.R., 14, E5.
Tregarth, L.M.S., 19, D2.
Trehafod, G.W.R., 8, B5.
Treherbert, G.W.R., 7, B5.
Trench Crossing, L.M.S., 15, E2.
Trenholme Bar, L.N.E.R., 28, F4.
Trent, L.M.S., 16, D4.
Trentham, L.M.S., 15, D3.
Trentham Gardens, L.M.S., 15, D3.
Treorchy, G.W.R., 8, B5.
Tresmeer, S.R., 1, B4.
Trethomas, G.W.R., 8, B4.
Trevil, L.M.S., 7, A4.
Trevor, G.W.R., 20, F5.
§*Trewythan*, G.W.R., 14, C4.
Trimdon, L.N.E.R., 28, D5.
Trimingham, N.S.J., 18, D2.
Trimley, L.N.E.R., 12, E3.
Trimsaran (Goods), G.W.R., 7, A3.
Trimsaran Rd., G.W.R., 7, A2.
Tring, L.M.S., 10, E1.
Troedyrhiw, G.W.R., 8, B5.
Troedyrhiew Garth, G.W.R., 7, B5.
Troon, L.M.S., 30, E3.
Troutbeck, L.M.S., 26, E1.
Trowbridge, G.W.R., 3, B4.
Trowell, L.M.S., 16, C4.
•Trowse (Norwich), L.N.E.R., 18, F3.
Troy (Monmouth), G.W.R., 8, A1.
Truro, G.W.R., 1, E1.
Trusham, G.W.R., 2, C3.
Truthall Platform, G.W.R., 1, F5.
Tub's Hill (Sevenoaks), S.R., 5, C4.
Tullibardine, L.M.S., 34, F3.
Tulloch, L.N.E.R., 33, B5.
Tulse Hill, S.R., 5, B3.
•Tumble, G.W.R., 7, A3.
Tumby Woodside, L.N.E.R., 17, C2.
Tunbridge Wells, S.R., 5, D5.
Tunstall, L.M.S., 15, C3.
•Turnberry, L.M.S., 30, G4.
Turnchapel, S.R., 1, D5.
•Turnhouse, L.N.E.R., 31, B3.
Turriff, L.N.E.R., 38, D3.
Turton, L.M.S., 20, A2.
Turvey, L.M.S., 10, C1.
Tutbury, **L.M.S.**/•L.N.E.R., 15, D5.
Tuxford, L.N.E.R., 16, B2.
Twechar, L.N.E.R., 30, B1.
Tweedmouth, L.N.E.R., 32, D2.
Twenty, M.G.N., 17, E2.
Twickenham, S.R., 5, B2.
Twizell, L.N.E.R., 32, D3.
Twyford, G.W.R., 4, A1.
Twywell, L.M.S., 10, A1.
Tycoch Jc., G.W.R., 7, A2.
Ty Croes, L.M.S., 19, D1.
Tydd, M.G.N., 17, E3.
Tyldesley, L.M.S., 20, B2.
Tylorstown, G.W.R., 8, B5.
Tylwch, G.W.R., 14, C4.
Tyndrum, L.M.S. & L.N.E.R., 33, E5.
Tyne Dock, L.N.E.R., 28, B5.
Tynehead, L.N.E.R., 31, C5.
Tynemouth, L.N.E.R., 28, B5.
Tyseley, G.W.R., 15, G5.
•Tytherington, L.M.S., 9, F2.

U

Uckfield, S.R., 5, E4.
Uddingston, L.M.S., 30, C1.
Udny, L.N.E.R., 38, E2.
Uffculme, G.W.R., 2, A2.
Uffington (Berks.), G.W.R., 10, F5.
Uffington & Barnack, L.M.S., 17, F1.
•Ulbster, L.M.S., 39, E4.
Ulceby, L.N.E.R., 22, E3.
Ulleskelf, L.N.E.R., 21, D4.
Ullesthorpe, L.M.S., 16, G4.
Ulting, *see* Langford.
Ulverston, L.M.S., 24, A4.
Umberleigh, S.R., 7, F3.
Union Mills, I.M.R., 23, B2.
Unstone, L.M.S., 16, A5.
Uphall, L.N.E.R., 31, B3.
Uphill, *see* Bleadon.
Upholland, L.M.S., 20, B3.
Uplawmoor, L.N.E.R., 30, D2.
Upminster, **L.M.S.**/L.P.T.B., 5, A5.
Upminster Bridge, **L.M.S.**/L.P.T.B., 5, A5.
Upper Bank, L.M.S., 7, B4.
Upper Batley, L.N.E.R., 21, E3.
Upper Broughton, L.M.S., 16, D3.
Upper Greenock, L.M.S., 30, B3.
Upper Jc. Goods (Greenhill), L.N.E.R., 31, B1.
•Upper Lydbrook, S.V.Y., 9, E1.
•Uppermill, L.M.S., 21, F1
Upper Pontnewydd, G.W.R., 8, B3.
Upper Port Glasgow (Goods), L.M.S., 30, B3.
Upper Warlingham, S.R., 5, C3.
Uppingham, L.M.S., 16, F2.
Upton (Ches.), L.N.E.R., 20, C5.
Upton & Blewbury, G.W.R., 10, F4.
•Upton (Yorks.), L.N.E.R., 21, E4.
Upton Magna, G.W.R./L.M.S., 15, E1.
Upton-on-Severn, L.M.S., 9, C3.
•Upwell, W.U.T., 17, F4.
Upwey, G.W.R., 3, F3.
Upwey Jc., G.W.R., 3, F3.
Urmston, C.L.C., 20, C2.
Urquhart, L.N.E.R., 36, C1.
Ushaw Moor, L.N.E.R., 27, D5.
Usk, G.W.R., 8, B3.
Usselby, *see* Claxby.
Usworth, L.N.E.R., 28, C5.
Utterby Halt, L.N.E.R., 22, G2.
Uttoxeter, **L.M.S.**/•L.N.E.R., 15, D5.
Uxbridge, G.W.R. & L.P.T.B., 5, A2.

V

Valley, L.M.S., 19, B2.
Van Road, *see* Garth, G.W.R.
Vauxhall (Gt. Yarmouth), L.N.E.R., 18, F1.
Vauxhall Fish Mkt., **L.N.E.R.**/M.G.N., 18, F1.
Velvet Hall, L.N.E.R., 32, D3.
Venn Cross, G.W.R., 8, F5.
Ventnor (I.W.), S.R., 4, G3.
Ventnor West (I.W.), S.R., 4, G3.
Verney Jc., L.M.S./•L.N.E.R./•L.P.T.B., 10, D3.
Verwood, S.R., 3, E5.
Victoria (London), S.R. & L.P.T.B., 5, B3.
Victoria (M'chester.), L.M.S. 20, B1.
Victoria (Mon.), G.W.R., 8, A4.
Victoria (Norwich) Goods, L.N.E.R., 18, F3.
Victoria (Nott'm.), L.N.E.R., 16, C4.
Victoria (Sheffield), L.N.E.R., 21, G3.
Victoria (Swansea), L.M.S., 7, B4.
Victoria Docks, L.N.E.R., 5, B4.
Vine Street (Uxbridge), G.W.R., 5, A2.
Virginia Water, S.R., 5, B1.
Vobster (Goods), G.W.R., 3, B3.
•Vowchurch, G.W.R., 14 F1.

W

Wadborough, L.M.S., 9, C3.
Waddington, L.N.E.R., 16 B1.
Waddon, S.R., 5, C3.
Wadebridge, S.R., 1, C2.
Wadhurst, S.R., 5, E5.
Wadsley Bridge, L.N.E.R. 21, G3.
Wadworth, *see* Tickhill.
•Waenavon, L.M.S., 8, A4.
Wainfleet, L.N.E.R., 17, C4.
Wakefield, L.M.S. & L.N.E.R., 21, E3.
Wakerley & Barrowden, L.M.S., 16, F1.
Wakes Colne, *see* Chappel.
Walcot, G.W.R./L.M.S., 15, E1.
Waldron & Horam, S.R., 5, E5.
Waleswood, L.N.E.R., 16, A4.
Walkden, L.M.S., 20, B2.
Walker, L.N.E.R., 28, B5.
Walkerburn, L.N.E.R., 30, E5.
Walker Gate, L.N.E.R., 28, B5.
Walkeringham, L.N.E.R., 22, G5.
Wall, L.N.E.R., 27, B3.
Wallasey, L.M.S., 20, C4.
Wall Grange, L.M.S., 15, C4.
Wallingfen, L.N.E.R., 22, D5.
Wallingford, G.W.R., 10, F3.
Wallington, S.R., 5, C3.
Wallsend, L.N.E.R., 28, B5.
Walmer, S.R., 6, C1.
Walpole, M.G.N., 17, E4.
Walsall, L.M.S., 15, F4.
•Walsall Wood, L.M.S., 15, F4.
Walsden, L.M.S., 21, E1.
Walsingham, L.N.E.R., 18, D5.
Waltham, L.N.E.R., 22, F2.
Waltham Cross & Abbey, L.N.E.R., 11, G3.
•Waltham-on-the-Wold, L.N.E.R., 16, D2.
Walton (Derby), *see* Barton.
Walton (Northants.), L.M.S., 17, F2.
Walton (& Anfield) (Lancs.), L.M.S., 20, C4.
Walton-on-Hill, *see* Tadworth.
Walton-on-Thames, S.R., 5, C2.
Walton-on-the-Naze, L.N.E.R., 12, E3.
Wamphray, L.M.S., 26, A3.
Wanborough, S.R., 5, C1.
Wansford, L.M.S., 11, A1.
Wanstrow, G.W.R., 3, C3.
Wantage Road, G.W.R., 10, F5.
Wappenham, L.M.S., 10, C3.
Wapping Wharf (Bristol), G.W.R., 8, C2.
Warblington Halt, S.R., 4, E2.
•Warboys, L.N.E.R., 11, B2.
Warburton, *see* Heatley.
Warcop, L.N.E.R., 27, E2.
Wardhouse, L.N.E.R., 38, E4.
•Wardleworth, L.M.S., 20, A1.
Ware, L.N.E.R., 11, F3.
Wareham, S.R., 3, F4.
Wargrave, G.W.R., 10, G2.
Wark, L.N.E.R., 27, B3.
Warkworth, L.N.E.R., 32, F1.
Warley, *see* Brentwood.
Warlingham, S.R., 5, C3.
Warminster, G.W.R., 3, C4.
Warmley, L.M.S., 8, C1.
Warmsworth (Goods), L.N.E.R., 21, F5.
Warnham, S.R., 5, D2.
Warren Hill Jc., L.N.E.R., 11, C4.
Warrington, L.M.S. & C.L.C., 20, C2.
Warrior Sq. (St. Leonards), S.R., 6, F5.
Warsop, L.N.E.R., 16, B4.
Warthill, L.N.E.R., 21, C5.
Wartle, L.N.E.R., 38, E3.
Warwick, G.W.R., 10, B5.
Warwick (Milverton), L.M.S., 10, B5.
Washford, G.W.R., 8, E5.
Washington, L.N.E.R., 28, C5.
Waskerley (Goods), L.N.E.R., 27, D4.
Wassand, L.N.E.R., 22, D3.
Watchet, G.W.R., 8, E5.
•Watchingwell (I.W.), S.R., 4, F3.
Waterbeach, L.N.E.R., 11 C3.
•Waterfall, I.M.R., 23, B2.

† The C.L.C. works into this joint station

Waterfoot, L.M.S., 20, A1.
Waterhall Jc., G.W.R., 8, C4.
*Waterhouses, L.N.E.R., 27, D5.
Wateringbury, S.R., 6, C5.
Waterloo (Aberdeen), Goods, L.N.E.R., 38, G2.
Waterloo (Lancs.), L.M.S., 20, B4.
Waterloo (London), S.R. & L.P.T.B., 5, B3.
*Waterloo Dock, L.M.S., 20, C4.
Watermoor (Cirencester), G.W.R., 9, F4.
Water Orton, L.M.S., 15, G5.
Waterside, L.M.S., 30, F2.
Watford, L.M.S./L.P.T.B. & L.N.E.R./L.P.T.B., 11, G1.
Watford North, L.M.S., 11, G1.
Wath-on-Dearne, L.N.E.R. & L.M.S., 21, F4.
Wath Road Jc., L.M.S./S.K., 21, F4.
Watlington, G.W.R., 10, F3.
Watten, L.M.S., 39, D4.
Watton, L.N.E.R., 18, F5.
Watton-at-Stone, L.N.E.R., 11, F2.
Waverley (Edinburgh), L.N.E.R., 31, B4.
Waverton, L.M.S., 20, D3.
Wavertree, L.M.S., 20, C4.
Wealdstone, *see* Harrow.
Wearhead, L.N.E.R., 27, D3.
Weaver Jc., L.M.S., 20, D3.
Weaverthorpe, L.N.E.R., 22, B4.
Wednesbury, G.W.R. & L.M.S., 15, F4.
Wednesfield, L.M.S., 15, F4.
*Wednesfield Heath, L.M.S., 15, F3.
Weedon, L.M.S., 10, B3.
Weeley, L.N.E.R., 12, E4.
Weeton, L.N.E.R., 21, C3.
Welbeck, *see* Creswell, L.N.E.R.
Welbury, L.N.E.R., 28, F5.
Weldon, *see* Corby.
Welford & Kilworth, L.M.S., 16, G3.
Welford Park, G.W.R., 4, A4.
Welham Jc., L.M.S., 16, G2.
Wellfield, L.N.E.R., 28, D5.
Welling, S.R., 5, B4.
Wellingborough, L.M.S., 10, B2.
Wellington (Salop), G.W.R./L.M.S., 15, E2.
Wellington (Som.), G.W.R., 8, E2.
Wellow, S.D., 3, B3.
Wells (Som.), G.W.R. & S.D., 3, C2.
Wells-on-Sea, L.N.E.R., 18, D5.
Welnetham, L.N.E.R., 12, C5.
Welshampton, G.W.R., 20, F3.
Welshpool, G.W.R./L.M.S & *W.L.*, 14, B2.
Welton (Northants.) ,L.M.S., 10, B3.
Welton (Som.), *see* Midsomer Norton.
Welwyn Garden City, L.N.E.R., 11, F2.
Welwyn North, L.N.E.R., 11, F2.
Wem, L.M.S., 15, D1.
Wembley (for Sudbury), L.M.S., 5, A2.
Wembley Park, L.P.T.B., 5, A2.
Wemyss Bay, L.M.S., 30, C4.
Wemyss Castle, L.M.S., 31, A4.
Wendling, L.N.E.R., 18, E5.
Wendover, L.N.E.R./ L.P.T.B., 10, E2.
Wenford Bridge, S.R., 1, C3.
Wennington (Lancs.),L.M.S., 24, B2.
Wensley, L.N.E.R., 27, G4.
Wentworth & Hoyland Common, L.M.S., 21, F3.
Wenvoe, G.W.R., 8, C4.
Wern Sdg., G.W.R., 19, F2.
*Wernlas, S.M., 14, A2.
Werrington Jc., L.N.E.R., 17, F2.
Wesham, *see* Kirkham.
West Auckland, L.N.E.R., 27, E5.
West Bay (Bridport), G.W.R., 3, F1.
West Boldon (Goods), L.N.E.R., 28, C5.
Westbourne Park, G.W.R. & L.P.T.B., 5, A3.
*West Bridge, L.M.S., 16, F4.
West Bromwich, G.W.R., 15, G4.
*Westbrook, G.W.R., 14, F2.

Westbury (Bucks.), *see* Fulwell, L.M.S.
Westbury (Salop), S.W., 14, C3.
Westbury (Wilts.), G.W.R., 3, B4.
West Calder, L.M.S., 31, C2.
Westcliff-on-Sea, L.M.S., 6, A5.
West Cornforth, L.N.E.R., 28, D5.
Westcraigs, L.N.E.R., 31, C2.
West Croydon, S.R., 5, C4.
West Derby, C.L.C., 20, C4.
West Dereham, *see* Abbey.
West Drayton & Yiewsley, G.W.R., 5, B2.
West Ealing, G.W.R., 5, B2.
West Felton, *see* Rednal.
West Fen Drove (Goods), L.N.E.R., 11, E3.
West Ferry, D.A., 37, E2.
*Westfield, L.N.E.R., 31, B2.
Westgate (Wakefield), L.N.E.R., 21, E4.
Westgate-in-Weardale, L.N.E.R., 27, D3.
*West Gosforth, L.N.E.R., 27, B5.
West Grinstead, S.R., 5, E2.
West Halton, L.N.E.R., 16, D4.
*West Halton, L.N.E.R., 22, E3.
Westham, *see* Pevensey.
West Hartlepool, L.N.E.R., 28, D4.
West Hoathly, S.R., 5, E4.
West Holmes Jc., L.N.E.R., 16, B1.
West Horsham, *see* Christ's Hospital.
Westhoughton, L.M.S., 20, B2.
Westhouses, L.M.S., 16, B4.
West Hove, *see* Portslade.
West Kilbride, L.M.S., 30, D4.
West Kirby, B.J. & L.M.S., 20, C5.
West Leigh, L.M.S. & L.N.E.R., 20, B2.
West Meon, S.R., 4, D2.
West Mill, L.N.E.R., 11, E3.
West Moors, S.R., 3, E5.
West Newport, L.N.E.R., 37, E2.
Westoe Lane, S.S.M.W., 28, B5.
Weston (Lincs.), M.G.N., 17, E2.
Weston (Northants.), *see* Ashley.
Weston Jc., L.M.S./S.D., 3, A3.
*Weston & Ingestre (Staffs.), L.M.S., 15, E4.
See also Ingestre.
Weston Coyney, L.M.S., 15, C4.
Weston-on-Trent, L.M.S., 16, D4.
Weston-Rhyn, G.W.R., 20, F4.
Weston-sub-Edge, G.W.R., 9, C5.
Weston-super-Mare, G.W.R., 8, D3.
West Pennard, S.D., 3, C2.
West Ruislip (for Ickenham), G.W.R./L.N.E.R., 5, A2.
West Rounton Gates, L.N.E.R., 28, F5.
West Runton, M.G.N., 18, D3.
West Marina (St. Leonards), S.R. 6, F5.
West Stanley, L.N.E.R., 27, C5.
West Thurrock Jc., L.M.S., 5, B5.
West Timperley, C.L.C., 20, C1.
*West Vale, L.M.S., 21, E2.
West Wemyss, L.N.E.R., 31, A4.
West Weybridge, S.R., 5, C2.
West Wickham, S.R., 5, B4.
*Westwood, L.N.E.R., 21, F3.
West Worthing, S.R., 5, F2.
West Wycombe, G.W.R./ L.N.E.R., 10, F2.
Wetheral, L.N.E.R., 26, C1.
Wetherby, L.N.E.R., 21, D4.
Wetheringsett, *see* Brockford.
Wetwang, L.N.E.R., 22, B4.
Weybourne, M.G.N., 17, D4.
Weybridge, S.R., 5, C2.
Weyhill, G.W.R., 4, C4.
Weymouth, G.W.R./S.R., 3, G3.
Whaley Bridge, L.M.S., 15, A4.

Whalley, L.M.S., 24, D1.
Whaplode, M.G.N., 17, E3.
Wharncliffe Coll., L.M.S., 21, F3.
Wharram, L.N.E.R., 22, B5.
Wharton, *see* Over.
Whatstandwell, L.M.S., 16, C5.
Whauphill, L.M.S., 25, C4.
Wheathampstead, L.N.E.R., 11, F2.
Wheatley (Oxon.), G.W.R., 10, E3.
*Wheatley (Yorks.), L.M.S./ L.N.E.R., 21, F2.
Wheatsheaf, *see* Gwersyllt.
*Wheldrake, D.V.L., 21, D5.
Wherwell, S.R., 4, C4.
Whetstone (Leics.),L.N.E.R., 16, F4.
Whifflet, L.M.S. & L.N.E.R., 31, C1.
Whimple, S.R., 2, B2.
Whippingham (I.W.), S.R., 4, F3.
Whissendine, L.M.S., 16, E2.
Whistlefield, L.N.E.R., 30, A5.
Whitacre, L.M.S., 15, G5.
*Whitburn, L.N.E.R., 31, C2.
Whitby, L.N.E.R., 28, F2.
Whitby West Cliff, L.N.E.R., 28, F2.
Whitchurch (Glam.),G.W.R., 8, C4.
Whitchurch (Hants.),G.W.R. & S.R., 4, B3.
Whitchurch (Salop), L.M.S./ G.W.R., 15, C1.
Whitchurch Down Platform, G.W.R., 1, C5.
White Bear, L.M.S., 20, A3.
White Colne, L.N.E.R., 12, E5.
Whitecraigs, L.M.S., 30, C2.
*Whitecroft, S.V.Y., 9, E1.
Whitedale, L.N.E.R., 22, D4.
White Fen(Goods),L.N.E.R., 11, A3.
Whitefield, L.M.S., 20, B1.
*Whitegate, C.L.C., 20, D3.
Whitehaven, L.M.S., 26, E4.
Whitehouse, L.N.E.R., 38, F4.
Whitehouse Jc., L.M.S., 24, F3.
Whitehurst, G.W.R., 20, F4.
Whiteinch, L.N.E.R., 30, C2.
*Whitemoor (Goods), L.N.E.R., 17, F3.
White Myre Jc., L.N.E.R., 31, A3.
White Notley, L.N.E.R., 11, F5.
White Rigg, L.N.E.R., 31, C1.
Whithorn, L.M.S., 25, D4.
Whitland, G.W.R., 7, A1.
Whitley Bay, L.N.E.R., 28, B5.
Whitley Bridge, L.M.S., 21, E5.
Whitlingham, L.N.E.R., 18, F3.
Whitmore, L.M.S., 15, C3.
Whitney-on-Wye, L.M.S., 14, F2.
Whitstable & Tankerton, S.R., 6, B3.
Whitstable Harbour, S.R., 6, B3.
Whitstone & Bridgerule, S.R., 1, A4.
*Whittingham, L.N.E.R., 32, F2.
Whittington (Derbys.), L.M.S., 16, A5.
Whittington (Salop), G.W.R., 20, G4.
Whittlesea, L.N.E.R., 11, A2.
Whittlesford, L.N.E.R., 11, D3.
*Whitton (Lincs.), L.N.E.R., 22, E4.
Whitton (Middlesex), S.R., 5, B2.
Whitwell (Derbys.), L.M.S., 16, A4.
Whitwell (I.W.), S.R., 4, G3.
Whitwell & Reepham, M.G.N., 18, E4.
*Whitwick, L.M.S., 16, E4.
Whitworth, L.M.S., 20, A1.
Whyteleafe, S.R., 5, C3.
Wichnor Jc., L.M.S., 15, E5.
Wick, L.M.S., 39, D4.
Wickenby, L.N.E.R., 17, A1.
Wickford, L.N.E.R., 6, A5.
Wickham (Hants.), S.R., 4, E3.
Wickham Bishops, L.N.E.R., 12, F5.
Wickham Market, L.N.E.R., 12, C2.
Wickwar, L.M.S., 9, F2.
Widdrington, L.N.E.R., 27, A5.
Widford, L.N.E.R., 11, F3.
Widmerpool, L.M.S., 16, D3.

†Widnes, L.M.S. & L.M.S./ L.N.E.R. 20 C3.
Widney Manor, G.W.R., 9, A5.
Wigan, L.M.S. & L.N.E.R., 20, B3.
Wigston Glen Parva, L.M.S., 16, F3.
Wigston Magna, L.M.S., 16, F3.
Wigston South, L.M.S., 16, F3.
Wigton, L.M.S., 26, C2.
Wigtown, L.M.S., 25, C4.
Wilbraham Road, L.N.E.R., 20, C1.
*Wilburton, L.N.E.R., 11, B3.
Wilby, L.N.E.R., 12, B3.
Willaston, L.M.S., 15, C2.
Willenhall, L.M.S., 15, F4.
Willerby & Kirk Ella, L.N.E.R., 22, D4.
Willesden Jc., L.M.S., 5, A3.
Willington (Beds.), L.M.S., 11, D1.
Willington (Derby), *see* Repton.
Willington (Durham), L.N.E.R., 27, D5.
Williton, G.W.R., 8, E5.
*Willoughby (Lincs.), L.N.E.R., 17, B4.
Willoughby (Warwicks.), *see* Braunston.
Willmcote, G.W.R., 9, B5.
Wilmington, L.N.E.R., 22, D3.
Wilmslow, L.M.S., 15, A3.
Wilnecote, L.M.S., 15, F5.
Wilpshire, L.M.S., 24, D2.
Wilsden, L.N.E.R., 21, D2.
Wilsontown, L.M.S., 31, C2.
Wilstrop (Goods), L.N.E.R., 21, C4.
Wilton, G.W.R. & S.R., 3, C5.
Wimbledon, S.R./L.P.T.B., 5, B3.
Wimblington, L.N.E.R., 11, A3.
Wimborne, S.R., 3, E5.
Wincanton, S.D., 3, D3.
Winchburgh, L.N.E.R., 31, B3.
Winchcombe, G.W.R., 9, D4.
Winchelsea, S.R., 6, E4.
Winchester, S.R., & G.W.R., 4, D3.
Winchfield, S.R., 4, B1.
Winchmore Hill, L.N.E.R., 5, A3.
Wincobank L.M.S., 21, G3.
Windermere, L.M.S., 26, F1.
*Windermere Lake Side, L.M.S., 24, A4.
Windmill End, G.W.R., 15, G4.
Windsor & Eton, G.W.R. & S.R., 5, B1.
Winestead, L.N.E.R., 22, E2.
Wingate, L.N.E.R., 28, D5.
Wingfield, L.M.S., 16, C5.
Wingham Town, E.K.R., 6, C2.
Winnersh Halt, S.R., 4, A1.
Winscombe, G.W.R., 8, D3.
Winsford, L.M.S., 20, D2.
*Winsford & Over, C.L.C., 20, D2.
Winslow, L.M.S., 10, D2.
Winson Green, L.M.S., 15, G4.
Winston, L.N.E.R., 27, E5.
Winterbourne, G.W.R., 9, E1.
Winteringham, L.N.E.R., 22, E4.
Winteringham Haven, L.N.E.R., 22, E4.
*Wintersett & Ryhill, L.N.E.R., 21, E4.
Winterton & Thealby, L.N.E.R., 22, E4.
Winton (Goods), L.N.E.R., 31, A5.
Winton Pier (Ardrossan), L.M.S., 30, D3.
Wirksworth, L.M.S., 16, C5.
Wisbech, L.N.E.R.& M.G.N., 17, F3.
Wisbech St. Mary, M.G.N., 17, F3.
Wishaw, L.M.S., 31 D1.
Wishford, S.R., 3, C5.
Wistow, L.N.E.R., 21, D5.
Witham (Essex), L.N.E.R., 12, F5.
Witham (Som.), G.W.R., 3, C3.
Withcall, L.N.E.R., 17, A2.
Withernsea, L.N.E.R., 22, E2.
Withington (Glos.), G.W.R., 9, E4.
Withington (Hereford), G.W.R., 9, C1.
Withington (Lancs.), L.M.S., 20, C1.

Withnell, L.M.S., 24, E2.
Withyham, S.R., 5, D4.
Witley, S.R., 5, D1.
Witney, G.W.R., 9, E5.
Wittersham Road, K.E.S.R., 6, E4.
Witton, L.M.S., 15, G5.
*Witton Gilbert, L.N.E.R., 27, D5.
Witton-le-Wear, L.N.E.R., 27, E5.
\ iveliscombe, G.W.R., 8, F5.
Wivelsfield, S.R., 5, E3.
Wivenhoe, L.N.E.R., 12, F4.
Wixford, L.M.S., 9, B4.
Woburn Sands, L.M.S., 10, C1.
Woking, S.R., 5, C1.
*Woking Cemetery (Necropolis Co.), S.R., 5, C1.
Wokingham, S.R., 4, A1.
Woldingham, S.R., 5, C3.
*Wolferton, L.N.E.R., 17, D5.
Wolfhall Jc., G.W.R., 4, B5.
Wolsingham, L.N.E.R., 27, D4.
Wolston, *see* Brandon.
Wolverhampton, G.W.R. & L.M.S., 15, F3.
Wolverton, L.M.S., 10, C2.
*Wombourn, L.N.E.R., 15, F3.
Wombridge (Goods), L.M.S., 15, E2.
Wombwell L.N.E.R., 21, F4.
Womersley, L.M.S/L.N.E.R., 21, E4.
Wonersh, *see* Bramley.
Wooburn Green, G.W.R., 10, F1.
Woodborough, G.W.R., 3, B5.
Woodbridge, L.N.E.R., 12, D3.
Woodburn, L.N.E.R., 27, A3.
Woodbury Road, S.R., 2, B2.
*Woodchester, L.M.S., 9, E3.
Wood End, G.W.R., 9, A5.
*Woodend, L.M.S., 26, F3.
Woodend Colliery, L.N.E.R., 31, C2.
Woodford (Essex), L.N.E.R., 5, A4.
Woodford & Hinton (Northants.), L.N.E.R./ L.M.S., 10, B4.
Wood Green (Middlesex), L.N.E.R., 5, A3.
§Wood Green (Staffs.), L.M.S., 15, F4.
Woodhall Jc., L.N.E.R., 17, B1.
Woodhall Spa, L.N.E.R., 17, B1.
Woodham Ferrers, L.N.E.R., 11, G5.
Woodhay, G.W.R., 4, A4.
Woodhead, L.N.E.R., 21, F2.
Woodhouse * (Leics.), *see* Quorn.
Woodhouse (Yorks.), L.N.E.R., 16, A4.
Woodhouse Mill, L.M.S., 16, A4.
Woodkirk, L.N.E.R., 21, E3.
Woodland, L.M.S., 26, G2.
Woodlesford, L.M.S., 21, D3.
Woodley, L.M.S./L.N.E.R., 21, G1.
Woodmansterne, S.R., 5, C3.
*Woodmuir, L.M.S., 31, C2.
Woodnesborough, E.K.R., 6, C2.
Woodside (Birkenhead), B.J., 20, C4.
Woodside (Halebank) Goods, L.M.S., 20, C3.
Woodside (Surrey), S.R., 5, B3.
Woodside Park, *L.N.E.R./ L.P.T.B., A3.
Woodstock, *see* Blenheim.
Woodvale, C.L.C., 20, B4.
*Woodville, L.M.S., 16, E5.
Woofferton, S.H., 9, A1.
Wookey, G.W.R., 3, C2.
Wool, S.R., 3, F4.
Woolaston, G.W.R., 9, F1.
*Wooler, L.N.E.R., 32, E3.
Wooley Coll., L.N.E.R., 27, D5.
Woolfold, L.M.S., 20, B1.
Woolston, S.R., 4, E3.
Woolwich Arsenal, S.R., 5, B4.
Woolwich Dockyard, S.R., 5, B4.
*Wooperton, L.N.E.R., 32, E2.
Wootton (I.W.), S.R., 4, F3.
Wootton Bassett, G.W.R., 9, E4.
Wootton Wawen Platform, G.W.R., 9, B5.
Worcester, G.W.R & G.W.R./ L.M.S., 9, B3.

Worcester Park, S.R., 5, B3.
Worgret Jc., S.R., 3, F4.
Workington, L.M.S., 26, E3.
Workington Bridge, L.M.S., 26, E3.
Worksop, L.N.E.R., 16, A3.
Worle, *see* Puxton.
Worleston, L.M.S., 15, B2.
Worlingworth, L.N.E.R., 12, C3.
Wormald Green, L.N.E.R., 21, B3.
Wornit, L.N.E.R., 37, E2.
Worplesdon, S.R., 5, C1.
Worsborough (Goods), L.N.E.R., 21, F3.
Worsley, L.M.S., 20, B2.
Worstead, L.N.E.R., 18, E4.
Worthing Central, S.R., 5, F2.
*Worthington, L.M.S., 16, E4.
Worthy Down Platform, G.W., 4, C3.
Worting Jc., S.R., 4, B3.
Wortley, L.N.E.R., 21, F3.
Wotton, L.N.E.R., 10, E3.
Wrabness, L.N.E.R., 12, E3.
Wrafton, S.R., 7, F3.
Wragby, L.N.E.R., 17, A2.
Wrangaton, G.W.R., 2, D4.
Wrangbrook Jc., L.N.E.R., 21, E4.
Wraysbury, S.R., 5, B1.
Wrea Green L.M.S., 24, D4.
Wrenbury, L.M.S., 15, C1.
Wressle, L.N.E.R., 21, D5.
Wretham & Hockham, L.N.E.R., 12, A5.
Wrexham,G.W.R.& G.W.R./ L.N.E.R./G.W.R., 20, G4.
*Wrington, G.W.R., 8, D3.
Wrotham & Borough Green, S.R., 6, C5.
Wroxall (I.W.), S.R., 4, G3.
Wroxham, L.N.E.R., 18, E2.
Wryde, M.G.N., 17, F3.
Wycombe Jc., L.M.S./ L.N.E.R., 16, D2.
Wye, S.R., 6, D3.
Wyke, L.M.S., 21, E2.
Wykeham, L.N.E.R., 22, A4.
Wylam, L.N.E.R., 27, B5.
Wylde Green, L.M.S., 15, F5.
Wylye, G.W.R., 3, C5.
Wymondham (Leics.), *see* Edmondthorpe.
Wymondham (Norfolk), L.N.E.R., 18, F4.
*Wynyard, L.N.E.R., 28, E4.
Wyre Dock, L.M.S., 24, C4.
Wyre Forest, G.W.R., 9, A2.
Wyrley, L.M.S., 15, F4.

Y

Yalding, S.R., 6, C5.
Yardley Wood, G.W.R., 9, A5.
Yarm, L.N.E.R., 28, F5.
Yarmouth (Great), L.N.E.R. & M.G.N., 18, F1.
Yarmouth (I.W.), S.R., 4, F4.
Yarmouth Beach, M.G.N., 18, F1.
Yarnton, G.W.R., 10, E4.
Yate, L.M.S., 9, G2.
Yatton, G.W.R., 8, D3.
Yaxham, L.N.E.R., 18, F5.
Yaxley & Farcet, L.N.E.R., 11, A2.
Yeadon, L.M.S., 21, D2.
*Yealmpton, G.W.R., 2, E5.
*Yeathouse, L.M.S., 26, E3.
Yeldham, L.N.E.R., 11, D5.
Yelvertoft & Stanford Park, L.M.S., 10, A3.
Yelverton, G.W.R., 2, D5.
Yeoford, S.R., 2, B4.
Yeoveney, G.W.R., 5, B1.
Yeovil Jc., S.R., 3, E2.
Yeovil Pen Mill, G.W.R., 3, D2.
Yeovil Town, G.W.R./S.R., 3, D2.
Yetminster, G.W.R., 3, D2.
Yiewsley, *see* West Drayton.
Ynishir, G.W.R., 8, B5.
Ynys, G.W.R., 19, F1.
Ynys-y-Geinon Jc., L.M.S./ G.W.R., 7, A4.
Ynysddu, L.M.S., 8, B4.
Ynyslas, G.W.R., 13, B5.
Ynysybwl, G.W.R., 8, B5.
Yockleton, S.W., 14, A1.
Yoker, L.N.E.R., 30, C2.
York, L.N.E.R./L.M.S., 21, B3.
Yorton, L.M.S., 15, D1.
Ystalyfera, L.M.S/G.W.R., 7, A4.
Ystrad (Rhondda), G.W.R., 8, B5.
*Ystradgynlais, G.W.R, 7, A5.
Ystrad Mynach, G.W.R./ *L.M.S., 8, B4.
Ystradowen, G.W.R., 8, C5.